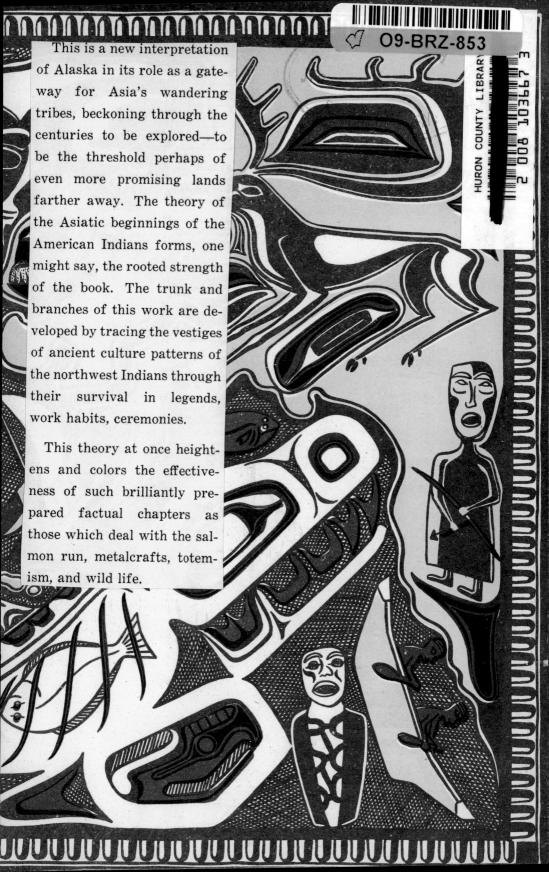

This is a new interpretation of Alaska in its role as a gateway for Asia's wandering tribes, beckoning through the centuries to be explored—to be the threshold perhaps of even more promising lands farther away. The theory of the Asiatic beginnings of the American Indians forms, one might say, the rooted strength of the book. The trunk and branches of this work are developed by tracing the vestiges of ancient culture patterns of the northwest Indians through their survival in legends, work habits, ceremonies.

This theory at once heightens and colors the effectiveness of such brilliantly prepared factual chapters as those which deal with the salmon run, metalcrafts, totemism, and wild life.

ALASKA BECKONS

*Ena-gwenee, Mighty One; Tall Man Odindza, his enemy; and
Kronaydin, the Wanderer, a dwarf* PAGES 18-24.

ALASKA BECKONS

917.98
B23

BY MARIUS BARBEAU

ILLUSTRATED BY ARTHUR PRICE

1947

The CAXTON PRINTERS, Ltd.

CALDWELL, IDAHO

The MACMILLAN COMPANY of CANADA

Printed and bound in the United States of America by
The CAXTON PRINTERS, Ltd.
Caldwell, Idaho
61700

To

William Beynon

Member of a leading Wolf clan
of the Tsimsyans

My chief interpreter and assistant for many years
in my research into the history and
ethnography of his people.

PREFACE

ALASKA may seem remote. On the map, it looks like
a closed hand at the northwestern end of our
continent, with the forefinger—the Aleutian Islands—
pointing to the heart of Asia. On the left, the Gulf of
Alaska is bent like a bow before releasing an arrow;
Bering Sea stretches forward between Alaska, the Aleutians, Kamchatka, and Siberia; and, to the right, lie the
vague expanses of the Arctic Ocean, on the roof of the
globe.

As its peninsula holds up the frozen seas, we are apt to
think first of its midnight sun in the summer, its sundogs
in midseasons, and its winter twilights, deep snows, and
cold blasts far below zero. Yet this impression of re-
moteness and frigid vacuity is far from justified; it can
easily be changed. The recent war has done much to
bring Alaska into the news. This northern country has
moved toward the hub of actuality, and is still drawing
closer.

We may remember that this immense land is no longer
forsaken and difficult of access. Its climate varies from
very moist and snowless the year round, at its southern
edge, to really cold in the long winters—almost as cold
as Manitoba and the states immediately to the south—
down to perpetual frost underground on the high plateaus in the interior. Its resources in scenery, minerals,
wild life, legend, and epic tales are immense, unfathomed.

From the immemorial past, it has always beckoned to

itself people of varied types beginning with the Siberian
tribes that never ceased to cross Bering Strait to hunt in
its free wilderness, the Slavs in their quest for booty and
furs, and the venturesome sea-otter and whale hunters.
Then it drew, like a magnet, the Hudson's Bay Company, which trespassed upon the jealously guarded preserves of the Russians; the white miners and "stam-
peders," on the gold trails of the Klondike; the explorers
and surveyors, tramping the uncharted valleys and hill-
sides; the big-game hunters, tracking the grizzly bear,
the Kodiak bear, the bighorn, and the mountain goat;
the mountain-climbers, scaling volcanic peaks, seeking
geysers and paradise valleys, or thrusting their spikes
into St. Elias, one of the highest mountains in North
America; and the Japanese and Americans, recently engaged, beyond the Aleutian Islands, in a death struggle
for its ultimate control as a highway to conquest or a
rampart for home security. People are hastily learning
now the extent of its potentialities and idle wealth for
the future, and its varied domains may no longer, as in
our blindfold past, be sparsely utilized or occupied.

It is with the Alaska of old, that once beckoned the
eastern Siberians to its wild shores and on its devious
highways, that this book chiefly deals. From their bridge-
heads on the Aleutian Islands and Cape Prince of Wales,
east of Bering Sea, these nomadic tribes took their fate
into their hands and started on a lifelong trek in search of
new fishing and hunting grounds, down the seacoast, up
the Yukon River, across the mountain divides, on to the
headwaters of other rivers, without an end ever in sight.

MARIUS BARBEAU

Ottawa, Ontario, Canada
March 19, 1946

ACKNOWLEDGMENTS

IN THE preparation of the materials and script, the author gratefully acknowledges his debt to:

THE NATIONAL MUSEUM OF CANADA, for permitting him to use the materials and knowledge accumulated in the course of a number of expeditions during the past twenty-five years of study among the Indians of the northern Rockies.

ARTHUR PRICE, artist, for preparing the illustrations, end papers, and jacket design.

JOY TRANTER, dramatist and poet, who studied and criticized his text from the point of view of the reader and helped him to revise it.

DOUGLAS LEECHMAN, archaeologist, National Museum of Canada, for further text improvements and proofreading.

LURTON BLASSINGAME, for expert advice and interest.

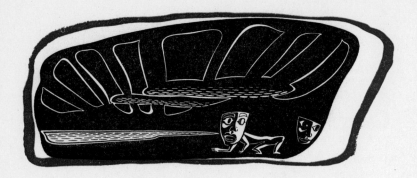

CONTENTS

LIST OF ILLUSTRATIONS

Page

ALASKA BECKONS

THE HIGHWAY

THE RECENT life-and-death struggle between the Japanese aggressors and the armed defenders of Alaskan soil brings to mind the Indian legend of Kronaydin, a wanderer without fire or homeland, who was going somewhere in the Déné country on the upper Yukon River, but knew not his next step.

This native legend out of the remote past, recorded in the far Northwest by the French missionary, Petitot, holds a symbol for us. Like Kronaydin, we are all on our way, but no one can predict exactly whither. Our only certainty is that the North Americans are determined to remain in full possession of their continent to the rim of the Arctic Ocean, and to achieve final victory in its protection.

Once, according to the Déné tradition, there lived, on the shore of Bering Sea facing Siberia, an ancient American, a nomad of the frozen tundras. His complexion was coppery, his hair lank and dark. His features were Mongolian—some would say Tartar or North Asiatic. In winter his warm outer dress was the caribou parka; his summer raincoat was made out of the transparent guts of the walrus; and his waterproof boots had been cut out of seal skin and sewn with sinew. The women sewing for him toiled, during long Arctic winters, in the pale light of stone lamps under the frozen dome of snow houses, or of earthen lodges with a ladder entrance through the roof. Self-supporting though he

was, living off the country as he went, he none the less
remained poor, wretched, hungry as a wolf, and sullen in
his misery. For the country that his wild paths crisscrossed was inhospitable and hostile. It was a barren
highway. People who were wont to travel on it from
west to east never lingered there very long.

Kronaydin, the Wanderer, fell into an ambush one day,
and became a captive in the hands of a hunter of his own
kind, who was bent upon reducing him to slavery, perhaps to crush out his life during the winter festivals.
In the darkness of a cave in the Porcupine Mountains,
the captive knew full well that he was no longer the
master of his own fate. In his distress he called upon his
guardian spirit, whose name was Ena-gwenee (Mighty
One Looking All Around at Once). Ena-gwenee, re-
sponding to the call, struck the mountain with his thunder, tore the cave asunder, and bade his protégé, the
Wanderer, go forth on his endless trek ever eastward.
But his advice was for him to move away from the salt
sea, where enemies surging out of the shades of sunset
were wont to trip on each other's heels and cut each
other's throats.

Before starting on his journey toward the sunrise, the
Wanderer turned to gaze at the kindly giant of the Far
North, and saw him walking on a bed of red-hot cinders.

"How fearful, Grandfather, are your ways!" he said
with awe and reverence. "Your trail is a bed of lava."

Mighty One reassured him, saying: "Be not afraid, for
it is not all lava that smothers lives, all burning trails that
lead to perdition. I am the hunter's own friend, the light
in the dark, your spirit protector. I do not freeze out the
people as the polar frost does, as also does my enemy, Tall
Man Odinza. I only save them, like the warmth of the

sun, when they fall upon evil, dark days. My abode is a
lofty crater, and the hot springs in the hidden valleys
overflow for my sweat bath. My secret resort is the
Valley of Ten Thousand Smokes. All this, for the moment, is my homeland, and you are my grandchild."

"Grandfather, today you have saved my life."

"As long as Tall Man stalks you and keeps creeping
upon you, Grandson, you cannot be sure of the morrow.
You know not whether this trail, open today, perhaps
blocked tomorrow, may lead you to its outlet or a dead
end. Nor am I safe anywhere within his reach, for he
is mighty and bloodthirsty, and the sworn enemy of all
but his own accursed breed."

"Then, Mighty One, let us travel together!"

"Yes, let us join forces together, for there is no one so
great on earth but he harbors the seed of his own death;
no one so small but he holds some hidden power. The
one rushes into combat wherein mortal blows are given
and received; the other escapes unnoticed or shoots his
arrow from below. Death may come both ways, glaring
from above, or unseen out of the ground. Ere long you
shall know the truth of my words."

The Wanderer, Kronaydin, and Mighty One, Ena-
gwenee entered a beaten trail up a vast river (the
Yukon) across the mountains of sunrise. But they were
ill-matched to walk together very long, for alone the
giant traveled at a fast pace. So Mighty One lifted the
Wanderer to his shoulder, set him there, and headed for
the wild lands of the interior and the plateaus. When the
air of Moonland was too chill for the little man, he would
hide him for awhile in the fur lining of his mittens, or
he would shelter him in the warm palm of his hand.
When they both were hungry, the giant, with his har-

poon, hunted the bear, the caribou, or the beaver for food, and he did all in his power to please his puny friend of the dark cave, whom he had found without fire or country. Thus the mighty at times are drawn in pure affection to the very small, and the puny are raised up to the heroes of their own worship.

This native legend, in the light of the recent Japanese onslaught and the forced exodus of the Aleutians from their islands to the mainland, reveals to us, first of all, an ugly ghost of aggression to Alaska from across Bering Sea. Tall Man Odinza, with greed and hatred in his simian chest, was already tramping forward on the beaten path of invasion eastward. He has not yet ceased tracking the Wanderer of the Arctic steppes. But his cruel story does not stop at the mere chase long ago, along a trail of geysers and sleeping volcanoes, of the fugitive and his guardian spirit, Mighty One. Once more, in our own time, it burst its smothered craters, to belch fumes and lava all over the land.

The Wanderer and Mighty One traveled on until, one day, the friendly giant paused and said: "Tall Man, my enemy, is drawing close. As his name, Yanakwi-Odinza, implies, his head proudly rubs the sky. So proud is he that he traces his descent from the heavens above; he claims to be the son of the gods. Pride and conceit have been his incentive from the beginning; they are bound to lead him to victory over all, or to his defeat and final ruin. Young men and women, ever swaying to his will, swarm around him; they are the fount of his true power. He means to kill you and me some day, in an encounter. If he does, my blood, like the breath of a volcano, shall stain the vault of the sky, stain it all over with the red clouds of sunset."

"How fearful, Grandfather, are your ways!" he said with awe and reverence. "Your trail is a bed of lava" PAGE 18.

Sitting on the shoulder of his guardian spirit, the Wanderer held his breath, and whispered: "Grandfather, let us go forth! Perhaps he may never overtake us. How could he guess where we are going, for we know not ourselves?"

"Too late, Grandson! I see him coming in the distance; my sight flashes all around. Soon he and I shall wrestle in the way long familiar to both of us, wrestle until one of us gasps his last breath, leaving the other full mastery over the land."

The Wanderer felt sad in his heart, for he could not find in himself the power to help Mighty One. The giant consoled him with a gift.

"Here is a beaver's tooth," he said. "Its blade is hard and sharp. A good tool, it may also be a useful weapon. Hold it firmly in your hand, while you hide there under the dwarf willows. Now I am bound to fight as never before in my lifetime."

The two giants, Mighty One, who was kindly and helpful, and Tall Man, whose head proudly brushed the sky, met in a life-and-death struggle that made the volcanoes belch flames and lava, and drew the sea up in a huge tidal wave. Two supernatural men, one good and the other bad, were now fighting to a finish.

Odinza, the fierce challenger, gave the first body blow, and made Ena-gwenee reel back several steps. Mighty One, who could not be downed easily, rallied aud thrust his solid fist into the face of his rival, who began to bleed and to moan. The tiny Wanderer, under his willow bush, heard the groan and held fast to his only weapon, the beaver tooth.

Long the enemies struggled; long they fought with bitter fury. The rocks in their paths were ploughed out of the earth and heaped up sky-high. Ena-gwenee, the good one, weakened finally, and the blood began to drip from his forehead, out of his veins. He cried: "Grandson, where is your weapon? It is now your time to help."

"Grandfather, here I am ready to join you in the fight for life or death."

"Brave little man! Come close, while I still hold him. Cut his leg tendon from behind. Cut it at the ankle."

The Wanderer severed the mighty leg sinew with the magic beaver tooth. This tooth had long been sharpened to cut down forests of tall trees.

He whose head had vainly rubbed the sky crashed to the ground, to rise no more. His body lay shivering amid the dead volcanoes and the steaming geysers.

"Well done, my grandchild!" shouted Mighty One, triumphant. And the Wanderer was overjoyed.

"The reward shall be yours. Your life now is safe on the trails back and forth," said the giant. "You need me no more, for this event marks the twilight of all giants, good or bad. We have come to the end of our wanderings together. Here is my parting word to you."

"Your parting word, alas!" whispered the Wanderer, with pain and regret.

"Keep this staff of manly power, and hold it close to your heart. It is my last gift to you and your kind. Remember!"

After Ena-gwenee, or Mighty One, had disappeared, the Wanderer remained alone and downhearted. He went on his way, discovering new lands and strange people, crossing swollen rivers, driving down precipitous canyons, scaling mountains that seemed to bar his way onward to the sunrise or a warmer sun, and spearing fierce animals which bit and clawed at his life.

Whenever in peril he planted his magic wand in the ground and cried, "Grandfather Ena-gwenee, come to me!" And his call to his unseen spirit helper was never in vain. Forever he traveled the earth onward, never retracing a step, for there is nothing to bar the way anywhere to whoever holds the staff of manly power close to his heart.

The wild paths of migration across Bering Sea—over Bering Strait, or along the broken chain of the Aleutian Islands—have long been tramped by the feet of countless Mongolian and Tartar nomads from the northern Siberian steppes, all of them advancing like Kronaydin, toward the sunrise into America. The land they had left behind, overflowing with restless people, had edged them out without pity. Conquerors of the brand of Genghis Khan, sword and burning torch in hand, had hounded them out of sight and scorched the earth behind them. As they had known no mercy in the forlorn land of their birth, they wasted none on their own victims, which they chanced upon on the trail.

These Siberian fugitives were none other than the wanderers of the legend recorded by Father Petitot among the Dénés of the Yukon and the Mackenzie rivers. Mighty One Ena-gwenee and his magic staff represent the tireless spirit of these rovers in search of food and booty and bent upon slaying the straggler in their path. The evil Odinza, whose head rubbed the sky, was the livid specter of prowlers close upon their heels, born robbers parading pedigrees that traced their questionable ancestry back to the high heavens, as the Japanese do.

Down to the time of the recent war, the direction of migratory feet away from Asia into Alaska has always pointed to the sunrise, never to the sunset. The trail itself leads only one way, wide open as it is from the west, and nearly blocked by the stubborn mountains to the east. The Japanese of our time had only to set ablaze a pitchwood torch to arouse frenzy, had only to pick up the sword fallen from the hands of the last warrior khan, and follow the age-worn path of migration across Bering Sea for fresh inroads and piracy. They have never been gifted with chivalry or inventiveness, and in them foresight is not a natural endowment. Their fate did not, indeed, differ from that of the evil Yanakwi-Odinza, the one whose head so proudly rubbed the sky. The Alaskan white wanderers standing across their path, with feet on the ground or wings in the air, wielding as a weapon the magic beaver tooth, soon sealed their fate. The beaver itself has long been a famous emblem on this continent.

The Déné legend of the Wanderer may be taken as prophetic by whoever glances at the annals of Alaska for the past hundred years. Here the Slavs, on the trail of the sea otter, stumbled upon natives and harnessed them into service. There the Russian American Company and the Hudson's Bay Company later crossed swords reluctantly, for they were neither real wanderers nor mythological giants. Yet they stopped at nothing short of international war.

All sorts of reminiscences awaken as soon as the map of the northern Rockies appears, with the brand new red stripe of its recently opened Alcan Highway from Fort St. John, past Fort Nelson, along the Liard River, past Whitehorse, Kluane Lake, Fairbanks, and the Big Delta, swinging twin lines down to Valdez and Seward on the salt sea. These reminiscences go back to earlier attempts to clear the path and open a roadway toward Asia.

With the beginning of World War II, the long-slumbering Ena-gwenee of the native legend awakened for a new encounter along the trail of geysers and extinct volcanoes extending from the Kurile Islands to the heart of Alaska, heretofore pointing only eastward. But, this time, something different happened. An artery, the new Alcan Highway, now began to throb from east to west and inject new life into the struggle. It bristled with might and roared with thunder. It helped to turn the tidal wave in the Pacific.

The story of how this highway to Asia so suddenly came into existence has already been written in high places. But it bears recalling here. Surely not all of it can be told overnight, as it was near a hundred years in the making. The forging of the last links in the chain alone is a work of epoch-making, almost miraculous, military achievement. The plans for a peacetime Alcan Highway, which had been hanging fire for some time before the war, at last became a war reality. Asia truly is now within the reach of America, just as America for countless milleniums had been the recipient of incessant Asiatic migrations.

Once before, in the 1830's and 1840's, a staunch effort was made to force an easterner's way westward through the northern Rockies into the Yukon and Alaska. Heroic deeds of pioneering and discovery, as a result, have unfolded an epic, too little known as yet.

Those were the days of the fur trader, when the Russian American Company had moved into the coastal areas. There it held not a few trading posts and military strongholds. Then the Hudson's Bay Company, who exploited by royal charter most of the northern expanses of this continent, would go on expanding as far as they could. They would not stop short of a full stretch, after having crossed lakes and prairies and run up gorges and canyons, until the headwaters of the great rivers flowing west into the Pacific had come within reach.

Alexander Mackenzie, of the North West Company, was the first, in 1792, to take his life in his hands and, with a small escort of French-Canadian voyageurs and half-breed canoemen, cross the Rockies proper while ascending the Peace River, that flows northeastward to the river now bearing his name. In his incredible journey he passed the point where Fort St. John later was to stand, a mere outpost in the wilderness.

Fort St. John, for long an obscure name, sprang suddenly into the war news. It is only a lap beyond the starting point, at Dawson Creek, of the Alcan Highway, undertaken in 1942 by the American government, with the consent of the Canadian government, to meet the Japanese thrust eastward along the prehistoric pathway from Siberia and the Aleutian Islands.

Why a military highway, to be built at top speed, should begin at this remote spot, east of the Rockies, about 1,600 miles from its destination in northwestern Alaska, is easily understood. A decision at that time had to be made in haste, for the Japanese already were pounding for a landfall at Dutch Harbor, near the mainland of Alaska at the far end.

Civil advisers in peacetime had advocated, on behalf of the American and Canadian governments, the shorter road, west of the principal chain of the Rockies, from Prince George northward along the Finlay River. A railway, joining up with the Canadian National Railways and the provincial railway from Vancouver northward, might sometime travel the whole way to Alaska; such a prospect more than once has figured in the news. Or a pathway, shorter still and closer to the coast, might have followed the old Indian trail which the Western Union Telegraph Company, in 1866, had made its own.

However, the Fort St. John, Liard River, and Teslin Lake route was the choice. Its builders labored under a defensive complex brought about by the dread of the Japanese, who had just shown their knavery at Pearl Harbor. A road farther west, so they feared, would be exposed to attack. The Canadian government already had blazed a trail through the air, with five air bases established and operating northward from Edmonton by way of the Liard River to Whitehorse. By March 1, 1942, plans and machinery were in readiness at Dawson Creek, and, incredible as it may seem, the symbolic ribbon opening the Alcan Highway to war traffic was cut officially at Kluane Lake on November 20, the same year.

What the American army accomplished in so little time, in a difficult and partly mountainous country, is little short of fabulous. Its feat evokes the Kronaydin legend of the same country, with its battle of giants, and its puny Wanderer armed only with a beaver tooth hamstringing the evil Odinza that had sprung forward from the shades of sunset. But the beaver tooth was magical, no less than the power of the road builders, whom no barrier could stop short of their objective.

The geographic obstacles strewing the line of vision seemed impassable. Some geologists, after exploring the mountains and the rivers, had declared that the muskeg at the foothills would bar the way, that the canyons of the Liard would baffle the engineers. Others, who had crossed that country, were not so pessimistic. Historians,

*"Brave little man! Come close, while I still hold him. Cut his leg
tendon from behind. Cut it at the ankle"* PAGE 23.

who forget nothing, whistled the old tune that the Hudson's Bay Company once had tried, during two or three decades, to clear the way for the fur trade from the Mackenzie River up the Liard and across the divides to the Stikine and the Yukon rivers, only to be defeated finally by natural impediments, because of dependence upon water transportation.

Who would think of surpassing the daring and courage of the great pioneers of the northern Rockies—Alexander Mackenzie, John McLeod and Paul Boucher, Robert Campbell, Louis Lapierre, John Bell, Alexander Hunter Murray—all of whom, in the service of the great company, had entered the wilderness at the risk of their lives and taken there a precarious foothold for later comers?

Enough can be found in the early journals of exploration in that territory to deter modern trail blazers from fresh futility, where their hardy elders, who could subsist on "tripe-de-roche" and shoe leather, had tried and failed long ago. But army engineers and contractors were not deterred in their pursuits by past experiences, nor by warnings of some geologists, who stressed the difficulties of muskeg close to the foothills. Without them this mysterious country never would have had another chance of being opened to outsiders. The grizzly bear, the moose, the caribou, the timber wolf, would have gone on forever roving the pristine trails outside the range of the motorist speeding on a highway. But now, thanks to them, the claybanks and the mud holes of the Sekani Chief, the Prophet, and the Muskwa rivers, the canyons of the Liard, the mountain lakes of the upper Yukon River, are throbbing summer and winter with the pulsation of heavy motors. Mount St. Elias itself recently was witness

to an unwonted event close to its lower reaches to the east
—the official opening of the road by delegates of the
American and the Canadian governments impressively
gathered to make speeches, and see their breath freeze
white as they spoke.

Now that the army engineers, with their wonder tools
and unflagging industry, have finished their job, we may
lean back and ponder over the phenomenal obstacles they
have overcome, which had once before checked their
elders of the fur trade. The pioneers of a hundred years
ago possessed dash and endurance, but they lacked the
beaver tooth of Kronaydin—that is, the modern tools
which no mountain barrier now can resist.

"Hutchison, who was McLeod's successor, arrived and
wintered at Fort Halkett" (above the Grand Canyon),
wrote Robert Campbell in his journal,[1] at the beginning
of a vivid description of the difficulties he encountered
on the upper Liard River, also called Mountain River.

Hutchison had been ordered to establish a post at Dease's Lake and
to explore as far as possible, that summer, down the west side of the
mountain. He started off to carry out his instructions, but had not
proceeded far when an alarm was given that hundreds of Russian
Indians were advancing on the camp to murder all occupants. A
panic seized the whole party and they ran down the bank pell-mell,
jumped into their canoes, and off they went downstream, never halt-
ing until they had reached Fort de Liard, where they stopped a few
days, and then proceeded down to Fort Simpson.... For some time
their narrow escape was the engrossing topic of the day.[2]

Robert Campbell was the only one to volunteer to go
back to Fort Halkett, which had been abandoned. In
1837 he wrote:

---

[1] Journal of Robert Campbell (1808-51). A ms. copy at the Library of the
National Museum of Canada.
[2] Ibid.

At Fort de Liard canoes had to be made, and birch-bark for this purpose had to be obtained. It was very hard to induce men, either whites or Indians, to make the journey up the river. The panic of the previous year had spread all over the district.[3]

By the middle of May, Campbell had engaged a crew of sixteen rivermen in all.

I could see that they were going into this enterprise in a half-hearted way. On the third morning after starting, during the night, some of the Indians had cleared out. The spirit of disaffection spread rapidly among the remainder. When we put ashore for breakfast, nearly half of the men said that they were so fearful of what awaited them that they had made up their minds to go no farther. So I resolved to put back to Fort de Liard at once and get refitted. I called for volunteers and explained that the trip had to be made, that the men engaged would, like myself, have to see it through to the end of the journey, that there was to be no turning back or flying from an enemy before he was seen; that, when he was seen, I would not ask any of my men to go and face him before I did; that if any of them showed signs of insubordination, it would be at the peril of his life. . . .

The summer freshet had come before we reached Hell's Gate. When the river is in flood no boat of any kind could ascend from the Gate to the Devil's Portage, as the current is not only very strong, but is full of rapids and rushes and whirlpools between perpendicular walls of rock two or three hundred feet high. Our progress was very slow and I was kept in constant anxiety lest the men would lose heart, as the croak of a frog or the screech of a night-owl was immediately taken for an enemy's signal. The imaginary dangers gave me more trouble and concern than the real ones.

At last we reached the Devil's Portage, where some of the men tried to alarm me. But I was up too early to be caught by their flimsy tricks. The evening before as we had arrived there, the men had carried some of the baggage part of the way across the portage, which is three miles long. As we were about to retire for the night, our dogs set off barking towards the woods. I attributed this to the presence of a bear or another animal, but some of the timid said, "There must be enemies prowling round." After a time the dogs quietened down, and we went to sleep.

I was up betimes in the morning as usual, and went quietly off

---

[3] *Ibid.*

with my gun to the farther end of the portage. In passing I noticed particularly how the pieces were lying, which, the previous evening, had been taken forward. On my way back I met my good old guide, Louis Lapierre, who reported to me that the men were all idle in camp, gun in hand, and that they declared they were surrounded by enemies and in danger of their lives.

I hastened on, but observed in passing that one of the bales had been shifted and was cut in one corner. I hurried into camp and, in no gentle terms, asked the men what they meant in wasting their time. They replied that hostile Indians were in a bush around them; this was made plain by the cut in one of the bales. I answered that before they had moved out of their blankets I had found the bale and was sure that they had done it themselves. Enemies are not in the habit of leaving clumsy marks of their presence. I had seen no enemy nor a trace of one anywhere. I ordered them to brace up and go back to work at once, if they were worth their salt.

After three days' hard work we got the canoes and cargo over the portage. Shortly after this we reached Fort Halkett, which appeared not to have been visited since abandoned, the previous year. And, curious to say, not an Indian, nor a vestige of any, did we see all summer, in spite of the fierce hordes my men constantly thought would swoop down upon us.

Fort Halkett is situated on the bank of Smith River and its confluence with the Liard, and, except in the river valley, is surrounded by rugged mountains whose hard rocky sides were beautified by green slopes, spruce, poplar, birch and tamarac, while small shrubs grew in profusion. Wild fruits—raspberries and strawberries, blueberries and cranberries—are very abundant.

In the neighborhood are some curious warm water springs issuing from the sloping bank of the river. The water, cold as ice in summer, is warm, though not hot, in winter. [This phenomenon has given rise to a presistent legend, that of a tropical valley. And, after this country was quite abandoned, a number of prospectors and explorers kept looking for it and bringing back tales from fairyland.] I determined to winter here.

But before the winter set in, I went on to Portage Brûlé, the spot which Hutchison and party, the year before, had evacuated hurriedly. On reaching there, we found the place just as they had left it. The goods were scattered about all the way down to the river's edge, just as they had been dropped by the men running to the canoes. Now everything was spoiled except such articles as ball, shot, etc. The provisions had been eaten by the wild animals.

After our return to the Fort I took the earliest opportunity of pointing out to the men the folly of their fear. My words, I think, had the desired effect and brought them back to their senses. We commenced to refit the place for winter occupation.[4]

On his way back from the headwaters in a later season, Campbell retraced his steps down the Liard River, and with his trusty Lapie proceeded downstream in a pine-bark canoe. He wrote:

It was by no means an ordinary undertaking for us to run down the strong and swift current of a river so full of rapids, whirlpools and other dangerous places, in a canoe of the frailest material. We trusted our guns for food.

At Fort Halkett, now abandoned, we changed our pine bark for a small birch canoe, which in the spring we had left there. We reached Devil's Portage the same day. Here we were overtaken by a heavy rain storm and sought shelter under the branches of a large pine tree.

Next day we were passing between the rocky cliffs and through the rapids leading for miles to Hell's Gate. Our canoe was so small that the waves kept dashing over it, and we shipped so much water that we had constantly to bail her out, or empty her whenever we could get a ledge or strip of beach to stand on. Some distance above Hell's Gate, when we were enclosed on both sides by high perpendicular walls of rock, with not a spot where we could land, our canoe sprung a leak. As we could see from the rate at which the water was coming, we thought we were lost. We would sink before getting through Hell's Gate.

In the midst of our anxiety, we saw a pine tree growing on a ledge near the water's edge. We made for it, succeeded in landing under it and, to our great relief, found pitch on the tree. Lighting a fire with flint, steel and touchwood, we turned up the canoe and pitched it. Later we safely got through the gate. . . . [5]

Many years after the Liard River had been abandoned as a trade route because of the great length of its difficult navigation, it was revisited, in 1871-72, by McCullough

[4] *Ibid.*
[5] *Ibid.*

and Thibert, the discoverers of the Cassiar gold fields.
And Emile Petitot, the French missionary, at that time,
wrote about it from hearsay (translated here) :

I have ascended the Liard River a few miles only, but all the
voyageurs who have had anything to do with it agree in their description of its frightfulness. Its mountains are precipitous; its swirling
waters and whirlpools rush through a narrow gorge between steep
walls that rise up to the sky. The only half-breed daredevils who have
descended these swift waters had themselves bound to their boats;
otherwise they would have been washed off by the foaming waves.

R. G. McConnell, the geologist who explored the Liard
watershed in 1887-88, came upon the old portage trail,
which was less than four miles in length instead of twelve
as he had been led to expect. And he wrote:

The trail is very difficult. It passes over a ridge fully a thousand
feet high, on both sides of which the slopes are exceedingly steep. The
old portage track was easily followed among the heavy timber for
some distance after leaving the upper end. But going east it became
overgrown with brushwood, and at last it disappeared. We were
obliged to cut out a new one for ourselves. As this track was cleared
out in 1871 by Messrs. McCullough and Thibert for the purpose of
hauling their boats across, it shows how active is the forest growth of
this region. The old trail was covered with shrubs and small trees
several inches in diameter.
This country forms a neutral ground between the Indians trading
east and west of the mountains, and the danger in navigating the
river makes it difficult of access. The absence of natives and the
immunity from hunting enjoyed by the moose, since the abandon-
ment of old Fort Halkett, has resulted in the great increase in their
numbers. The beaver are also abundant, and, like the moose, appear
to have thriven in the absence of their natural enemies. Grizzly
bears are especially common on the Devil's Portage. . . . This probably is the best moose country in North America. Everywhere we
landed, we observed fresh tracks in abundance. We killed one at the
mouth of Rivière des Vents, and another farther down near Crow

River, and could have shot a number of others. At the "Rapids of the
Drowned" we scared three into the river. They unfortunately attempted to swim the rapids and were drowned.[6]

Once the difficulties of the Devil's Portage were overcome—after six days—this geologist and his party found
it impossible to cut out a track and haul their heavy
wooden boat over the steep hills, and took the risk of
running the rapids.

Below the Devil's Portage, for thirty or forty miles the river flows
through what is called the Grand Canyon. It is more correctly a
succession of short canyons, with expanded basins filled with eddying
currents. In the season of high floods, the water forcing its way
through the throat-like contractions is thrown into a commotion
too violent for any but the staunchest boats to stand. The canyon
was supposed to have been run in two hours, at the rate of about
eighteen miles an hour, an astonishing velocity, but the time was
probably underestimated. It took us several days to get through, as
we were obliged to make a number of short portages, one of these
over three miles in length.

We launched our new canvas boat and, on the 16th of July, commenced the descent of the Grand Canyon. As we proceeded, the
bordering banks became higher and steeper, while the current ran
with increasing impetuosity until, rounding a bend, it broke into
foam against a barrier of rocks intercepting its course. We passed
this by a small portage and then continued our headlong course
down the river, but were soon stopped by a succession of bad
riffles. In the next couple of miles we ran through a number of wild
places, the canvas boat gallantly riding the waves. We were forced
to make two more short portages. Then we entered a deep, gloomy,
defile, walled in by black vertical cliffs. Part way down the canyon
a couple of islets, with steep rocky banks, divide the stream into
several channels. These we soon left behind, and hurrying through a
second narrow pass we came out on a wide part of the river. The
current is still swift, running at the rate of seven miles an hour, but
the navigation is easy. . . .

At the end of this reach the river bends to the north and it strikes

---

[6] Montreal: Geological and Natural History Survey of Canada, *Report on an
Exploration in the Yukon and Mackenzie Basins.* 1891.

violently against sombre cliffs lining the left bank. There it is deflected again to the east with the formation known as Rapids of the Drowned. Here, at one of the most dangerous spots on the Liard, the water plunges with its whole force over a ledge which curves outwards and downwards from the left-hand bank, into a boiling *chaudière*.

The name of Rapids of the Drowned commemorates the drowning at this point of a Hudson's Bay clerk named Brown and a boat-load of voyageurs. The boat had plunged into the *chaudière* to be drawn under.[7]

All this would have been cheerless reading to the engineers burning the midnight oil over their plans for the Alaskan Highway. But, brushing aside explorers and historians, they relied only upon the wings of their aerial surveys and the bucking power of their bulldozers, just as the fabled Wanderer once had trusted his beaver tooth. And both of them were right, beyond common sense.

The Alcan Highway has spanned the mud holes of Nelson River, cut a clean swath in the flank of virgin forests and mountain slopes, crossed and recrossed the Liard above the Grand Canyon. Without pausing a day or a night, it has swung at great speed west and north again, jumping off from the headwaters of a river flowing east over the divide to another flowing northwest, toying much of the way with the seemingly impossible.

With a startling lack of introspection, its makers never laid stress on the gravity of their responsibility or the immensity of their undertaking. No one among them stopped to put into words the puzzles which must have beset them at times; no one seems to have let his feelings or anxieties gain the better of him, although some of these pioneer workers, as they went about their

---

[7] *Ibid.*

task, took grave risks and paid for them with their lives. No song perhaps has uttered the anguish of their souls in the crisis. Modern man, now wed to the machine, no longer gives vent to poetic outbursts, nor lapses into the language of the gods; he no longer cares a whit whether posterity ever knows of the birth pangs of the present or of the herculean tasks of its pathfinders. Hopes are no sooner expressed than they are fulfilled.

Mechanized power has taken the whole field to itself, coldly dislodging humanity from its former estate. The battle of the Alaskan giants Odinza and Ena-gwenee could no longer be renewed in our age. The Wanderer at their heels would let his beaver tooth become the whole story.

The tale of the building of the Alcan Highway, as we now read of it in the magazines, is all prose and statistics, with only a dash of humor and futility thrown in. The mosquito and the no'see'em figure more widely in the rambling reminiscences of the workers than the scaling of mountainsides or of the running of canyons. "Yarns" far more than tears mark the impression which nature has left upon the foremen shouting orders and the laborers doing the work.

Coming across the Beaver and the Sekani Indians of the Liard, a Negro batallion would yell, in a body, "Hello, Paleface!" and the so-called Paleface would retort, "Hello, Black-Face White Man!" This "yarn" can be found in semi-official accounts on the progress of the highway. But it lacks the tang of novelty. Look for its *première* in the century-old records of the Comanches and the Mohaves of the western plains!

The other 1942 "yarn" about Henry Moberly and his grizzlies on the Peace River hardly bears long scrutiny, should any one claim it as original. At least a score of years ago it was commonplace on the Skeena River and elsewhere. Moberly, a great bear killer, used to say, "Wait till the grizzly is about six feet from you, throw your hat at him, to get him to rise. Then, shoot! If you miss at this distance, you shouldn't be there. Probably you won't be."

Just as the ancient Wanderer from Siberia found no great barrier to impede his progress across Bering Sea, into Alaska, so did his modern followers, the Japanese, at a leap reach Dutch Harbor, late in 1941, and expect to land in force on this continent. Had they succeeded in their first attempt, they might have found self-justification in prehistory. For this would not have been the first invasion of this continent from the northwest. But the Dutch Harbor garrison parried the first blow and held off the landing force, which never had happened before. Now it devolved upon the Americans and the Canadians to keep their back door bolted against renewed raids from that quarter. Reinforcements, equipment, munitions, and fuel, were instantly expedited from the east by sea and overland via the Alcan Highway.

This new artery, vital though it was for the time being, was merely a breach through forest and mountain. The war machine, once geared to aggression, forged ahead hammer and tongs. The highway to Alaska and Tokyo did not rely solely on such a route, the main function of which at first was defense rather than attack.

The Edmonton and Liard River highway was winterbound part of the year, although the snowdrifts were not as bad as might have been expected; in the first winters, they did not prevent traffic. The early summer freshets and the rain storms did not, as was expected, sweep away the trestle bridges over the mountain rivers and their tributaries. The claybanks in the cuts or on the mountainsides did not for long fill the ditches or block the way. But its chief handicap was that it remained a long, devious route through a country which is virgin wilderness, the most inaccessible on our continent.

Most of the war equipment and munitions from Washington, Oregon, and California was not sent that way. It would have had to cross the Rockies eastward into the western plains and then westward at the northern end of this mighty range before reaching the Yukon watershed.

Thus no overland route was as yet available between the American states and the Canadian province west of the Rockies; all the traffic there had to be carried, as formerly, over the exposed coast waters.

The continued lack of an overland route for the regions west of the Rockies still leaves the problem where it was before the war, and calls for the eventual opening of a connecting road from Prince George in northern British Columbia, via a tributary of the upper Peace River, to Fort St. John, where it would join the Alcan Highway.

Should a direct road be opened for service from south to north, operating all winter outside the regions of sub-zero weather and deep snows, the results might soon compensate for an additional outlay. Such a road might be valuable as an added tourist asset, and it would connect the coastal towns and valleys with an inland roadway.

The only gap still left there between improved motor

roads already in existence north and south is about 400 miles wide as the crow flies. It extends through a mountainous and rainy country, along valleys and gorges, from a point north of Hazelton, on the Canadian National Railways in northern British Columbia, to Teslin Lake, where the new highway veers towards Whitehorse.

The gold rush of 1859 and later years opened the Caribou road up the Fraser River to Quesnel, Barkerville, and the Omenica. The "Poor Man's Route" of 1898, from Ashcroft to the Klondike, extended it along old Indian trails to the Skeena River and beyond. All this distance north of the American frontier is now covered by an improved and scenic motor road. And the remainder northward, within easy reach of the coast, with little zero weather in the winter and less than a foot of snow—as in Hazelton—as a possibility might follow the old trail adopted, in 1865-66, by the Western Union Telegraph line, the most practical of all. The Western Union Telegraph trail once was a topic almost as vital in world news as is now the Alcan Highway.

It is not generally remembered that the earliest attempts at laying and operating an Atlantic telegraph cable, in 1857, 1858, and 1859, did not meet with success. It was only in 1866 that Cyrus West Field, the American originator of the project, achieved his purpose in establishing a permanent telegraphic communication between the old and the new worlds.

An alternative in Field's scheme, should the failure of the oceanic cable be permanent, was to build an American telegraph line overland, then across Bering Strait, through Siberia to Europe. This enterprise was the first attempt to open a route from east to west across Bering Strait. It is in the reminiscences of "old-timers,"

Indian and white, mostly on the Skeena River, that one is apt still to hear of the "talking wire."

The magnitude of the enterprise at the time was colossal. The wire would run several thousand miles across wild stretches in British Columbia, Alaska, Bering Strait, and Siberia; relay stations were to be established at many points; and an army of linemen would have to keep the line in working order. For, along telegraph lines on the British Columbia trails, down to ten years ago, cabins with two linemen each were maintained every thirty miles, and revictualing the cabins was the unfailing business every summer of a pack train—Catelina's first, and then Byernes', his successor, both of Hazelton.

The construction, in the middle 1860's, of the Great Western Union across the mountains of British Columbia, has left indelible traces in the memory of the oldest surviving Indians and pioneers. For them it was a landmark in time. When asked about their age and the date of certain events, the Indians usually reply, "I was a child, a young man, at the time the Talking Wire came through this country," or "It happened before [or after] the coming of the Talking Wire." Although no white man at that time had settled along the Skeena River, the local tradition about the Great Western Union persists among the old people on the whole upper Skeena River.

The date of the placing of the wire along the Bulkley and Skeena rivers is given as 1865. The late J. B. Charleson of Ottawa (who died an octogenarian in 1920) was in charge of construction, a Mr. Conway was the civil engineer, and a Captain Butler controlled the supply party. An old man named Morison, still surviving at Mission Point in 1920, who was about twenty years of age in the 1860's, remembers how a telegraph operator named McCutcheon cried out, one day in September, 1866, "Boys! Our work is finished." The news had come that the laying of the Atlantic cable was a success.

The copper wire and other equipment were stored on the Kispayaks River, a tributary of the Skeena, and the work was given up. This booty soon fell into the hands of plundering Indians, who used some of the wire to build picturesque and shaky suspension bridges over the Kispayaks River near its mouth, and another bridge over the Hagwelget Canyon, which collapsed about twenty-five years ago.

The difficulties encountered by the builders were considerable. For equipment at the time was still fairly primitive, and the untamed natives along the way had to be won over or appeased. A Carrier Indian, named Skoakum-House-Tom (Jail Tom) — a very old Indian in 1920—related how he crawled near on all fours and killed two of the cattle in the herd which the party drove along for food. When asked if he were not afraid of being shot by the herdsman, he replied, "Oh, no! Not many white men in the country, that time."

"I was twenty or twenty-five years old, a newly married man, when we heard that the Talking Wire was coming through our land," said old Dog-of-the-Sky, a Hazelton chief of the Grizzly-Bear clan. "We were picking berries on the flat near Scouring-Rush camp, now Glen Meadow, or Hankin's Ranch, five miles above Hazelton. My cousin New-Woman came from the Hagwelget Canyon and gave us warning, 'Now the Talking Wire is coming down the river to Getenmaks [now Hazelton]. It has leaped across the canyon.' This was great news. I gave up picking berries and went to see the marvel. But the white men were on the move all the time. They came along with the Talking Wire and camped here, at Scouring-Rush. We were quite surprised, for we saw for the first time many things that were new to us: a herd of cattle, which we called goats of the sky; ovens [Dutch Ovens] to bake bread, and a Chinese cook. My people, quite afraid, would not stay so near the danger; they ran up to the hills, a safe distance off. The reason why most men would keep away was the fear that the Talking Wire would tell everybody about their secret affairs with strange women. And they would meet with trouble from their home fire-keepers. But I was interested. I stayed near the Talking Wire, for it has been my lifelong habit to make presents to the men in power. I gave the white chief a large basketful of huckleberries, which I had cleaned with care, and the Chinaman cooked the berries.

"The large herd of cattle was a constant marvel to me. A cow was butchered close to the camp, and cut with an axe right open down the back. The butcher gave me a piece of meat, and I brought it to my people in the hills. Only a few of the men were brave enough to eat a little of it. The women would not have any, because the cow was a strange animal. Only one woman dared to taste it, and she had only a mouthful. This was not good for her. She fell sick, and the people in derision threw it in her face.

"The white men took kindly to me and gave me the job of bringing wood and water to them. After camping two nights at Scouring-Rush, they moved with the wire and put up camp near Hiding-Place [Kispayaks] village. There I followed them. But as, after three days, they moved again, up the Kispayaks River to Gitang-

Now that the army engineers have finished their job, we may ponder over the phenomenal obstacles they have overcome PAGE 31.

walk at the headwaters, I found I had gone far enough;
I returned to my people."

The most direct route across British Columbia and
Alaska to Bering Strait is the one that was located and
followed without great difficulty, in the years 1865 and
1866, by the surveyors and engineers of the Western
Union Telegraph Company in the service of Cyrus
Field, of Philadelphia. Other road builders in our time
might tear from the book of those early pioneers a page
that is worth rereading now.

Under their guidance—derived from the practical
knowledge of the Indians who have crisscrossed this
country for generations—they would do well to switch
their bulldozers into renewed action northward along
the lower-level Grease Trails close to the seacoast. Here
they would proceed from Hazelton up the Kispayaks
Valley, across the low-lying headwaters of the Cranberry River, which empties into the Nass River close to
the southern Alaska border, almost within reach of Portland Canal.

Once the upper Nass River is crossed, a short distance
above the mouth of the Cranberry, the Indian trail
would lead them north along the outlet of Medziadin
Lake. This lake is the best spawning resort of the sockeye
salmon anywhere. Moving farther up this tributary of
the Nass River, called the Bell Irving River, along the
ancient trail of Déné migrations from Alaska, they
would pass the height of land between the Bell Irving and
the Iskut rivers, this last river being a tributary of the
Stikine River to the north. The height of land here lies
less than 1,500 feet above sea level, and seems to be the
greatest elevation on the whole route skirting the sea-

coast, whereas the Alcan Highway along the Liard River travels sometimes at an elevation exceeding 4,000 feet and through a much colder and snowier country.

North of this point, at Ninth Cabin, the Nass-Stikine trail ties up with the Yukon telegraph trail, only recently abandoned because of a radio substitute to the sixty-year-old wire service. Telegraph Creek, on the upper Stikine, is only a short distance off, at the terminus of a river-boat service in the summer.

The gap as the crow flies from Telegraph Creek north to the Alcan Highway, at Teslin Lake, is about 160 miles; and from the terminus of the improved provincial road north of Hazelton to the Highway the actual distance is less than six hundred miles, whereas the much greater distance of the Alcan Highway was cleared through trail-less forests and mountain tracks in less than a year!

The climate along this coastal road is on a par with that of Hazelton, which is situated 176 miles from the mouth of the Skeena River, and is eight hundred feet above sea level. The snowfall throughout the winter at Hazelton is light; it does not exceed 12 inches, and the temperature seldom drops, for brief periods, to 15 below.

Once the coast road is open from Hazelton north to Teslin Lake, and the remainder of the existing provincial highway from the American frontier is widened and improved north to Hazelton, the communications would be much shortened. They would be thrown open be-tween the states west of the Rockies and Alaska, and made less costly and far easier throughout the year.

The plan once adopted by Cyrus Field to link up Washington with Paris and London via Alaska and Bering Strait would be reborn for an epoch-making purpose under a new star.

The permanent defense of America would then carry its brand victoriously to the core of a spurious Oriental empire on the rampage and, like the beaver tooth in the hand of the ancient Wanderer of the steppes, cut off at the ankle the sinews of wanton aggression forever.

EAGLE STRIKES

THE CANOELOADS of native Alaskan migrants that once landed at Naha from the north built their village on one side of the lagoon, facing the village of Laranows on the opposite shore. For, among the Alaskans, it was the custom to have their villages in pairs, or divided in halves. A clan invariably associated with another of different extraction with whom its members intermarried, bartered, and exchanged ceremonial services.

This partnership between the clans always began with a treaty of alliance, comparable to a marriage of convenience. Both parties, bound to each other by mutual interest and various needs, usually managed to live side by side in peace and contentment. For the maintenance of justice and social equilibrium they had to follow a code of ethics, and any breach of custom or etiquette was liable to cause friction, bring about demands for redress, and sometimes bitter feuds. As if to invite complications among some of the Tlingit tribes, a third band lived in the neighborhood and had close dealings with the first two on the same footing. Here the "eternal triangle" was apt to appear on the stage for a crisis and a dramatic denouement, as happened many times in more than one place—for instance, at the beginning of the story of the Na'as of Naha Bay, near the present Loring, some twenty miles north of Ketchikan.

The Na'as — whose name means "People," in the

language of the Na, or Déné of the north, whence they
had come—seem to have been of mixed extraction, although they considered themselves as blood relatives,
firmly knit together. Marriage between their members
was barred as incestuous. Some of them were seal hunters who, like all true sea folk of the Far North, built
traps for seals in the coves; others, of inland origin,
erected salmon traps in salt water to catch salmon before
the fish had entered the river for the "run" up to the
spawning grounds at the headwaters.

As the villagers of Laranows, their allies across the
lagoon, were all a fresh-water people, their fishing stations and hunting grounds extended up the main river
and in the valleys branching off amid the mountain
ranges. Their former country was that of the wolf,
the bear, and the caribou, on the wide expanses called
On-Prairie (Larh-wiyip) of the high plateaus, to which
they went back yearly for hunting, fishing, and trading
with their nomadic kinsmen and friends.

The Na'as and the Laranows allies were not the only
ones to occupy Naha Bay. After they had journeyed
from the north and arrived there, they had encountered
the Kanhaades, a band of earlier occupants in the neighborhood. The Kanhaades, a seacoast people, like a part
of the Na'as, hunted seals and whales and fished for salmon. In common with them, they knew the ancient
tales of the supernatural Raven, or Creator, and of Adee,
the Thunderbird. A new alliance from that day bound
them all three together for good or ill, and they were as
if wed. Exogamy was enforced within each unit—that
is, its members were obliged to marry outside, into one of
the two other groups. Na'a suitors sought brides among
the Laranows or among the Kanhaades, or the reverse.

*They were paddling with all their might on the way down the coast
toward the harbor of refuge of Leesems* PAGE 56.

Now that these migrants from the north were three-fold at Naha Bay, the stage was set for their everyday life. As the Na'as and the Laranows had just arrived upon the scene and previously had long been acquainted with each other, the Kanhaades could not help but consider them intruders. In spite of their new pledges, they often fretted at the invasion. Touchy and jealous, the earlier occupants of the country required especial courtesies, in their quality of local hosts. They were not without an inferiority complex, which had resulted from earlier encroachments upon their territory by hungry raiders from the frozen tundras to the north.

It was agreed at first that the Laranows from inland would intermarry with the Na'as of the salt waters, and would share with them in the catch of salmon from the fish traps below the lagoon. As this agreement was scrupulously observed, all went well for a time between the partners. But, one day in the summer, a dispute arose among the elders on both sides over the salmon catch up the river, which the inland Laranows jealously reserved to themselves. These ancient river folk would not slacken in their resolve to keep the salt-water Na'as out of the fresh water. Still, in spite of the chief's chicanery over fishing rights, the young people went on courting and falling in love with each other as of old.

Every day a highborn suitor from Laranows crossed the suspension bridge over the river, near its mouth at the lagoon, to woo the beautiful niece of the head chief of the Na'as at the salmon weirs. And they would have married during the winter festivals had not the princess's uncle given her away, much against her inclination, to a young Kanhaade chief not too far off, to spite his up-river neighbors.

Even after the loss of his sweetheart, the Laranows
lover kept crossing the bridge to Na'a, but now at night,
in secret. Whenever her Kanhaade husband was out
hunting overnight, her lover would come over, and go
back only at dawn, when the birds twittered. Instead of
summer birds after a few moons, it was the crows and
the ravens of the long winters that awakened the be-
nighted lovers, who had between themselves defeated
the schemes of their sulking uncles.

As the husband met poor luck in the hunt, he knew
that his wife must be unfaithful. But he was not clever
enough to catch her while wrongdoing. She was ever
on the alert, and her ear and her eye were as keen as those
of the eagle; his own, in comparison, were only like the
raven's or the crow's.

To discover the cause of his failure in the hunt, he
cut a hole through the side of the lodge next to his
wife's couch, and left only the loose bark to hide a wide
opening. And, before taking off in his canoe, he bade
her, "Keep the fire burning while I go around my trap
line, I expect to catch a lone wolf." As wolves were
scarce so close to the seacoast, she knew that danger was
now near at hand, but could sound no warning to her
lover, who had seen the hunter starting on his way, with
much equipment as if for a long outing.

As soon as the Laranows night visitor had heard the
words whispered to him by his sweetheart, "The hunter
is fast on the trail of the wolf," he stood up, took his
leave, and went back home unmolested. Yet the
slighted husband, who had hastily come back by way of
the hills, was watching him through the hole in the wall.
Smarting under the insult, he refrained from an impul-
sive retaliation on the spot, for this would have aroused

the Laranows, whose superior might he cared not to defy. After sunrise, he only taunted his wife's brother, who was her keeper in his absence: "Is this the way the Na'as keep their solemn pledges?"

Touched to the quick, the brother instantly killed his sister, and taking her body over the bridge which her constant lover had so often crossed at night, he cast it off on the far side of the stream. Aware of the significance of this desperate deed, the head chief at once called his advisers in council, and, before the sun had set, he sent word to the Na'as across the lagoon:

"To blot out this smirch upon our honor, we now grant to our partners opposite the right to erect salmon traps up our river, provided they do not block the avenue to ours wherever they stand."

Quite satisfied with this concession which they had coveted for many years, the Na'as erected their traps just below those of Laranows, but their catch fell far short of their anticipation. So, at night, they moved up their traps a little at a time. The hosts were not so idle as to let the newcomers creep upon them and cut deeply into the run. They tried to push them back down the river, but to no avail.

A Na'a chief was overheard saying, "The stranglehold of the Laranows on this river has now been loosened for ever"; and another went on, "I am not yet consoled for the loss of my niece because of the inroads of a wolf in the night." In spite of these assertions, which were like straws in the wind, the river folk could not help dislodging the new traps after dark, and casting them adrift in the swift waters. The next morning, the angered Na'as had to swallow their discomfiture only because of their smaller numbers in the face of the hostile Laranows.

Even in their own village at the lagoon, the Na'as, who were in the minority, were chary of any open challenge to their neighbors opposite. Any exchange of swift blows might turn against them, and once more send them wandering down the coast. Yet in spite of all, blood revenge is an urge that cannot be stilled, save in dire extremities. And the Na'a people, in their past migrations, never had known a dead end; forever they had been on the move.

One night a brother of the beautiful young woman who had been slain crossed the river to Laranows, cut off the head of the guilty lover of his sister, and took it back home as a trophy.

This bold attack meant war, and the river folk made ready for the fray. The Na'as realized that their fate now lay in their hands; they must fight or take to flight in their dugout canoes.

The only harbor of safety for them now seemed to be the Kanhaade village, a short distance to the north. There they would tighten the alliance with their neighbors, in an effort to induce them to join in the retaliation against a common enemy. But the Laranows, aware of their intentions, swiftly attacked them, headed them off from the Kanhaade village, killed many of them, and drove the survivors to the south.

In their predicament, the Na'as dodged their pursuers, came back by stealth at night to their deserted village at the lagoon, loaded on to their large dugouts all their movable possessions, and silently prepared for a long flight down the bitter waters to save their lives. They carried on board with them a large eagle carved out of stone, and a wooden eagle. In their new trials these effigies would be like charms, as they belonged to their head chief; the stone eagle serving as an anchor, and the wooden bird having stood on his house front. They also saved their large copper shields, which, more than anything else, meant wealth and treasure. They were paddling with all their might on the way down the coast toward the harbor of refuge of Leesems—of which they had often heard in their southbound migrations, but which was still far out of sight—for they knew that they would be pursued by their powerful enemies until the craving for revenge had been appeased.

Similar trials were in store for the Na'as, now called Eagles, and the Laranows, whose name had become Wolves, after they had once more settled side by side, on the opposite sides of the creek called Tsooneh, in Tlingit territory, near the present Cape Fox in southern Alaska. The Na'a people, in a new treaty, agreed to share in halves with their new Laranows allies the seal and the salmon catches out of their traps. And they settled down once more to live in peace next to each other.

Friction very soon arose between them as to who, of the two, enjoyed the first rights over Tsooneh Creek. And disputes marred the harmony to the point of arousing anger and resentment. The chief of the Wolves, whose wife was an Eagle of the highest rank, came back home one day fuming with anger, and, as his dinner was not ready, he clubbed her over the head and wounded her right arm with his spear.

Much weakened, the Eagle woman was only able to drag herself out of the house, over the bridge, across to her own people's lodge, where she sought refuge and protection. After having accused her husband of cruelty in the presence of her uncle, Wa'amak, she fell dead.

The torch was lit over her head, and she held it up while her husband retired to his couch PAGE 67.

Her body was hidden, and word at once went around, "Hush, do not weep! Keep it all a dead secret!" Her brother went across the creek to her husband's cabin, and said, "Rest assured! My sister is on her way to prompt recovery. But she wants her carved chest from the far corner." And he went back with the box, while all eyes were turned on him.

Another brother, who closely resembled the slain woman, cut her long hair, made braids out of it, and tied the braids around his head. Out of caribou skins he had tight-fitting garments sewn for himself, within which he hid a deadly double-bladed knife. Over these he placed his sister's blood-stained dress, and he smeared his face with red ocher and gum, to have it look like his sister's after the assault—their features being quite similar, and their build the same. Then he lay down, as his sister would have, slowly to recover of the wounds inflicted by her husband. His name, Larh-kae, has been remembered to this day.

As the people of her tribe had suppressed all signs of grief after disposing of her dead body, the guilty husband, much reassured, sent two slaves with small gifts to console her and find out how soon she would come back. She looked comfortable, sitting in her corner, although her face seemed badly battered, while her uncle fed and entertained the messengers, who went back home without suspecting the deceit.

"The woman is well on her way to recovery," they reported cheerfully to their master.

They went back, a few days later, carrying armfuls of caribou furs and copper shields in compensation for the breach of etiquette, and were glad to hear the Eagle chief say to his niece, "Woman, your injury has been

wiped out. You may go back to your husband, as if
nothing had happened."

Larh-kae, the brother, impersonating her to perfec-
tion, went to her habitual couch, which had been made
ready and sprinkled with eagle's down, meaning peace
and good will, and he lay down as if exhausted. At night
the husband slept quietly beside him, but not for very
long. For the disguised intruder cut off his head with
the double-bladed dagger and silently remained for a
while fixing the pelts. He raised the blanket cloaks to
simulate the actual bodies of the estranged pair, just as
if nothing had happened to them after their reunion;
then he slipped away into the stillness of a dark night.

The household, after awakening in the morning,
moved about quietly to avoid disturbing them. But
their strange stillness finally aroused attention. Before
midday, the truth dawned upon them all, and their fury
instantly cried aloud for revenge.

The brave Larh-kae, being the Eagle chief's eldest
nephew, put on his armor of tough sea-lion hide and, over
it, his costume of white ermine. In the opposite village,
meanwhile, the eldest nephew of the Wolf chief donned
his Grizzly-Bear cloak, surmounted by the bear's head,
whose eyes and ears were of haliotis shell from the deep
sea.

The two young warriors then faced each other across
the creek, while their chiefs and tribes stood behind them
clamoring. The murder, according to an ancient custom, could be expiated only by single combat between
the bloodthirsty champions now standing on the bridge.

After a hair-raising battle over midstream, the Eagle
overcame the Wolf, cut off his head, and picked up his
fallen headdress, with the shrieks of a bald eagle sub-

duing its prey. And his tribe joined him in wild shrieks,
as was their own privilege. The victor in that memorable duel had won for himself and his posterity the
famous Grizzly-Bear hat adorned with opalescent shells
which, until then, had been the appanage of the proud
Wolves of the Alaskan rivers.

In the fight that followed for days between the two
warring tribes, the Eagles slowly gave way to greater
numbers and made ready for one more flight down the
coast. They built a large raft, on which they loaded
their most valuable possessions: the carved post representing the fin of the shark, the large stone eagle, which
they placed behind the large round stone egg of the
eagle, the smaller stone eagle, and the four nests of live
eagles raised by the chief's household and kept as pets
on the four corners of the house. The house, for this
reason, was called the "Eagle's Nest House." After they
had lashed these totems together on the raft, the people
took to their large dugout canoes, towed the raft after
them, and started on their renewed flight toward the
famed Leesems.

The intermittent fighting between the Na'as, the
Laranows, and the Kanhaades went back to a number
of causes that usually lay dormant, as if under warm
ashes. When, at times, friction broke out anew, it
kindled somber fires of hatreds and led the underdogs to
resume a flight that was like a habitual pattern to them—
a flight blindly aiming at a destination to the south,
where wealth and blessings awaited them at the end of
countless trials.

As all these migrants retained haunting recollections
of an earthly paradise where their ancestors had enjoyed

a golden age, they always hoped to return to a blissful existence, even though they were all the time drifting farther and farther away from the cradle of the race. Their "good land" of yore made them only the more anxious to reach, some day, the bountiful country which, they were told, was lying ahead like a promised land.

They were not always pursued, but felt drawn ahead while migrating southward. This was emphasized by the old Niskae chief, Mountain, when he said, "Our people often are called 'Fugitives.' But it does not mean that they were fleeing enemies. They were only looking for Leesems."

The fear of an enemy hot on their tracks remained a great stimulus, even though that enemy was a former ally, mostly of their own blood and language. The feuds of the Na'as and the Laranows were the latest episodes in a series of dog fights that harked back to the dim past. Other episodes out of their epic traditions will presently help to clarify their collective mind as to the fairly uniform trends of their drift from the north, along the seacoast or down the rivers to the coast.

The Na'as at Larhsail, who were called Fugitives and deserved the name, were forced into flight because of their witchcraft practices. Wa'amak, their head chief, had bewitched his ally the Kanhaade chief and caused his death by sorcery. The clan of the victim made ready for retaliation. As Wa'amak's supporters were in the minority, they had no choice but to embark in search of another foothold somewhere else. The Na'as of other families, who dissociated themselves from the affair and would not join in the flight, suffered the consequences.

The three clans that had halted along the salt waters below the mouth of the Stikine had previously dwelt side by side at the head of this mountain river. There they had lived long enough to lapse into intrigue, such as was familiar to them, and to fall out with their allies. A quarrel was blamed upon the Kanhaades, who in those days resented the superiority of the Wolves, the greatest of all inland hunters.

The power of the Wolves rested upon the countless pelts which they secured in the hunt and on the salmon catch out of the main river in the neighborhood of Water-of-Big-Stream—now Thuya Creek. Far from generously sharing their possessions with their allies as they might have done, they edged them off their hunting grounds and their fishing stations. They would not even let the Na'as stationed on an inland creek come too near, save for the barter of furs and commodities.

Driven together for a common cause by their opponents, the Kanhaades and the Na'as made a secret pact against the greedy Laranows clan.

The next winter, when the Wolf chief, Kalowt, and his nephews went around their trap lines they found no fur-bearing game, but only fresh blood on the snow. Meat and blood, but no furs! This happened repeatedly for several moons, until the Wolf hunters seethed with rage while trying to discover the shadowy robber of their trap line and deadfalls. Kalowt would have no pelts for barter that year, and his reputation as the best hunter in the country would suffer; deep humiliation and even ridicule would descend upon him. Gritting his teeth, he grumbled to his nephew, "A thief in the dark has laid his foul hands upon my traps, but I'll find his tracks and pounce upon him."

After his traps were reset, Kalowt went into hiding
behind a cliff near one of them. A mink was caught, one
morning, but for several days no one appeared on the
trail, and the waiting was dull and painful. But at last
his patience was rewarded, as a Na'a hunter—not a Kanhaade as he had expected—tramped forth in the deep
snow, took up the mink, skinned it, threw back the remains, and walked away muttering, "The pelt for me;
only the meat for Kalowt!"

No sooner had Kalowt come back home than he
summoned his nephews and told them, "The eagles
always have preyed upon wild rabbits in their warrens;
our upriver neighbors likewise. I have seen one of them
steal a mink pelt out of my trap. It shall be his last."

An experienced warrior like Kalowt, to make doubly
sure of victory, never rushes into a fight. So he explained: "The Na'as and the Kanhaades are trying to
provoke us into a fight for which they have prepared.
Let us bide our time! They are now close together in
their winter quarters. In a few moons, when the buds
sprout, the Kanhaades are bound to move out to their
own streams, and fish by themselves. Then will be the
right moment to look for them."

But the young men would not listen to slow wisdom.
They said, "The thieves with a crooked bill have fouled
our traps. The power is ours, their punishment must not
wait another day!" This turn was exactly what the
plotting allies had hoped for and foreseen.

The next morning, before dawn, the Wolf warriors
fell upon the Na'as, whom they expected to find sound
asleep. Instead, they were up and waiting. While the
fight was on, the Kanhaades, who spied a chance, raided
the Wolf camp, broke into the lodges, slaughtered the

occupants, captured some women, and set fires everywhere. Alarmed by the warning given by a few fugitives, the Wolf warriors up the river left off in the
middle of the battle, swiftly took to their dugouts, and
fled downstream.

The victorious Na'as followed on their heels, until
they all arrived within sight of a huge glacier bridging the
river, under which the water flowed through a cave-like
tunnel. The least daring in the caravan decided to
tramp their way overland through the mountains toward
the Leesems headwaters. But Kalowt, his oldest nephews,
and some of his nieces plunged headlong through the ice
passage and reached safely the smooth waters beyond it.
They did not pause very long at their camp below the
glacier, but went down to the tide flats, where they sojourned for years and joined in hunting the sea otter
with the coast tribes.

After a while they moved down the water front to
Larhsail—now Cape Fox—and then still farther, to join
the tribe of Work Channel in the Tsimsyan country,
and later the Killer-Whale tribe on an island between
the mouth of the Skeena River and the Queen Charlotte
Islands. And this was only one of a number of clans
drifting down in a ceaseless trek toward the midday sun.

After their easy victory over Kalowt on the upper
Stikine, the Na'as fell out among themselves over the
spoils. A branch of the clan (the Men'esk faction) left
the village, journeyed over the hills and back to the
river, where they built canoes and traveled down it
until, in their turn, they came to the great glacier. There
they stopped, terrified. But, as they were pursued by
their own tribe, they must go forward or perish. So
they re-embarked in their canoes and, confronted with

*The northern nomads have swept southward, all of them in the
direction of a better land* PAGE 71.

death, they paddled their way through the whirling
stream to safety.

Another tradition of the Na'as, that of the Salmon-
Eater clan in the three northern nations of the coast,
takes us to a legendary period as far back as memory can
reach—that is, to the time of the flood. It begins with six
canoeloads of people sailing out of the ocean into calm
waters, at the edge of what is now called Bering Sea. As
soon as the wind began to blow, the mists vanished, and
land came into sight. This land must have been the
Aleutian Islands, at the southern rim of Bering Sea. The
people then set foot ashore, established their first camp,
met the Grizzly-Bear people who occupied the country,
made friends with them and took them as allies or partners, and found existence here much to their liking.

Their camp grew into a village, and Salmon-Eater
(Githawn), the chief, had a cap of cormorant made for
himself out of the skin and feathers of cormorants, and
for many years he wore it on his head whenever it rained.

After the Salmon-Eater tribe had learned the language
of the new land and relinquished its own, the people
mingled more freely together. The nephew of Ka'it, the
head chief of the Grizzly-Bear clan, aspired to marry
Salmon-Eater's niece, Selarhkons, the first princess in the
land, and sent messengers with a proposal for her. No
sooner had the chiefs agreed about the marriage than
Ka'it prepared for the event.

As she was of high standing, messengers went for her
with twin canoes. She proudly sat on the boards laid
across the top of the canoes and was brought by sea to
the home of her suitor's uncle. There the messengers
placed her near the bridegroom, and gave her fresh food.

Everyone admired Selarhkons' beauty and the splendor
of the raiment she had brought with her: a wide robe of
sea otter, a fine robe of young sea otter, a chief's all-over
parka, and a robe of smooth leather decorated with valuable tsik shells from the sea. As the attire of a woman of
distinction, in those early days, consisted of breeches only
and four robes to be worn over them, her breeches were
made of soft leather with a golden tan.

Female attendants combed her hair, which was fine
and glossy, and spread out a couch for her near that of
the bridegroom, the prince of the Grizzly-Bear tribe,
who would be there all night to keep her company.

In the house of the bridegroom, at night, she was
bidden to sit down and hold up a pitchwood torch. The
torch was lit over her head, as she held it up while her
husband retired to his couch. When all others but
Selarhkons had gone, he went to sleep without seeming
to be aware of her presence. There she sat motionless
overnight, and the pitchwood torch slowly burned down
to the level of her hand. To shield her hand from the
slowly burning fire she had to cover it with her robe,
which, this night, was the one adorned with tsik shells.
She kept pulling her robe up and rolling part of it
around her exposed hand to protect it, until the upper
end of the robe was scorched like the torch. Then she
took off her robe altogether, and lay on it the rest of
the night, with the ashes of the burned torch beside her.

When Ka'it sent for her in the morning, she put on
her second dress and went to her father-in-law's house
for a meal, while her husband slept far into the day.

"Why do you, fool, so abuse your bride?" the chief
asked his nephew. "Her uncle, Salmon-Eater, cannot be
insulted with impunity. I predict more tribulations for
us than we can foresee, because of your rashness."

The nephew ignored all warnings until, after the fourth night, Selarhkons' last robe was burned, and Ka'it had another hastily made for her in the simple style of his own Grizzly-Bear clan. This homely robe she refused to wear, and she preferred staying naked in the proud nobility of her birth.

When, on the fourth morning, Salmon-Eater and his attendants came over with trays of food for the marriage feast according to the *lugyin* rule, they beheld the noble Selarhkons still holding up the remnants of the dead torch near the sleeping bridegroom. Incensed by her humiliation, they returned to their village and prepared for revenge. During their absence, Selarhkons disappeared by enchantment.

The war broke out with fury between the two tribes— the first, which had come out of the ocean, and the second, the Grizzly-Bear tribe. After torrents of blood had been shed on both sides, the survivors scattered into the forest, and the Salmon-Eater clan began to search the woods for their princess. Far away they found a tall granite statue in her image, standing over a creek at the head of an island lake, her legs planted one on each side of the stream. Of this stream she was the source.

Struck with awe in her presence, they prayed to her as they would to the spirit of the lake, which was alive with trout. Salmon-Eater's eldest nephew, Kawm, donned his uncle's cormorant cap, as was the privilege of a nephew in line for his succession. But the aged uncle warned him, "This cap should no longer be worn, for it may not be to your grandmother's pleasure. A new danger, I feel, is now in store for us."

The story of the curse brought down upon this lake near Bering Sea by the cormorant cap forms part of the lengthy tribal traditions that have come down from the dim past to the present day. In the course of blistering trials, spirit frogs with copper eyes and mouths leaped out of the campfire, and Salmon-Eater's nephews were about to board their canoe in flight when a flash of lightning stopped them short. Selarhkons, now changed into a supernatural woman, walked out of the mountains that were ablaze. In her underlip glowed a wide labret, and in her hand she held a staff with a carved frog for a handle. Salmon-Eater's niece, who had become an impersonation of the fire and the frog, cried out, "Because of your rashness you shall die."

So it came to pass. The only survivor was Las, a nephew of Salmon-Eater, who dodged the sight of the fiery statue, as he was hiding at the bottom of the canoe. In his flight he went back to his people at the edge of the sea and spread the tale of destruction in the path of the Volcano Woman of the inland lake.

While the Na'as slept one night, a huge fireball descended upon their village and reduced it to ashes. The people perished, all but a princess, who, like the other maidens of her rank, stayed in her puberty seclusion on a hill, hidden in a hut made of copper shields. Her only food, in a prolonged fast, was dried halibut and a little whale blubber, and her only beverage was spring water sipped through the hollow leg bone of a crane. After the destruction of the village, she walked down the heights and over the ruins, to find only stone axes, adzes, and stone pots in the warm ashes. Heartbroken, she gathered them and heaped them up in a pile. A short distance below the village, she saw that the seven canoes of her uncles were still intact and covered up with green boughs. There she sat and cried her heart out.

She was still sitting there when an old woman approached the ruined village and intoned a dirge, "Yeanawhaw—our war canoe travels over the ocean."

As she sang, her head remained covered down to the eyes with a wide-brimmed hat of split spruce roots. On top of her hat sat a copper frog, and the hat was trimmed all round with small frogs. In her hand the woman held a staff carved with human faces; the handle of the staff was of copper. The dirge was the frog mourning song, which is still preserved among the many descendants of Salmon-Eater down the Alaskan coast to the Skeena River: "Our war canoe travels over the ocean."

As the princess still sat entranced near the canoes, she gazed out to sea. There, a long way off, she beheld a sail made of matting—an *ahlarom-skane*. A canoe approached, and six hunters—one of whom was an old man and another a slave—landed in the cove, where they were dismayed to find only brownish ashes. The village they had known existed no longer. Before re-embarking, they discovered the princess. They wanted to take her along with them, away from this scene of desolation. But she refused to leave her uncle's canoes behind. Yielding to her wishes, they dragged them out to tidewater and towed them along. In one of these canoes the princess sat by herself wearing the cormorant cap, which she had saved. All along the way she sang the dirge of the Frog Woman: "Selarhkons is the volcano spirit to whom my people owe their fate."

She was married to Kyem-neak, the chief of the tribe that had rescued her. She bore him a son, who upheld the leading name of her uncle, Salmon-Eater; then a daughter, named Skya'an; and eight other children, who safeguarded the posterity of Salmon-eater.

Wherever the Na'as came from, down the rivers or along the seacoast, they have preserved in their oral traditions significant traces of the past, like those contained in the episodes of the Naha lagoon and Tsooneh Creek, of Wa'amak at Larhsail, of the intrigues against Kalowt on the upper Stikine River, and of Salmon-Eater and his niece, Selarhkons. Although these samples are only fragments out of vast backgrounds, they tell an unmistakable story: the northern nomads have swept southward, as the rain runs down from a roof, all of them in the direction of a better land, and the origin of their race, language, and culture was Asiatic.

The exogamous moieties of their ancestors in northeastern Siberia—the Chukchee, the Koriaks, the Gilyaks, the Kets, and others—continued in existence among their nomadic kinsmen after they had crossed Bering Sea into America.[1] Everywhere the Na'as of Alaska stood in pairs with the Laranows; they traveled more or less together. Or, in places, their choice was between two alternatives, as they were often confronted with the Kanhaades, a third group, who had been the early occupants. All these people, Siberian and American, were non-totemic—that is, their names were not totemic, and they knew of no mystic connection with patronymic totems or heraldic animals. It is only after the newcomers in Alaska had journeyed far and long that their outlook underwent a change and they began to assume symbolic crests in the manner of the European nobility.

As in Siberia, some of them were a coast people by heredity, hunters of whales and sea otters and experts at maneuvering skin canoes or bidarkas and large dug-

---

[1] Roman Jakobson, "The Paleosiberian Languages," *American Anthropologist,* Oct.-Dec., 1942, p. 607.

outs. Others were inland folk and forest hunters, roving the tundras of the hinterland along the valleys. They built weirs for seals in the coves, as did the Na'as of the Naha lagoon; in their skin canoes they hunted whales with harpoons and floats made out of sea-lion stomachs; and they relished blubber and seal grease—like Selarhkon's daughter, whose diet, when fasting, included "a little whale blubber," along with dried halibut and smoked salmon.

Among the Paleosiberians, marriage was arranged by the parents according to their rank, their means, and the interests at stake; the suitor met with tests at the hands of the bride's parents; and the infidelity of the wife brought down blood revenge, unless the honor and pride of the husband were well restored by compensations.

Grievances between tribes often were settled by single-hand combats between selected champions—as in the case of Larh-kae, who donned an armor of sea-lion hide, whereas his opponent on the bridge wore a Grizzly-Bear cloak.

Witchcraft and the black arts of shamanism were prevalent, although not professional, as in Siberia.[2] The episode of Wa'amak, who had bewitched a Kanhaade chief, might have happened in Siberia, just as it did in Alaska. Dreaded and resented, sorcery was secretly practiced by individuals on both sides of Bering Sea.

The custom of falling upon an enemy when he was sound asleep, as in the attack of Kalowt against the Na'as on the upper Stikine, was the usual method of warfare among the Dénés and everywhere in the sub-Arctic regions.

A racial inferiority complex prevailed among the

----

[2] *Ibid.*

Paleosiberians; it was the result of repeated invasions and defeats suffered at the hands of the ever expanding Mongolians and Tartars. The crucial period for them had been during the depredations of the Tartar, Genghis Khan, in the early thirteenth century. This famous conqueror, the greatest of all time, overwhelmed them and chased their remnants away from the center to the edges of the continent in the northeast toward Kamchatka and the Arctic. Some of the Fugitives of Alaska were an offshoot, one of the most recent, of the same primitive stock, then broken up into isolated bands and cast adrift close to Bering Sea.

The fears of the Fugitives—which, during the winter, among the Dénés of the North, had degenerated into blind terror and hallucinations—were everywhere coupled with the haunting dream of a golden age now lost and a longing for the bountiful land to the south. This land of promise for Genghis Khan (much nearer the source) was the Celestial Empire of China, whereas for the Na'as and the Laranows, closer to us, it was Leesems, down the seacoast.

Salmon-Eater and his band, sailing out of the ocean onto a coast inhabited by the Grizzly-Bear tribe, were among the latest to leave Asia for America, only a few hundred years ago, not long before the Russians invaded eastern Siberia in force.

The cormorant cap which Salmon-Eater wore under the rain at the edge of the sea, the sea-otter robes of his niece, Selarhkons, and her tanned leather breeches and dress decorated with shells, were waterproof parkas of the type familiar to the prehistoric traders across Bering Sea. These garments were normal for a northeastern Asiatic, yet to the less cultured Grizzly-Bear

tribe of Alaska they were wonderful. When destroyed
by fire they could not be replaced. Those offered in
replacement to Selarhkons were not acceptable. She
refused them, preferring to remain naked in the sight
of all, and, in her utter distress, to turn to stone in the
forest.

The boards laid across the top of two canoes as a seat
for the bride, in the Salmon-Eater tradition, remind one
of the *pirogues doubles ou liées*—double dugouts, or dugouts lashed together—of which Father Petitot speaks in
his *Dictionnaire de la langue Dènè-Dindjié*[3] These double
canoes, unknown on this side of Bering Sea except in the
traditions of the northernmost Dénés, were a common
device in coastal navigation on the Asiatic side of the
Pacific Ocean as far south as the tropical seas.

The sail made of matting which the recluse princess,
at the time of the volcanic eruption, saw coming to her
from the sea was also an unfamiliar object on this side
of the ocean. The prehistoric American natives never
used sails of their own, and the one which brought the
saviors of the recluse seems to have been a sail woven of
bulrushes, common along the seacoast of Japan, China,
and other countries to the south.

The conical hat, woven of split spruce roots, of the old
Frog Woman is a very ordinary headdress in Asia; it is a
Mongolian cultural feature. Later it was used deriva-
tively among the North Pacific Coast nations.

The mythical frog in the Selarhkons story, coupled
as it is with the starfish among the Tlingits and the Tsimsyans, is an Asiatic concept. Although the frog is not
found in sub-Arctic Siberia, the Siberians have borrowed it from the south, where it is familiar. Jochelson,

---

[3] P. xxxi.

the Russian ethnographer exiled in Siberia, found frogs
represented there in carved amulets, as a theme in Yukaghir mythology, and in the form of decorative designs,
among the Gilyaks and the Chukchees. But the ancestors of the Salmon-Eater clan are more likely to have
acquired this frog concept nearer its sources, on the seacoast of Japan or China.

Selarhkons changing to a tall granite statue and giving
birth to a creek, which henceforth issues from her, is not
American, but strangely reminiscent of the theme of
divine rivers in Asia and in classical Europe. This motive
to this day has remained un-American among the natives.

The stone axes and adzes which the recluse princess
picked up in the ruins of her burned village belong to a
stone age more typically American than Asiatic. Yet
the Paleosiberians were a Neolithic people who knew of
copper and iron, which they hammered in a cold state.
The stone dishes in the ruins carry us back to the
stone dishes and lamps of the Eskimos of northern
Alaska and the Aleuts of the Bering Sea islands.

Dirge songs commemorating a tragic event, and sung
at the death of the chiefs to whom they belong, are
Buddhistic in character. They have remained unknown
to any American tribe save in a small area in the far
Northwest. An echo of rituals for the dead, they have
been introduced from outside into the Tlingit, the
Haida, and the Tsimsyan country. They presuppose the
transmigration of souls to the other world and their
eventual rebirth into a new body in the same family.

Selarhkons herself was none but the legendary Copper
and Volcano Woman very well known all over the
North. She was the mythical person who, according to
the native belief, used to cross the sea and bring red

copper and iron to the American natives. One day, according to Father Petitot, the Dénés had ill-treated her, and she had ceased to come to them. Finally she had sunk underground amid volcanoes belching fire and lava, and leaving traces of her blood in the form of copper nuggets. Not only has the fame of this supernatural ancestress traveled to most of the Dénés west and east of the Mackenzie River, and even to some central Eskimos, but it has also escorted the Na'a people of the same racial and linguistic stock across Alaska to the south. It has traversed the Tlingit country southward, to take root among the Haidas of the Queen Charlotte Islands and the Tsimsyans of the Nass and the Skeena rivers.

The cluster of cultural features embodied in the Salmon-Eater traditions plainly shows that here we are confronted with a seacoast people whose original focus once belonged somewhere on the eastern coast of Asia and was in the outlying parts of the Mongolian world.

The most direct and easiest path of migration for these newcomers into America was the unbroken chain of Aleutian Islands, onward from Bering Island close to Kamchatka. And earlier rings in the chain of antecedents can be traced back southward to the Kurile Islands, north of Japan.

The twin canoes, the sail of matting, the cap of cormorant, the sea otter, the volcano, copper, divine river, and frog themes, the Buddhistic dirges, the Chinese-like hats woven of split spruce roots, the dentalium shells, the preferences of the princess for "a little whale blubber" along with dried halibut, in the Selarhkons narratives, are one and all like pointers in the sole direction of the balmy Asiatic coast within the periphery of an ancient Chinese culture.

"On my way down from Aks-taqhl, the face of the Thunderbird floating about on the waters never ceased to escort me" PAGE 83.

Significant details in this cultural cluster are drawn from the Aleutian region rather than from the more remote and frigid northern route of entry into America via Bering Strait, trodden by the Chukchees, the Dénés, and the Eskimos of the northern tundras and frozen seas.

Where did Salmon-Eater obtain the cormorant skins out of which his headdress was made? Certainly not at East Cape, on the Siberian side of Bering Strait, for none of the four existing varieties of cormorants exist there. The only resort of the famed spectacled cormorant (extinct for nearly a hundred years through extermination) was Bering Island, much farther south, close to Kamchatka and the westernmost Aleutian Islands. The three other varieties of smaller cormorants (double-crested, pelagic, and urile) are quite at home in the Aleutian Islands and Kamchatka; the double-crested is found no farther north than the islands, and the last two fall short of the strait. Their northernmost representatives stop at Norton Sound.

This was also true of the sea otter, and of the other geographical and cultural features, like the dentalium shell ornaments, contained in the Salmon-Eater's narratives. Had this ancestor and his niece, Selarhkons, originated in the Arctic Circle and crossed the sea at Bering Strait, they would not have donned garments of cormorant and of sea otter decorated with dentalium, as they did, to the wonder of the Grizzly-Bear natives of the new world. They would have worn reindeer parkas instead, as in northern Siberia, or they would have readily accepted their equivalent in caribou.

These newcomers upon Alaskan soil could not have been of pure Eskimo, Chukchee, Koriak, or Tartar stocks of the Far North and the interior, as were those migrants who were in the habit of crossing Bering Strait and moving into the Yukon River basin eastward. For they were squat, short, and bowlegged, like hereditary canoe folk. Their features were strikingly Mongolian, as they still are along the North Pacific coast as far south as the Fraser River. And they lived off the sea, hunting seals, sea lions, and whales, eating shellfish, seaweed, dried herring eggs, and using kelp. Their canoes were made of wooden frames, with skin covers in the north, or dugouts, according to the natural resources of the coast.

Should they have crossed the sea at Bering Strait, they would not have known of twin canoes and sails of matting, for these belong only to the Asiatic coast below Kamchatka; their memories would not have been haunted by reminiscences of live volcanoes, as they were apt to be in the Aleutian region. The suitor of the princess, Selarhkons, besides, would have been a caribou or polar-bear hunter rather than a member of the Grizzly-Bear clan. The resorts of this bear are the forests, mountains, and northern barren lands, rather than the frozen moss-beds of the sub-Arctic wastelands.

In the treeless region of Bering Strait there would have been no resinous torch made out of spruce bark at the bedside of the Grizzly-Bear bridegroom, who was obviously of mixed extraction, just as the Aleutians all were—partly Kamchatkan, Mongolian, Eskimo, perhaps with an element of Chukchee and Koriak. His wish to sleep while the light was burning overnight was an Eskimo and Aleutian trait—Eskimos never sleep in the darkness: this would mean death. But to his wife and her people, this imposition on her to hold up a burning torch to produce light, in the absence of a self-feeding stone lamp, meant offense and cruelty; it led on to disaster.

For us all these details definitely establish the respective
identity of the Salmon-Eater and the Grizzly-Bear allies. They belonged to the Alaskan mainland in the
neighborhood of Kodiak and the Mount St. Elias area.
And their island pathways into America were the same
as had previously led other coastal fishers from Asia,
step by step, in small groups onto the Kurile Islands
north of Japan first, onward across the Aleutian chain,
all within sight of each other, until they had set foot
on the mainland to the west, and had pursued the same
course southward as Salmon-Eater and his canoeloads
of Leesems-seekers.

Once on their trek down the American seacoast, the
scattered Na'a bands met with experiences that are
recounted in epic tales (called *adaorh*), most of which
have assumed allegorical forms. Here, as elsewhere, we
find many haunting vestiges of the past in Asia, and, if
our numerous records of these recollections differ in
detail, they agree in substance.

The Na'as were of two or three branches. Some came
from the northwest, some down the coast, others inland
over the tundras. On their path south, not a few stayed
behind—some near the lakes at the headwaters of the
White River, others in the many villages of the Tlingit
from Yakutat down to Prince of Wales Island.

One of their leading clans, that of Salmon-Eater and
Selarhkons, proceeded to the Queen Charlotte Islands
and beyond. It played a leading part in the activities
and the arts of the Haidas and the Tsimsyans. Perhaps
the majority of these sea folk sought their way into the
promised land of Leesems, which to them was the Nass
estuary, where, every spring and summer, shoals of

candlefish and salmon rise from the depths. More of the Na'as, the true fugitives from the North, hastened beyond the Nass and established themselves at the Gitsalas canyon of the Skeena River and elsewhere. And, last but not least, an offshoot of this most recent Siberian horde journeyed as far south as Vancouver Island, palming itself off as of royal blood. Stone-Cliff (Legyarh) and his henchmen belonged to this venturesome band. They were to play a leading role in the history of New Caledonia and British Columbia.

The last phase of the Na'a trek unfolded itself after the coming of the white man, in the latter part of the eighteenth century and in the early nineteenth. Vanguards on the move thrust forward with the help of firearms secured in the early fur trade. Belated elements, from 1850 to the present, went on peacefully infiltrating the nations to the south. Some Tlingits, for instance, moved hundreds of miles south to the Kwakiutl country in the neighborhood of Alert Bay. George Hunt, the well-known informant and interpreter, belonged to one of their intrusive families; and Paul, a Haida silver carver of the present generation there, presumably is a kinsman of the educated Tlingit leaders of the same name and ancestry in Alaska.

After the Eagle pursuers of Kalowt had passed under the glacier in their descent of the Stikine River to the ocean, they met with experiences which are still remembered by their descendants on the upper Nass (in the Men'esk households), and they acquired new totems or emblems. Contrary to our current notions, these Na'a people until then had not possessed any heraldic symbols; in their customs and outlook they had been wholly non-totemic.

Their explanation of the late origin of these innovations, in one of many traditional narratives, is: "When the Men'esk canoe of the Na'as reached the salt water, the paddlers beheld a monster on the shore; and they stopped in front of it. It was the Kyae-alren, a fantastic bird standing in shallow water. The insides of its open wings were human-like faces."

The beholders of this supernatural being broke into dirge songs for a commemoration, and they took this giant bird for a crest. Then they went on their way farther down the coast.

They lost their breath soon again, at the sight of a huge house surmounted by a great eagle with outspread wings. The Haida chief, North-Wind, and his folk, who owned it, were moving in and out of the doorway. They came forward and invited the newcomers to come in, saying: "You, too, are Eagles. For this reason you are welcome to dwell with us here." Drawn ashore, the river folk entered the Eagle household of their coast relatives.

The Eagle hosts and their guests soon fell out, and the upriver newcomers who had accepted hospitality, were forced to take flight. Farther south they landed at the mouth of a creek, where they built a salmon trap. They were joined by Neesyoq, an old ally of the Laranows moiety.

When the Neesyoq Wolves were caught pilfering the salmon traps of the Eagles one day, they pretended to be Grizzly-Bear spirits, and, to save their face, they murdered the Eagle fishermen who had caught them red-handed. That day they emptied the salmon traps. This crime, as soon as discovered, called for revenge.

Eagle fishermen disguised themselves as women, wear-

ing skirts and bosom wrappers. In the morning, when
a Wolf spy wearing the skin of a grizzly approached the
chief's house, an Eagle dressed as a woman walked out
and clubbed him. Inside the bear armor he uncovered
the dead body of a Wolf chief, and, standing over his
body, he composed a dirge. This deed entitled the Eagles
to assume Grizzly-Bear-Man as a crest.

The coast in this neighborhood was too barren to
provide these rovers with a good living, and they suffered poverty and starvation. On the move again and
looking for Leesems, they came upon new supernatural
experiences that furnished them with dirges and symbolic crests. The famed Gyeabelk, or spirit of the
Thunderbird, was the first and foremost. A dirge
marked its entry into existence as a totem. And, at the
death of Men'esk—the head chief at Village-of-Lagoons
on the upper Nass—this dirge still commemorates the
unique apparition. It consists of the words: "On my way
down to Aks-taqhl, the face of the Thunderbird floating about on the waters never ceased to escort me."

Men'esk, still in the presence of the Thunderbird,
summoned two of his nephews to draw its picture so
as to preserve it in paint. These craftsmen, after several
days of effort, produced the likeness of the bird by
painting its head, wings, and tail, and covering the
wings inside and the fanlike tail with childlike faces. It
was the spirit of the deep sea. As soon as they had
finished, the exultant chief proclaimed: "This shall be
my totem." And so it has remained ever since.

Forever in search of Leesems, the fugitives next encountered on the seacoast the royal bird with two heads
back to back on a single body—the split eagle. They
also adopted it as an emblem.

From the Men'esk *adaorh* we now pass to the tradition, still more explicit, of the old chief, Mountain, on the lower Nass River. Asked fifteen years ago to explain the totem pole of the Eagle at the deserted village of Gyeetiks, the tallest in existence (eighty-one feet high), Mountain named from memory the fifteen heraldic figures carved one above the other along its tall shaft, and he told with great exaltation—he almost chanted it —the story of their origin. A part of this epic is:

"Six canoes loaded with our ancestors once landed outside Klawaq [on what is now Prince of Wales Island, in southern Alaska]. They meant to settle down there, but they failed to make a living. Not knowing where they were at the time, they decided to go on moving down the coast until they would find Leesems. During their migration in the canoes, some of them died, others were born. For two moons they paddled, and arrived at Saneenae, a place which other people before them had left vacant, having drifted farther off toward the sun.

"While they sojourned at Saneenae, Aitl, one of the young men, went down, at ebb tide, to the shore for shellfish. A big stone, with cavities under it, stood exposed. With a long stick he poked into the holes that were filled with water, to see whether any fish happened to hide there. Something snapped at the stick. He could not pull it out, as a huge devilfish with many suckers, and very powerful, was holding it fast.

"To make sure of not missing it, Aitl tried to capture it with his hands, but the monster with his mighty tentacles caught him instead and tried to pull him in. To protect himself he held with one hand the rock near him, but the two valves of a large shellfish—a *kal'un*—

clinging to the crevices in the stone at once closed on his fingers. When a man finds himself in this predicament, he knows that he is lost, for the *kal-un* is large and deadly; it never gives up its prey.

"The tide was already rising when his brothers, noticing his plight, came down to his rescue. They stood there, awe-stricken, at a loss what to do, as the arm of their kinsman was caught fast. In haste they soaked a seal stomach pouch, inflated it, and attached it to him, to serve as a float on the rising tide. In despair, he spoke to them in Tlingit, as this was then the language of our ancestors, 'Cry for me!' These words he kept on repeating in the face of the on-coming sea. They have, in the Tlingit language, become a dirge for us: '*Hiyanawhae* . . . Cry for me!'

"While the drowning Aitl and his clan were singing this dirge, the tide rose past him and he was lost. When it fell back, his body, removed by force, was burned on a pyre, and his ashes were buried on the shore.

"This calamity made the people re-embark in their canoes and paddle more doggedly than ever on their way. In their flight toward the unknown, they toiled with their paddles day and night, as they had no sail. Now they arrived at Ahlk-nebaeh, south of the Stikine River. Then they by-passed the Tongas Narrows.

"As, at the Narrows, the salmon were plentiful, the sockeye most of all, they caught some and roasted them on the beach. The day was sunny and warm. It was so fine that the Fugitives, for the first time in many days, relaxed, and Gunas, a young man, went into the water to swim. A giant halibut rose from the bottom and swallowed him. After he had disappeared, his family searched for him, but without finding the slightest

trace of his body. An eagle swooped down to the edge
of the water, looking for fish, and the fishermen saw a
huge halibut rising there to the surface, as if to meet the
bird. They caught the halibut and cut it open. In its
stomach they found the body of Gunas, their dead relative; his flesh had already decayed. A copper shield surrounded his neck like a collar. Gunas' uncle stood at the
head of the fish and began to lament his nephew's death.

"Here are the words of his dirge, which have become
traditional in the Fugitive clan: 'This is the place where
we encountered the supernatural halibut.'

"Gunas' body was cremated, his ashes were buried on
the shore, and the flight down the coast was resumed
with frenzy. Near Aks-taqhl, now Cape Fox, a large
body of tidewaters, the Fugitives beheld Man-Underneath, a monster of the sea, with long hair. This supernatural being was like a statue holding a fish by the tail
in his hands. According to other accounts, Man-Underneath held two king salmon, one with either hand.
Sitting on the ocean, he was eating the salmon, while
the people marveled at him and decided to take him as
an emblem—Man-of-the-Sea, or Man-Underneath.

"A frightened canoeman sitting in the stern urged,
'Let us flee from here; Man-of-the-Sea will devour us
all!' While the canoe was turning, he asked his brother,
who faced him, 'Is he still eating the salmon?' 'Yes, he
is eating it.' These words were never forgotten, to this
day. They are repeated in another dirge used at the
death of chiefs in our family.

"The Fugitives approached Aks-taqhl in fair weather.
There they beheld Bull-Head, a large fish, and hastened
ashore, inside a small island. From this vantage point
they gazed for a long while at the monster, whose body

was covered with human faces. So impressed were they that they decided to have him as another emblem. Like the others, it has been represented since on a number of totem poles. Seeing the monster, an old man wondered, 'What is it I behold? What is the being there whose body is alive with human faces?' And these words are embodied in traditional dirge.

"At the other end of Aks-taqhl, the people went ashore, where Larhsail now is, and joined the tribe already living there, to be their allies. Together with these earlier occupants, our ancestors formed the village of Larhsail, the present Larhsail in southern Alaska. Ka-Shaiks of Saxman [near Ketchikan] is their head chief and our close relative.

"A young man and his sister, soon after, went out in a canoe. The young man wore on his head an Eagle cap with a stuffed eagle's head. Their canoe capsized, because of a strong wind suddenly rising from the sea. The man was drowned, but the sister was saved, and their chief, dressed in his finery, walked down to the beach, lamenting the loss of his nephew.

"Then a halibut, looking like an eagle, rose to the top of the water. The chief in mourning touched his long earrings of leather adorned with squares of haliotis shells as wide as two fingers and longer than his hand, and he said, 'The prince whose canoe capsized shall wear my earrings.' To him the supernatural halibut-eagle in the water was no other than his nephew, now transformed. The words of his lament became a fourth dirge. We still preserve it: 'Dear boy, after your death wear these earrings.'

"His chant no sooner was ended than a strange canoe landed with the body of his nephew. Standing near it he cried out, 'Dear son, the Eagle cap still sits on your head.' And these words are part of a fifth dirge. The eagle-halibut had become one more emblem for our clan. The body was burned and buried there, at the village of Larhsail, and the people once more decided to move toward Leesems.

"They went around Cape Fox and stopped at Tongas, where they saw many canoes filled with Fugitives. Here they became acquainted with the grandfather of La'ee, the chief of another Eagle clan; also the grandfather of Sagya'mas, the Eagles' ally, the chief of a leading Wolf clan. Other Eagles and Wolves had preceded them in their migration. They did not stay anywhere very long, but started with La'ee, Sagya'mas, and their people on their constant search southward. They traveled through the narrows, and, without realizing it, cut across the bay at the mouth of the Nass.

"They made two camps at the place now called Tsem'ateen, on both sides of the inlet at its head near the mouth of a river; and they built a fish fence across the river, with a trap to catch salmon. The salmon here were plentiful—the spring salmon, the humpback, and the dog salmon, but no sockeye.

"La'ee, the chief of the other Eagle clan, and some of his men left in a canoe soon after, to look for Leesems, their destination. They paddled away, and this time discovered it. After they had gone back for their tribe and brought it along, they built a new village at Leesems and called it On-Bundles, on account of the bundles of smoked salmon with which the earlier occupants presented them upon their arrival.

"Our story, which we knew well because it is often repeated, halts at On-Bundles, near the mouth of the

Nass. The emblems which our ancestors acquired on
their way down the coast are carved on the totem poles;
formerly they were only painted *(qawah)* on the house
fronts.

"Our people, together with La'ee and Sagya'mas, who
had gone ahead, joined the Git-rateen tribe. In that
town on the Nass, the earlier occupants were the Raven-
Frog people, the Killer-Whales, and some Wolf people,
who had recently arrived. But Salmon-Eater, the important Eagle chief from the far north and the Queen
Charlotte Islands, had not yet made his appearance in
this country.

"The quest for food, according to season, took our
people to various places. They went back every year
to the inlet, on what is now called Portland Canal. In the
spring they caught candlefish for grease, at Fisbery Bay
on the lower Nass. At other times, in the summer, they
went to their salmon streams elsewhere. In this bountiful
Leesems they never lacked food.

"Some of the Leesems Eagles journeyed once more to
join the coast Tsimsyans. Because the salmon was plentiful on the Nass some of them went up to the canyon.
Kudzaw'ee settled down at the salmon weirs in the
estuary of the Skeena. Demhaa'de, our close relative,
never paused very long until he had reached Gitka'ta, a
long way south of Skeena.

"Before these people had come down from the North,
while they sojourned at Saneena and elsewhere, they
mingled with the Tlingits and spoke their language. For
this reason the words of our dirges to the present still
are Tlingit. After the Eagles had settled on the Naas
they did away with that language, but could not change
their dirges. To this day they remain unchanged.

"The Niskae, in the early days, was spoken only at On-the-Lagoons, up the river at Anse-ma'isk, on the Nass. This language of the country spread down the river to the newcomers, the Wolves and the Eagles.

"At Git-larhdamks or On-the-Lagoons, up the river, dwelt two allied clans, the Kyaerh and the Tsirh-kan, who held on resolutely to the Niskae because from time immemorial it had belonged to their homeland. These natives claim that they taught it to the newcomers, after they had welcomed them. This they had told them, 'Henceforth you shall speak a new language— *she'algyarh*, the Niskae.' The chief of Git-larhdamks who declared it became known under the name of Hunt-after-Language—Sen'algyarh. It was conferred upon him in a great feast by the Fugitives from the Far North."

There ended the narrative of the old chief, Mountain, accounting for the origin of his totems and of the adoption of the Niskae language by his Eagle clan. And other narratives, from other sources, also stand in corroboration.

More truth is hidden behind these native allegories than is at first apparent. The growing distance which the advance of the Na'as, or "People," toward Leesems had placed between them and their Asiatic cradle did not materially alter their outlook nor dim their ancient lore. They remained true Asiatics, in a constant search for food and opportunities. Their starving souls preyed upon novelties and excitement in their new path; their skillful hands, long trained in varied crafts, turned to fresh devices and inventions. In their audacity, born of pressing needs and instinctive fears, they were driven into unforeseen danger and, when cornered, they risked their lives in a fight or a hazard because they could not help it.

Their culture, now reduced to great simplicity, once had drawn its fundamentals from rich ancestral backgrounds on the outskirts of the Mongolian world. As their recollections of the past endured through the generations, they proved to be the most venturesome and adaptable of all the American Indians. Throughout their wanderings in the new world, they remained inveterate prowlers, living off the sea and ever dreaming of bounty and wealth which, to their forebears, had been the Celestial Empire and its fabulous treasures.

Farther and farther though they strayed from their original moorings, they continued to cremate their dead and speed their souls on to the upper world to the west for reincarnation. At the funeral pyre they sang Buddhistic dirges, which were exclusive family possessions, several of them in a former language. Along their way they associated with casual allies, whom they could not dispense with, yet with whom they quarreled and fought. In a feud they resorted to duels between appointed champions. When they wanted a float or needed a raft to lift or carry heavy burdens on the water, they could, like the whale hunters of the Bering Sea, inflate a sealskin and use it. Like the other migrants of Asiatic extraction, they knew how to appease the sea or the dead by casting precious earrings into the deep; or they might whip the stormy waters into submission. They revered the bear spirit and sang prayers to it, as their forebears had done when successful in the bear hunt; and a group of their forerunners had assumed the grizzly as a name, and later as an emblem. And they stood in awe in the presence of the Thunderbird, which was as famed in Asia as in prehistoric America. The name of "Adee" for this mythical bird was the same, in some places, on both sides of Bering Sea.

The outstanding achievement of the Na'as and their imitators, however, was the development of totems out of foreign elements, and the extraordinary use made of these totems in their pictorial and plastic arts. Never were the heraldic arts anywhere pushed to such extremes and significance.

Their Thunderbird, or Gyaebelk, was a supernatural eagle, and as soon as some of them, in their trek into new territories, beheld the great eagle of North-Wind, a Haida forerunner, sitting on the front gable of a large house, they adopted it as a symbol. The double-headed eagle of the Russians, a while later, completed the trilogy of their earliest totems. These have remained fundamental in the crest system of the whole North Pacific coast.

The Thunderbird, the great eagle, and the split eagle clearly merge into a single heraldic concept subsequent to the Na'as' shift from their earlier coastal footholds (the Aleutian Islands) to the islands south of the Stikine River, in Alaska. And the Haida chief, North-Wind, must have preceded them in claiming the great eagle, since it was already sitting on his front gable, and, being of the seacoast, he was surely in contact with the Russians.

As the double-headed eagle was the emblem of the Russian American Company since its inception at the end of the eighteenth century, it had become a towering symbol of foreign might and power to the oppressed natives. Of the two Russian ships plying the northwest coast, in the days of Baranov, one was the *Eagle*, presumably with a carved eagle figurehead in the familiar style. Long before this, the Russian imperial crest had entered the country by way of the Aleutian Islands, and the spread eagle of the sea-otter traders had swayed the whole population through plunder and massacre and made it rock on its foundation. In the wake of the Russian conquest the Haida chief North-Wind had, for some unrecorded reason, appropriated the eagle, just as Stone-Cliff (Legyarh) later took on the beaver gnawing a stick, which was the badge of the recently arrived Hudson's Bay Company.

The eagle totem and crest go back to Russian prototypes on the Aleutian Islands, where the Russian traders were stationed before 1800, just as the separate Eagle clans in southeastern Alaska were born after the adoption of the eagle symbolism. All careful observers, like J. R. Swanton and Lieutenant G. T. Emmons, are agreed that the Eagle clan system among the Tlingits is of recent adoption. Among the Tsimsyans, it is the latest of all social developments, in the wake of Tlingit innovations. The Thunderbird and Eagle totem poles of the Kwakiutl at Alert Bay, better known though they may be than any other Eagle totems, are about fifty years old, and like the earlier ones they go back to the Russian imperial incentive.

The early Russian occupation of Alaska has, indeed, left cultural elements behind it, some of them still active as far south as Vancouver Island, and even beyond. The recent meaningless totem poles of the Nootkas and the Salish, down to the Fraser River, are the latest extension of the same upsurge, the beginnings of which were outside this continent.

That the adoption of the eagle crest by the Tlingits may not antedate the year 1800 is shown by the inclusion of two other totems during the same migration: the devilfish and the shellfish, neither of which were known in North Pacific waters.

The devilfish is a gigantic octopus, often twenty feet broad and twelve feet long. It is found in the warm American waters off the California coast and elsewhere. The giant clam *(Tridacna gigas)* is the largest of all mollusks living in shallow water, from the Philippine Islands and the East Indies. It may exceed three feet in diameter and weigh more than four hundred pounds. The starting point for Aitl's experience, from which the crests were derived, need not be fictitious or supernatural. A devilfish or a giant clam may, in similar circumstances, overcome a man and bring about his slow death.

How the Na'as in the neighborhood of Cape Fox and Portland Canal in southern Alaska could have secured actual knowledge of these two monsters of the tropical seas is a question that cannot be definitely answered, because of two alternatives.

The first alternative is that the information may have come through the Kanakas, or South Sea Islanders, then in the employ of European and American fur traders on the northwest coast. These islanders, like some white sailors, at times deserted their harsh masters to seek refuge among the coast Indians. This was true of a parent or a grandparent of the best Tsimsyan craftsman, Oyai, on the Nass River; and Oyai was the carver of Chief Mountain's tall totem pole containing the devilfish and the giant clam.

The second alternative is that some North Pacific

Coast Indians—Haidas or Tlingits—may have inherited this knowledge from ancestors who had originated on the balmy coast of China and migrated northeastward over the Aleutian Islands to the American mainland, as they have inherited from them other cultural features of the past. Or it might be that they were taken for the sea-otter hunt in California by the fur traders and brought back home via the South Seas on the triangular trip from and to Bering Sea. In these long journeys they may have seen devilfish and giant clams at close quarters, and brought back home vivid descriptions of their huge size and strange power. The starting point for new totems has always lain in exactly such natural phenomena, which, to the Indians, bordered on the supernatural.

WOLF IN FLIGHT

THE RIVALRY between the Wolves and their allies, on the upper Stikine and elsewhere, was as constant as their renewed efforts to look for new partners after shifting their abode, and to resume living side by side with them in a precarious peace. The ancestral custom requiring two moieties to intermarry and exchange vital services made them mutually indispensable—so that Kalowt and his Wolf band, as soon as they had passed in flight and terror under the glacier, were glad to make friends, at the mouth of the river, with the first villagers of good will they encountered.

Before Kalowt, in the recent past, had occupied the upper Stikine—or perhaps after—another band of like blood, belonging to the nomadic Tahltans in the interior, drifted down from the north to the same headwaters and also hunted wild game over the grassy plains of the high prairies. Among them a child grew up whose name was Doubtful-Chief (Labaraet-Sem'oiget). His odd trait from childhood was his wearing a conical hat woven out of spruce roots and topped by ten flat disks strung together in a pile, a hat claimed to this day as an exclusive family possession.

Now a family crest, this hat is a reminder of the days long ago when the child, trying to keep up with his elders, would stumble and cut his face on the sharp blades of the tall grasses on the prairie. To protect his head, his mother had fashioned for him a hat with a wide rim all around, shielding his eyes and cheeks. As he grew up she kept weaving larger hats to suit him, until he became known by his headgear, the shape of which went back to an obsolete style. This hat after a time was considered a mark of high rank, and its native name alluded to its large size—so large, indeed, that it was also "He-Walks-Toward-His-Hat," as if he had been smaller than his hat.

After these people had settled and lived for a time at Dehlden on the upper Stikine, Doubtful-Chief quarreled with an elder on the opposite side and, suddenly blinded by anger, killed him outright. In the feud that flared up, his tribe, quite outnumbered, had to seek safety in flight and to hasten down the river in six canoes, chanting mournful songs on their way.

These Wolf fugitives journeyed together downstream until the huge glacier, spanning the river, seemed to block all avenues of escape. Other Tahltan fugitives— the Na'as and the Kalowt faction—at other times were also confronted with the glacier barrier of the lower Stikine.[1] They stepped out of their canoes and stood on the shore, wondering in their distress what to do.

Training their eyes upon the narrows, where the seething waters seemed to dive under the glacier, they saw an arch cut through the ice in the manner of a bridge. To probe their chances of a safe passage under it, they took a small tree with all its branches and dropped it into the swift waters, thinking, "If the tunnel is too narrow or too low, it will break off the branches."

The tree sped down and came out intact, on the far side, with its green boughs swaying in the air. Some

---

[1] See Franz Boas, "Tsimshian Mythology," *31st Annual Report, Bureau of American Ethnology*, p. 354.

fugitives who had crossed the glacier to look for it
reported their observation to the others standing on
the shore above the ice cave. Doubtful-Chief intoned,
in the manner of a dirge: "The ice bridge is safe for us,"
and led the first boatful past the barrier. The others
followed, one at a time, all of them to emerge safely, and
soon to reach the salt waters below. Doubtful's dirge,
commemorating the hardships of their flight, is still sung
in Tlingit, even among the Tsimsyans, after the death of
his leading descendants who remember him as the bold
leader who took them through the terrific passage of
Stikine Glacier.

They halted at a place in the estuary of the Stikine
and, finding it to their liking, they decided to live there.
They gave it the name, in the Tlingit language, of
Chief's-Hill *(Garanows)* to honor Doubtful-Chief. And
this new name has since become the leading name of the
highest Wolf chief, through the following generations,
among the Tlingits and the Tsimsyans.

After wintering by themselves at Chief's-Hill, they
decided to move on farther, to look for allies, whom they
had missed since their exodus to the coast had begun.
They came upon a village called Stikine, where dwelt
a Wolf people akin to themselves, and a boatload of
fugitives here went ashore to join them, whereas the
majority of the Chief's-Hill band decided to proceed
farther down the coast.

The news came to their ears of the battle of Naha
Bay, where, sometime before, the Na'as and their Wolf
allies had fought over the infidelity of a young Na'a
wife to her Kanhaade husband while he was out on the
hunt. As both the Na'as and the Wolves were still
driving in flight and pursuit down the coast, the Stikine

Doubtful Chief intoned, in the manner of a dirge: "The ice bridge is safe for us," and led the first boatful past the barrier PAGE 98.

fugitives themselves did not deem it safe to tarry here;
their own Kanhaade enemies might likewise be following
them with a score to settle.

Just as the Na'a wanderers to the south had already
discovered the Thunderbird with a long crooked bill and
assumed it as a crest, so did the Stikine fugitives come
upon the monster with human faces over its wings and
around its neck, and they likewise adopted it as their
own emblem, but with a difference. As the Thunderbird had, since its first appearance, fallen into decay,
and its long beak had come off, they called their own
replica of it "Rotten-Thunderbird." It has since remained under this name, one of their own outstanding
coat-of-arms.

The Chief's-Hill fugitives, enriched by this new find,
landed at what is now Tongas in southern Alaska, and
they found a local tribe there under the name of Tlingit-
Wolf. Only a part of their group joined the earlier occupants in the hunt of the sea otter far out to sea, which
for them was a novelty. The remainder of their kinsmen, in their canoes, journeyed to other points, and
could not make up their minds about a permanent
abode.

Some of them stopped at Salmon River (Kalaen), at
the head of what is now Portland Canal, but disliked it
and soon left for Gitzawhl, in the present Alice Arm on
Observatory Inlet. And they did not tarry there very
long, as they were drawn like most others by the abundance of food—particularly of candlefish—promised to
them at Leesems. A part of them at last permanently
settled among their kinsmen who had arrived previously
at Fish-Weir-Village, the present Grenville, whereas
the remainder, in two canoes, shifted for themselves and

joined the Tsimsyan tribe of Salmon-Weirs on what
we know as Work Channel (behind Port Simpson). The
bearers of the Chief's-Hill name, however, preferred to
accept the welcome of the Gitlaen tribe a short distance
to the south, near the mouth of the Skeena River.

The last branch rose in little time to the leadership
of the Wolf newcomers, because two sisters of Chief's-
Hill became the wives of local head chiefs, and brought
to their own kinsmen the prestige and power of their
husbands. Quickly they changed from the Tlingit language to the Tsimsyan. The oldest son of one of them
inherited the title of Chief's-Hill and eventually became
the head chief of the whole Gitlaen tribe, a large one.
Yet his new house was called Tlingit-Word, in souvenir
of the maternal language just relinquished.

The restless descendants of these Wolf fugitives would
not all stay forever at Gitlaen, for they were of a nomadic
breed, ever on the lookout for a new abode somewhere
ahead of them. Their ancestors had been Tahltan hunters on the inland prairies to the far north; then they
had become villagers on the upper and lower Stikine
rivers and at Tongas; then, soon after, they became
Niskaes on the Nass, and Tsimsyans at the mouth of the
Skeena farther south. An offshoot from the branch at
Gitlaen eventually moved to the present Porcher Island,
where it was received by the Killer-Whale band of
Chief Tsyebassae and incorporated in his seafaring tribe.

But the offspring of the Wolf predators of the North
never were wholly satisfied with their lot. Envious and
grasping, they ever craved for more in their perpetual
quest for food, booty, and power. Invariably they
stumbled upon obstacles that brought strife, wherever
they went. To use the words of present-day natives:

"They mingled with the Salmon-Weir tribe, the Gitlaen, and the Killer-Whale tribes of Porcher Island; they intermarried with them. Indeed, their children or their nephews were part Tsimsyan, of the old stock. Yet they had brought in something new and different. They were a great people to kill outsiders. The life of others meant little to them. They were always brewing trouble."

One evening, for instance, they stabbed to death a Killer-Whale girl who was digging up clams on the beach or Porcher Island, and they left her body there, unburied. Her people, pretending to ignore the crime, waited for their chance to get even, until one day they slew a girl of the offending clan, and also left her body lying in the open. Realizing that hostilities on a larger scale would follow, the Wolves hastily took to their canoes and paddled south, day and night, until they reached Tiyawkl on the north side of Queen Charlotte Sound, where they could no longer see the land beyond.

Bound as they were in their descent toward the sun, they dashed across the wide salt waters to Bella-Bella, and past it to Bella-Coola, down the main mountainous coast. Once they had reached Wigyaenoh—now Rivers Inlet—they camped on the point there and were satisfied that they had traveled far enough. As the deer were plentiful, they killed them and feasted upon the tender flesh, as their ancestors had done in all their past existence on the northern tundras, and they made the *wanh* (the deer) into their own symbol.

The Thunderbird with outspread wings and threatening beak, of Alert Bay and elsewhere, and the Wolf emblem on some of the modern totem poles in the same district, among the Kwakiutl tribes, no doubt go back to the Rotten-Thunderbird of these Wolf predators from Alaska and the Yukon. Some of their descendants, indeed, still abide on this rainy and balmy coast and form part of the old stock, into which much new blood has been infused. There they have fomented their own restlessness in others, introduced their traditions, and contributed their notions and skill in painting and carving totems, as the Na'as or Eagles and the Wolves had been doing elsewhere for some time, under the stimulus provided by the Russians.

Not a few of these southern Wolves eventually became once more dissatisfied with the mountain ranges where they had hunted the deer for some time, and they decided to move from Tiyawkl back north to the lower Nass, where their Wolf kinsmen had established their prestige over the other clans, even the Na'as or Eagles. And, as they were taken back into the fold, the name of these former Kwakiutls among the Niskae to this day has remained Tiyawkl-People.

The story of the passage of Doubtful-Chief under the glacier is far too striking and circumstantial to be of no significance in our search for dates in the past migrations out of the North, and more remotely from Siberia.

The passage is familiar enough in the traditions of the Eagle and Wolf clans not to be a mere episodic pattern in a folk tale devoid of historical contents. Experts—the late John Muir, explorer and geologist, the late Forrest A. Kerr, and George Hanson, geologists versed in the formation of the Stikine region—all accept the Indian narrative as a fair indication of what the Stikine Glacier must have been at one time, not so long ago, when the Indians were confronted with it in their drives down this river. It has now receded a very short distance from the Stikine River, perhaps less than a mile, after having somewhat pushed it out of its course.

From two to four hundred years ago, the arch under the glacier probably looked as it is described in the Indian narratives. But, in Hanson's opinion, glaciers of similar formation in the same neighborhood have receded far more speedily than the Stikine Glacier, if Kerr is correct as to approximate dates. The rapid rate of recession of the Tide Lake Glacier, between the Stikine and Stewart to the south, may throw some light on our problem.

Hanson has written of Tide Lake:

Trappers brought out stories of a lake, forty miles north of Stewart that was subject to change of level from year to year, and to very rapid changes of level of as much as 100 feet in one summer. Someone facetiously remarked that there must be high tides at that place; hence the name Tide Lake (recorded on the map).

The writer saw this lake in 1927, when it was at a low level, and visited the district again in 1931 when the lake had almost entirely disappeared. In its place was a clay plain covered in the upper part by a thin mantle of dry sand that drifted in the breeze. As the lake was fed by streams coming from glaciers and bearing glacial silts, the sands are varved and seasonally banded. . . .

This lake was held up by the Frank Mackie glacier which enters the Bowser River valley from the west. At its highest level, 500 feet above the bed of the lake, it drained north along the edge of the ice. When the ice receded, a moraine (or mass of debris) of the glacier formed a dam across the river, and a gap was cut in the moraine, which is 780 feet wide at the level of the lake bottom, and 160 feet high. And the lake was finally drained. . . .

At its highest stage, the lake had been six miles long and one mile wide. . . . The disappearance of the lake was due to a slight retreat of the glacier and to the cutting of a channel through the moraine. The retreat of the ice-front caused the outlet stream to have a steep gradient and thus enabled it to cut a deep channel. . . . It is not known how long since the lake stood at or near the highest level, but the freshness of the shoreline suggests that it cannot be more than a few hundred years at the most. . . . In 1905, the ice appeared to have been nearly up to the moraine. In 1927, it had receded about 200 yards from the moraine, and the outlet stream flowed along the edge of the ice. In 1931, the glacier had receded somewhat farther. . . . [2]

As the glacier there is now vanishing fast, to the point where it may disappear in about twenty-five years, according to Hanson, we may surmise how a similar glacier of larger size on the Stikine may have appeared to the natives canoeing down the river in their migrations to the sea. The arch under which the waters flowed and the canoes passed safely are not a mere fancy of native imagination, but a historical probability. Not so long ago, a similar arch may have existed at the edge of the Tide Lake Glacier, and a stream may have flowed under it. Yet the lake is now of the past, and the glacier is soon wholly to disappear.

Of the "Big Stikine" Glacier John Muir has written:

Around the beautifully drawn curve of the moraine, the Stickeen River flows, having evidently been shoved by the glacier out of its direct course. On the opposite side of the canyon another somewhat smaller glacier, which now terminates four or five miles from the river, was once united front to front with the greater glacier, though at first both were tributaries of the main Stickeen glacier which once filled the whole grand canyon. After the main trunk canyon was melted out, its side branches, drawing their sources from a height of three or four to five or six thousand feet, were cut off, and of course became separate glaciers, occupying cirques and branch canyons along the tops and sides of the walls. The Indians have a tradition that the river used to run through a tunnel under the united fronts of the two large tributary glaciers mentioned above, which entered the main canyon from either side; and that on one occasion an Indian, anxious to get rid of his wife, had her sent adrift in a canoe down through the ice tunnel, expecting that she

[2] "Varved Clays of Tide Lake, British Columbia," *Transactions of the Royal Society of Canada*, 1932, pp. 335-36.

would trouble him no more. But to his surprise she floated through
under the ice in safety. All the evidence connected with the present
appearance of these two glaciers indicates that they were united and
formed a dam across the river after the smaller tributaries had been
melted off and had receded to a greater or lesser height above the
valley floor.[3]

The "Big Stickeen" Glacier had been described previously, in 1863, by the American geologist William P.
Blake.[4] In his word picture we find the glacier as it
stood, close to the river, about eighty years ago:

At a point a short distance above the Scoot [River] there is an
Indian village. These Indians are quite different from the Koloshes
of the coast, and are evidently of the great Chippewyan family.
They offered skins of the sable for sale or barter, and had several fine
skins of cubs of black bear recently killed.

The glacier above presents a splendid appearance in the sunlight,
and extends for about two miles along the stream. The background
is formed by beautiful snow-covered peaks, from between which
the glacier issues, but its source cannot be seen. The slope of the
glacier is very gentle, and the vast body of ice appears to be unbroken
until it reaches the valley of the river, where it breaks down in
massive ledges and pinnacles of the purest crystal. The foreground
along the stream consists of an ancient moraine now covered with
trees, among which willows and poplars are conspicuous in their
delicate green foliage of spring. Some very large blocks of granite
standing in the river bear witness to the vast transporting power of
ice and to a much greater extension of this glacier in former periods.

From this part of the river a line of high and rugged peaks is
visible on the right or eastern side of the valley, and at a considerable
distance from the stream.

The accumulations at the foot of the glacier have evidently pushed
the river outward, and they have acted as a dam to the waters, which
above the moraine are quite deep and flow smoothly.[5]

The reference in this glacier tradition to sea-otter

---

[3] *Travels in Alaska*, pp. 47-48.

[4] Ms., Library of Parliament, Ottawa. (From *Executive Document 177, Part
2, 40th Congress, 2nd Session*, Washington, 1868.)

[5] *Ibid.*

hunting, after the Chief's-Hill fugitives had reached the salt water and joined a coast tribe, is another detail suggesting a historical date. Intensive sea-otter hunting developed only after the Russians and other sea traders began to press the natives, from the Aleutian Islands down to the Tlingit country, into their service; that is, less than two hundred years ago.

The passage under the glacier may not be much older than two hundred years. For the Wolf fugitives no sooner had crossed the Tlingit country, and entered the Nass River to the south, than they experienced a fantastic cataclysm, which deeply impressed itself upon tribal memories. They were smothered by poisoned fumes and thrown back by a volcano in full eruption.

Vivid recollections of the activities of the Lava Lake Volcano, fourteen miles south of the present deviated course of the Middle Nass River, are still preserved by all the Niskae elders, and the observers, including Hanson, who has visited the craters, agree that the last eruptions have taken place about one hundred and fifty years ago, probably a few generations only after the passage under the glacier.

Before the eruption (according to Grandfather-of-Slave, of the Lagoon-people) two tribes occupied a stream in the neighborhood. This stream, called White-Spring-Salmon, circled the mountains northward, and expanded into a big lake, which has since disappeared.

"The people, one winter, heard a strange rumbling in the mountains. Day after day, the rumbling was always the same; sometimes it stopped altogether. It lasted for three years. As the people could not grasp its meaning, they thought that it was supernatural. Spirits dwelt on the mountaintop."

According to another narrative: "The rumbling was heard once, and soon the ground began to shake. Standing outside their houses, the people saw the flames gushing toward them in huge swift currents, and they took flight, in sheer terror. Their village and the whole place was burned to cinders.

"The blame for this disaster was placed upon some young men, who, late one summer, had shown disrespect to a humpback salmon caught in the river. They had aroused the wrath of the salmon spirit standing over his kind.

"Soon after, a new and larger volcanic eruption occurred. At first, only smoke spread over the countryside. It was as if a huge house on the mountaintop was burning fiercely. The people beheld a large fire. The fire spilt down the mountainside in their direction, but not as fast as a forest fire. It moved down slowly, very slowly.

"It was strange, frightful, and awe-inspiring. Fumes spread ahead, and those who crossed them were smothered. Their bodies stiffened, hardened like rock. Terrified, the people of one tribe dug deep holes, like underground lodges, and hid within, scared as they were of the mountain spirits. The tribe opposite also dug itself in, but this did not keep the refugees from dying of the fumes, mostly in the lower of the two hiding places.

"As soon as the smoke dispersed, some people ran away. But a great many others stayed on, and did not suffer any more from the smoke. The fire then rolled down like a river and filled the lake. For a time the water was a bed of flame. The stones there were red hot. As far as the river of flames spread it burned the forest. It had started from the river away up, where

Before the volcano had pushed the Nass out of its bed and formed the canyon, the lake is believed to have been full of fierce and squirming animals—frogs and lizards PAGE 115.

the people had fished salmon, and slowly spread down to the place (fourteen miles to the north) where the canyon now is, at the end of a large plain, still treeless and desolate.

"Nothing was left of the salmon river at the time—not even a streak of water. The people who had escaped the fumes moved away, out of the country, some of them overland to the Skeena River. But my own family and others remained in the neighborhood of the volcano.

"The water came back, after a few years, to the place where the lava had blocked the stream of the White-Spring-Salmon. A large lake had formed behind the lava obstruction, between the mountains to the south. It was called New-Lake. To the white people now it is Lava Lake. A small stream soon began to flow out of it northward, and it ran into the Nass that had been pushed away quite a distance. This small river is New-Water.

"No salmon ran up the new river at first, but, after a while, some of them made their appearance. Year after year their numbers increased, until they were plentiful, as they are now. My granduncles, who never had renounced their country in spite of fire hazards, took possession of New-Water, also of New-Lake. These are still ours, from the past, and the New-Water became as valuable for fishing as had been White-Spring-Salmon. The woods around the lake were good hunting grounds for us, until the white people, some years ago, made their appearance, and, with their guns and poison spread destruction all around. My forefathers and their tribesmen, at the time of the volcano eruption, were very numerous. We now have dwindled in numbers until some of our families have nearly disappeared."

"When the lava fire rolled down the mountain," according to some, "the big lake in this vicinity turned to stone. The whole country was laid waste by the poisonous smoke, which killed many people."

The unknown date of the volcano eruption of the Nass seems to coincide with the appearance of the first sailing ships of the white navigators on the North Pacific coast. Old Grandfather-of-Slave, describing the eruption, explained that his father had died when very old, and the volcano terror was one of his favorite stories. He would say: "About one hundred and fifty years ago, the people in this country never had seen any white men. The first time they heard of a Pealed-Log, which is the name for a white man, was when a ship came astray (presumably Vancouver's) and entered Observatory Inlet." Then followed the vivid description of the volcano. The late Rev. J. B. McCullagh, who spent much of his life on the Nass River, also came to the conclusion that the eruption had taken place, as he puts it, "in the beginning of the last quarter of the eighteenth century."

After the survivors had settled along the Nass, at the northern edge of the lava fields, they suffered new losses at the hands of foreign raiders from the seacoast. So they moved up a short distance to a place called the Fortress at the edge of the lagoon marshes.

Some of the raiders came down overland from the north, others up the river from the coast. The most dreaded among them were the Haidas of the Queen Charlotte Islands, who had no salmon river of their own, and were looking for fishing stations. Every spring, the Haidas fished for eulachon or candlefish on the Nass, and some of them wanted to stay there the entire year.

That is why they were trying to dislodge the earlier Niskae occupants, all of them of the Wolf and the Kanhaade clans. The Eagles came in only later.

A few Haida raiders first attacked the Canyon tribe, who lost two of their women at their hands. But one of the Haidas was killed, one night, by his captive, who used a sharp mussel-shell knife to cut his throat, and then ran away. The raiders went back to their island, but they soon reappeared, now much more numerous. Aware of danger, the Canyon people moved up to the Fortress, where they joined the Volcano tribe. In those days, small marshes almost surrounded the Fortress in the rear, and the Niskaes for greater security dug two trenches at the bottom of the slope and flooded them. The main river washed the foot of the steep cliff to the south.

On the four sides at the top of the Fortress, around the palisade, they fastened large logs, which they would cut loose and roll upon their aggressors, if they were bold enough to approach.

The next year, a large party of Haidas arrived in their dugouts, from which they landed and several times attacked the Fortress as if they had been sure of victory. But they were beaten back. Logs rolled upon them, and sharp hemlock spears, hurled from above, pierced holes in the bottoms of their canoes at the foot of the cliffs. If the defenders fell in numbers, many more of the raiders rolled back into the river or were slaughtered. It was a great battle, lost to the Haidas, who took to flight and never came back. The Wolves, with the help of their allies, the Kanhaades, had saved the day. They remained supreme in the Nass, from its mouth upward to its headwaters.

As Sispagut, in his canoe, passed in front of Laderh's house, the door opened, and a gun was fired at him. He fell down, wounded in the arm PAGE 132.

Real crests or totem poles, in those days, were not known to the Nass River folk. Yet there were house-front paintings and, in places, a few carvings. A Kan-haade chief on the lower Nass once stood in front of his lodge, during a battle with the Haidas, just to keep them from taking away or destroying the large raven's beak, a wood carving that was his own emblem. At the time of the volcano eruption, a woman there chopped off one of the bear statues from a carved pole, put it in a bag, packed it on her back, and thus saved it from the fire.

But the rows of fine totem poles that, to our knowl-edge, stood near the Fortress or below, all along the lower Nass, were put up much later, from fifty to ninety years ago. One of them, the pole of the Frog and the Lizards, is of peculiar interest, since it is one of the only two which was saved from destruction in 1918, and now stands in the splendid staircase of the Royal Ontario Museum at Toronto. And it carries the mind back to the remote antecedents of the race, as the Frog spirit or totem is a clear Siberian reminiscence.

The woman fugitive of the Nass River Kanhaades who killed the Haida warrior at the canyon belonged to the Frog clan, and, like her captor, although remotely, she was of a lineage of raiders and plunderers from the Far North. Bold like them, she did not fear to retaliate. Her family did not at first belong to the Canyon or the Volcano tribe, though it had settled there with the natives some time ago, presumably after the volcano eruption.

The lizards on the Frog pole of the Lagoons are a symbol used nowhere else. They illustrate the name of the Canyon tribe whose village stands at the northern end of the lava expanse, their name being Lizard-People. Before the volcano had pushed the Nass out of its bed and formed the canyon, the lake is believed to have been full of fierce and squirming animals (frogs and lizards), and its gaseous stench was forbidding. Perhaps the gasses were a foreboding of the volcano eruption. The lava flow stamped all this out of existence, the lizards with the rest. But the Canyon tribe was named after them, and the Frog and Lizard pole holds the image of two of them.

Although the Stikine fugitives, who passed under the glacier and were later thrown back by the volcano, are usually called the Wolf people, it does not follow that the name of Wolf now applied to them is really ancient, or that the wolf has been their totem for very long.

No collective totemic name is given them in Alaska where they originated—that is, nowhere are they known there under the name of the Wolf. The only denomination recorded by J. R. Swanton for them all among the Tlingit was Sitqoedi, which now is meaningless. Nowhere can we find the wolf totem in large heraldic paintings or carvings, except among the upriver tribes of the Nass and Skeena to the south, and these are modern.

Among the Tsimsyans, the name for these Tahltan and Tlingit fugitives is On-the-Wolf, and they share the wolf myth of the Sedzan household. The wolf, according to this myth of a southern Tsimsyan tribe, once appeared in the form of a spirit and protected some people in need, who henceforth had him as a crest. But this event is recent, as it has not had the time to spread far from its source.

In the mountainous district south of the Skeena estuary, not far from the present salmon cannery of Inverness, where the wolves still are plentiful in the wooded valleys of Rock-Slide, the hunter Lugyedaw was painfully traveling in the deep snow away from his camp, in search of food, while his family was starving.

Suddenly he encountered a large wolf, which, like himself, was about to die of starvation. Its mouth was open and, as it approached him, it seemed to beg for help. Deep in its throat a bone caught crosswise made it impossible for it to swallow any food or water. The hunter fearlessly grasped the head of the beast, and with his finger pushed aside the bone and made it loose.

This wolf happened to be no common animal, but the wolf spirit, the chief of the wolves. So glad was he over his good fortune that he began to speak to the obliging hunter in a language that was quite understandable. "Lugyedaw!" he howled, "I shall call you, when in your turn you are in need. As soon as you hear my call, come up to me in the mountain, and I shall guide you to food —the mountain goat and the mountain sheep." And the wolf spirit ran off into the woods.

While the dazed hunter still remained under a spell, he heard another voice call "Lugyedaw," and at once he started uphill in the direction of the voice. As he was weak and exhausted, he could not make much headway in the deep snow. A large wolf, different from the first one, ran down the slope toward him; it was the nephew of the animal whom he had saved. And, as this spirit of the mountain stopped in front of him, he said, "Sit on my back and I will pick you up." The hunter was no sooner astride the wolf than he was taken up the mountainside and brought to the midst of a grassy slope where mountain goats were grazing. He was left where he could, in little time, kill plenty of meat for himself and his famished kinsmen below.

Once he had recovered his strength, Lugyedaw loaded himself down with fresh meat and carried it to his tribe. The people climbed the mountain with him and camped in the midst of the wild meat, which they had never been able to find by themselves. There they camped for many days, enjoying their good fortune.

The Skeena River, close to the salt waters, however, was not quite to their liking, as they had always been by preference an inland people. They decided to rejoin their kinsmen on the Nass River to the north, and to look for wives there among the Kanhaades. On the Nass, they associated in the hunt with the People-of-the-Salmon-Weirs and camped at the head of the Gap-of-Tseraret. Lugyedaw succeeded to a Wolf chief akin to him there, and he sang a Stikine dirge over his dead body, the traditional dirge of the glacier common to both. And, after the two families had been merged into one, he inherited his hunting grounds on the upper Nass.

The influx of the Wolves up the Nass River increased in time until this bountiful river had become, as it is still, a Wolf center, like a springboard for inland invasions to the south. Soon the Nass River Wolves spread to the upper Skeena River, which eventually fell under the sway of the wolf emblem and its associated crest, the grizzly bear.

Even the powerful Chief's-Hill, heading the Gitlaen tribe at the mouth of the Skeena, and the Rivers Inlet Wolf band likewise, fell back eventually in their own tracks and sought renewed bonds with their former kinsmen, in preference to their new holdings in a coastal

environment never wholly congenial to them. For their
ancestry, like that of the wolf, was of the northern forests up the rivers far inland. Wolves never quite adapted
themselves to coastal regions, never ventured across the
wide tidal waters to the Queen Charlotte Islands, where
they are virtually unknown except from hearsay or in-
tertribal contacts.

The red cedar, out of which is carved the beautiful
Niskae pole of the Frogs and the Lizards, evokes remembrance of the Stikine flight of the Wolves, of their trials
at the volcano, of the Haida invasion, and of the siege
of the Lagoon Fortress.

This pole, a few years before I purchased it for the
Royal Ontario Museum, stood close to another native
fortress, at the edge of the vast lava field still bare of
trees and vegetation on the middle Nass River. The
natives, by their incantations, had tried to stop the flow
of the lava which was poisoning and burning some of
their people and burying their best salmon stream.

Their descendants were now about to forget that
event of the dim past. Of the Fortress nothing remained but a high, rocky spur. More than once it had
been besieged by raiders, and it was finally abandoned
only after the recent arrival of the white man in the
country.

But the Indians I met there, who had strange tales to
tell, traced back their ancestry to warlike bands that
once had tramped down the trails from the north.
Their forefathers were raiders and conquerors. Like
others in the land, they had forced their way into this
country because it was rich in food, although already
occupied by other tribes. Everywhere this was their

story. After a while I wished to hear of the other side—
that of the earliest occupants, who were massacred, or
simply subdued or pushed away. But few among them
cared to speak of a low extraction, or to remember defeats in battle or a meek acceptance of overlords. Princes
pretend to remember only their pedigree.

Some remnants of those earlier people, I surmised,
might still survive up the rivers, in the interior, hemmed
in between mountains, lakes, and glaciers—for instance,
the Volcano tribe up the Nass River. Even now, their
district was not easy of access for an outsider like me.
The only way to find out was to penetrate their wilderness and learn the truth from them. So, at the end of
the summer of 1927, I used my first opportunity to
break in, and I planned to travel up the Nass to the
Fortress, a short distance above the canyon, and to explore the lava fields. A volcano in the northern Rockies,
even if dead, seemed more thrilling than a brooding
Vesuvius, which any tourist may visit with a railway
ticket. For here, just beyond our own doorstep, was the
challenge of the unknown.

The Canyon natives of the Nass are the only ones able
to navigate their treacherous river, but they seldom
attempt it in midsummer, when the sun thaws the snows
on the mountains and floods the valleys. One early
morning at the end of August, I packed up and left the
Arrandale cannery on the rising tide, on board a tunnel
gas boat which the half-breed Stevens used as a mail and
freight carrier up the river, past the canyon to the
Lagoon.

For hours we traveled in a haze which reminded me
of the legend of Temlaham of the Tsimsyans—the story
of their own Paradise Lost. A heavenly spirit once had

landed among their ancestors at dawn, when everything was screened in a white mist, and all they could hear, after his arrival, was hammer blows and mysterious voices from above. The veil tore up at midday, and the people had a vision of heaven on earth; brand new lodges erected on the heights, on the front of which shone the totems of the Sun, the Moon, the Rainbow, and the Stars. These bright new emblems were painted on their house fronts, and later carved on the totem poles.

Mystic hammer blows no longer startled this solitude, but the roar of our gas boat awakened the seals on the sandbars, as we left the sea behind us and screwed our way up the estuary of the Nass, and the sea gulls screeched over our heads. While traveling cautiously through the tide flats, we came close to shore, and a fringe of wind-blown evergreens pierced the fog. Two eagles sat proudly side by side at the top of a hemlock, much like the wooden eagles we were soon to see on huge totem poles at the deserted Indian village of Gyeetiks. A moment later, as the mist began to lift, we found ourselves stranded for a while on a sandbar. The sun peered at us through a rift above our heads: we now anticipated a fine day. Pushing ourselves off with long poles, we resumed our advance upstream and left behind us a trail of foam and bubbles.

A high promontory rose out of the water to our left and, on its smooth face, symbolic pictures were engraved and painted with red ocher. No one knew their meaning, for they had always been there, in so far as the present-day rivermen can tell. Yet they were reminisment of a fight which had taken place in this neighborhood. A number of shields in the native style were drawn in a row on both sides of a human face.

What could these intriguing pictographs commemorate if not the contest, not too long ago, between the Eagle chief, Stone-Cliff (Legyarh), a dreaded outsider, and the old local families of the Killer-Whales? Ancestors of Stone-Cliff, the Eagles once had arrived from the north and managed to gain a foothold here. But they were not the first, for the Wolves of the Stikine had preceded them. And, before them all, the Frogs, the Killer-Whales, and the Grizzly-Bears had occupied the valley. Now we were following a trail of conquest by invaders and of defeat for the earlier occupants.

Though the painted figures on the cliff before us may not have symbolized Stone-Cliff's victory over the others, they nonetheless suggested its memory, the more so since we were soon to pass Red Bluffs and Fishery Bay. These former resorts for springtime fishing used to accommodate the Eagle clans of the southern Tlingits and of the quarrelsome Haidas.

We passed Fishery Bay, which at this season was as empty as a seashell cast by the high tides upon the shore. Yet its vacant cabins were a feeble reminder of the days when Fishery Bay was the main thoroughfare of Indian life on the North Pacific coast. The natives from far and wide always tried to gain a foothold here, to share in the bounties that made life easy and prosperous. This salmon and candlefish river had been like a magnet to the tribes far and wide. The candlefish, for one thing, provided huge quantities of fat that was a staple of the whole country, in the interior no less than on the coast. As an article of trade, it was in great demand along the "grease trails" inland, north and south—so much so that everybody within measurable distance migrated for the spring run at the mouth of the Nass, and put up stores of fish oil or grease in large wooden containers. For miles on both shores we could see the camp sites of five or six contiguous tribes. This is where strife often broke out among them, and where cultural exchanges took place between nations.

Not so many Indians now look for candlefish in the spring; their numbers have dwindled, and the present-day survivors care little for anything, either one way or another. The past is a dead letter for them, no less than for most of the white people in their neighborhood. On our way farther up the river we passed Angyadae, a deserted village, whose totem poles were half buried in a new forest growth, and our gas boat worked its way up toward the canyon.

To our growing excitement we saw, in the distance, an islandlike spur riding in midstream, while the water danced wildly around it. We were approaching the lava beds, and a gap in the forest growth, to our right, extended for miles south of the river, in a huge semicircle of tableland, to the mountains with snowy peaks.

Place-of-Lizards, the canyon village, stood in front of us, astride the rock spur. A few modern houses, such as the Indians now build, were mostly empty. Their occupants had not yet returned from the salmon canneries.

Our boat suddenly swerved to the right into midstream, where it snorted in twisting currents, and then bravely fought its way ahead. We were thrilled, yet not quite sure of our security. And, a while later, we were relieved to land on the sandy beach to the right, close to a clump of cottonwood trees. Our elderly native guide led us into the woods only a few hundred feet from the shore, and we beheld a totem pole that was nearly buried under the trees; then a second, a third, and the lower section of a fourth pole—all of them lost in this forest. Yet they were less than forty years old. Oblivion had befallen these stately carvings.[6] Our guide looked for a fifth pole somewhere, but could not find it.

Just before the volcano eruption, while they were fishing salmon along a small stream to the south, some members of a Wolf clan had been smothered by the fumes. The totems stood here in their memory—the tall totems of the Wolf and the Grizzly-Bear clans.

The Wolf clan, one of the oldest, had associated, in the same village, with a Fireweed tribe of the interior, the Temlaham tribe that once had visions of spirit dwellings on the heights. On the front of these ancient dwellings had shone the Sun, the Moon, the Rainbow, and the Stars, which were to become the clan emblems of the Fireweed tribe. Here, on modern totem poles quite well preserved, we saw carved images of the Sun, the Moon, and the Rainbow. As the forest had reclaimed its ground around them, we had to swing axes to clear avenues up to them. Otherwise it was impossible to see them and take photographs. Before the afternoon was late, we moved upstream, past the boiling waters of the canyon. Though danger threatened, our Indians enjoyed it. We, the strangers, dropped our cameras to the bottom of the boat, squatted on our heels, and watched the dark boulders ahead, nor forgetting those left behind in the foaming waters. We entered the gorge, where the lava bore impressively the mark of a cataclysm.

Black lava might have tumbled over us as our boat hugged the edge of the ragged cliffs. After we had

[6] Two of these have since been purchased for the Museum of the American Indian; they now stand in Bronx Park, New York City.

covered a mile or so in this deep gorge of the Frog and Lizard Canyon, we bucked once more the hostile current, and our riverman pressed his motor for more speed. It stalled and stopped dead.

For a while we drifted down, but were reassured by the stolidity of our native host. He did not mind, but went on unscrewing bolts and pulling off electric wiring. The trench was deep, the water dark and smooth, without rocks in midstream. The volcanic wall beside us once had squeezed the river northward for miles, till it had encountered a ridge in its path. It was still bare, except for a tuft here and there on its stark baldness. Huge blocks of porous lava were cracked; some of them had slumped into the river, causing eddies and whirlpools.

We secretly remembered the wild dance of the stream below the canyon and the scattered rocks all about, like the bones of dead giants. But Stevens, the riverman, was not worried; he knew the place well. Looking upward toward the lava beds, he explained with a grin how some white prospectors from the south had entered this district, one winter, and had marveled at the large expanse covered with snow and bare of trees. Mistaking it for a huge Indian ranch, they had staked it for themselves while the going was good. But how deceived they were after the snow had disappeared! A graveyard this was, the graveyard of a dead volcano. The stillness of death had remained unbroken ever since the volcano had emitted its fumes and vomited torrents of molten rock. The flow had rolled down the valley into the flat bottomlands of the Nass, and filled huge empty spaces. It had pushed the river northward for many miles—about sixteen miles from the craters on a width of a few miles along the present river front.

Before we had floated down to the lower end of the canyon, the motor throbbed again, and we resumed our journey onward, soon to reach the upper shoulder of the lava wall. The river here turned a sharp corner and swirled on itself, forming a dangerous whirlpool. A whirlpool of this nature, I realized, could suck down objects, as if it were alive and greedy.

Stevens, whose tunnel boat had until now hugged the wall on our right, suddenly turned to the left—that is, as soon as he had reached the elbow of the river. Thrown back around the bend with a breath-taking swing into midstream, we found ourselves in no time at the outer rim, close to the north shore. There we steadied ourselves, to renew the upward struggle step by step, amid boulders and water spouts.

The worst was yet to come—the riffles, which we saw in the distance and were slowly approaching. The rustling of countless pebbles in shallow water, and the white crest of the dreaded riffles around a half-circle, seemed to warn intruders away, as if in an enchanted folk tale. The stream, wide at the top, rushed from a broad upper shelf, which we could not see from below, into a narrowing funnel. The climb was so steep that our motor seemed presumptuous even to measure its small strength against the might of nature.

The fight was on in earnest. The engine roared its best; the tunnel at the rear vomited fury. The riffles combed their strands of white hair with a swish past us down the stream. For a while we did not make any headway, though the prow of our swift river craft kept close to the shore on our right. It was touch and go, with the odds apparently against us. As if to relieve tension, Stevens turned to us and told a story.

"Here," he said, nodding to the left, "Neeskail, last year, coming back from the cannery, drowned with all aboard. Pushed to his left, he rolled over. Pop, he goes!"

But we did not roll over after all, and, that day, we reached the Fortress, now called the Lagoons, before sunset.

The main object of this expedition was to find Indians of a different kind, natives belonging to an old stock that had dodged invasions and remained unscathed. But soon I had to renounce any hope of finding really unmixed people, with a pure ancestry. Two Eagle clans, a Raven clan, a Wolf clan, and a Fireweed clan were now represented at the village of the Lagoons; they formed the majority of the tribe. The ancestors of some of them, according to their own traditions, had come up the river, others had moved in from the upper Skeena or the interior; many of them, long ago, had migrated overland from the north. In search of food, they had all found this territory, as others had before them. It was the same story as elsewhere: the invasion of west coast salmon streams by hungry roving Indians from the north or the interior.

Like the others, the early occupants here had found villagers in possession of the fishing streams and the hunting grounds. They had made friends with them, had become their allies, and had joined forces against common foes; or they had forced their way in. Ancient warfare and invasions were as much in evidence here as elsewhere. A proof of it was the Fortress, just below the modern village of the Lagoons, the high cliff standing out into the river like a watch tower as a shield protecting the village behind it. The Lagoon tribe in the old days used to resort to the Fortress in time to ward off attacks from below. There they stood a siege by the Haidas of Queen Charlotte Islands, not so long ago. The bold Haidas had ascended the river in huge dugouts. Interior nomads, the Tsetsauts, previously had tried their spears and their arrows against it.

The Fortress consisted of a natural pyramid of rock and dirt, with steep sides and an abrupt cliff on the water front. It used to be reinforced at the top by a palisade. In case of attack, a number of tree trunks attached to short posts were released upon the besiegers when they attempted surprise by creeping around at the rear, only to encounter flying stones and rolling logs. How some of the attackers were crushed in that way is still remembered. And this was not the only native fortress where rolling logs were released upon invaders. This type of defense was common all over the North Pacific coast, even to the far distant South Seas, where such fortresses were called "hippahs."

An interesting point, in the recollection of the local elders, was the arrival of some of their Indian ancestors at this place before the volcanic eruption, and of others afterward. Down the river, the Fireweeds and the Kanhaades were the earliest occupants, and the Killer-Whales their contemporaries. Later comers, about the time of the volcanic eruption, were the Wolf fugitives of the Stikine and of the high prairies. The last to arrive were the Eagles, who had made their appearance only a few generations ago, but have never failed since to avail themselves of all opportunities to dislodge others and go forward.

The rise of the Wolf clan here was not spectacular, but the result of slow pressure from within upon the earlier occupants, and occasionally of swift blows aimed at whoever challenged their might. The local feuds, in which they usually had the upper hand, or the repeated transgressions from outsiders, which they succeeded in repelling, are the subject of stories far too long to be repeated here. Illustrations only can serve as samples of the ways and means of the Wolves to achieve their aim when in search of a livelihood, and the power necessary to ensure them.

An old chief, Mountain, of the Kincolith tribe on the Portland Canal, lifted the veil for us on recent rivalries and contests for leadership, in a story he gave to me at much greater length, a few months before his end at an advanced age.

The Eagle pole standing in the wilderness at Gyeetiks on the lower Nass, near the tidewaters, was the tallest and almost the finest I had seen anywhere—81 feet high, without counting the heavy butt underground. Nearly seventy years it had stood for something memorable in the life of many Indians of this northern country. For sheer stateliness it may be unsurpassed anywhere, and I was anxious to save it from destruction before it had fallen before the wind and disappeared in the rank vegetation without leaving a trace. The proud eagle of the mountains and the Thunderbird sat defiantly at its summit. The forest around them was reclaiming its rights, after the native villagers, many years ago, had departed for other haunts or had died out.

To prepare for its acquisition by a museum, and assisted by Barton, a skillful interpreter, I approached the old chief, who lay on his couch. He had been an invalid for years, blind and hard of hearing, at the mission village of Place-of-Scalps.

I explained to him what an honor it was for his pole to be singled out as one of the finest, and to be removed to a museum and preserved; all this, of course, for a material consideration. The strange old man, whose long white hair flowed down his back, could not quite understand at first. When it dawned upon him that someone wanted to buy the monument erected to his ancestors, he had a ready answer. To him no one ranked higher than his forebears, whereas Douglas, he admitted, had been foremost among the white people in the past. Douglas was a fur trader of great prestige and the first governor of Rupert Land or British Columbia, about a hundred years before. With this in mind, his reply was: "Give me the tombstone of Governor Douglas, and I will give you the totem of my granduncles."

Then he gratified my wish to hear his *adaorh,* or the traditions of his clan, an Eagle clan of the North closely allied to the Wolves of the Stikine, that once had traveled in large dugout canoes down the Alaskan coast, had fought monsters, and had conquered a tribe of wild men. The story which he related at great length was an epic in grand style. And it was illustrated in the splendid totem pole of the Eagle-Wolf of Gyeetiks. The pole itself stood as a memorial, like a tombstone, to commemorate a famous granduncle to whom he had succeeded. This must have been his last telling of his *adaorh,* for he died during the winter. The following summer I bought the pole from his nephews. It has since been seen by many people, in the central rotunda of the Royal Ontario Museum, in Toronto.

Carved with animal figures from top to bottom, this Eagle-Wolf pole was more than a set of heraldic symbols or an illustration of mythical tales in wood.

Its stylized designs impressed us with their bold force-
fulness as works of art. Barbaric in the extreme, the
eagles and beavers on the tall shaft, the killer-whale
whose tail was clutched by a man, the grizzly bear whose
teeth bit viciously at a large native shield of copper,
dovetailed so well into each other that they were part
of a compact column rising superbly from the earth to
the sky. No white sculptor had ever done as good a job
out of a tall stick like this, with over thirty figures of
birds and animals, one on top of another, all blending
into a firm unity, with refinement and grandeur.

This Eagle-Wolf pole did not simply chance to be
the tallest of its kind: from the start it was meant to
surpass all others for all time. It stood as a symbol of a
powerful clan of invaders and conquerors that brooked
no opposition in the land. Until its erection, the size of a
pole had not of itself indicated the rank of the owners.
But from now on the size would assume a new significance. It would silently proclaim the power of Sharp-
Teeth, and of his bosom friend Laderh, who had borne
with him the cost of its construction.

Laderh and Sharp-Teeth belonged to different clans
on the Nass; the first was of the highest Kanhaade or
Raven-Frog clan, and the other of the proud Eagle clan.
Singly they might not be able to overcome their many
rivals on the Nass, particularly those of the Killer-
Whale clans and their chief Sispagut. But together,
shoulder to shoulder, they might rule the country. So
once more the contest was on for supremacy.

The Killer-Whale chief, Sispagut, who headed the
faction of the earlier occupants on the river, announced
his determination to put up the tallest pole ever seen in
the country; its name would be Fin-of-the-Killer-Whale.

As if to throw candlefish grease upon the smoldering
fires of jealousy, he selected Oyai of the Canyon to carve
the pole, not Laderh, whose vested right it was to per-
form this duty for him. Laderh, who felt slighted,
brooded for many a day over this insult, and finally
made a clean breast of it to his friend Sharp-Teeth. The
Wolf and the Eagle here were closely allied, as they
were both from the upper Stikine River, and at one time
allies.

Sispagut, on his side, having selected the largest red
cedar he could find on Observatory Inlet, had it felled
and towed home, a long way. Then he summoned Oyai
to come and begin his work for him.

The stage was set for a feud. Laderh, sure of the
support of his powerful friend Sharp-Teeth, prepared
to fight his enemy to the knife. As soon as Oyai had
begun his work, Laderh bade Sispagut to shorten his
pole by many arms length: it was far too long! Sispagut,
who was strong and very tall, a real giant, ignored the
protest. But Laderh was insistent, and soon he resorted
to threats. He would shoot down Sispagut, unless he
shortened what he derisively called his "walking stick."

Because of this threat, the tree remained under cover
on the shore, uncarved, for a few years. Oyai later returned to his carving, and, when he had finished it,
during the candlefish season in the spring, Sispagut sent
out invitations far and wide for the erection of his
"walking stick." This was another challenge to whoever might oppose him.

He intoned the dirge song of the Killer-Whales, one
morning, and stood in his dugout canoe in midstream.
As the canoe drifted down, he sang the dirge in front of
the village. One of his wives sat at the stern with a

paddle, and the other at the bow. The dirge meant that all the villagers were to be present at the forthcoming celebration. But, as he passed in front of Laderh's house, the door opened, and a gun was fired at him. He fell down, wounded in the arm.

A nephew of Sispagut on the shore ran to Laderh's house for instant retaliation, but he arrived too late. Laderh had already disappeared. The young brave cried out, "Why should he hide like a coward, when he is bold enough to kill?"

Ready though it was for erection, the totem pole rested on the ground for another year. But the next spring Sispagut announced a new date for the pole-raising festival. He felt in honor bound to redeem his word. One night he was betrayed and shot dead by one of his own nephews.

Sharp-Teeth, the Eagle-Wolf chief, had just adopted Laderh into his clan and taken him under his wing. Both of them, in league together, could more easily defeat the challenger, Sispagut. To further their aims they had bribed the eldest nephew of their rival, knowing that he was jealous of his uncle and wanted to usurp his power. They had whispered into his ear: "Shoot him down like a muskrat and we shall make you a chief, his worthy successor."

Sharp-Teeth encountered more trouble than he expected from Sispagut's powerful clan, who refused to ignore the conspiracy and accept a new leader imposed upon them. They defiantly erected the pole of the Fin-of-the-Killer-Whale in memory of Sispagut, their courageous leader, thus winning the first round in the battle for supremacy between the Killer-Whales and the Eagles. Their totem pole, the Fin-of-the-Killer-

Whale, for a time was the tallest on the river. The Eagle and Wolf newcomers in their midst had been thrown back into their own tracks.

The quarrel now was on in earnest, as Sharp-Teeth's own prestige was at stake, no less than that of Laderh. The Eagles, the Wolves, and the Kanhaades together must show their mettle, now or never.

Sharp-Teeth, in the summer, searched for the largest red cedar he could find, on Portland Canal and Observatory Inlet. The inlet, in those days, had the finest stand of red cedars in the district. He found a giant at what is now Granby Bay, had it felled and towed down the inlet to the village of Gyeetiks, ninety miles below.

The leading carver, Oyai, once more summoned, began his work in the autumn, to finish it if possible in the early spring, before the candlefish season. To achieve this he, his nephews, and four other helpers had to keep on carving the huge tree throughout the winter. Some old men still remember having seen them at work from dawn to sunset, day after day.

Invitations, during the winter, were dispatched in all directions, to the tribes at home and abroad—up the Nass River, on the Skeena, westward to the Haidas of the Queen Charlotte Islands, and northward to Tongas and Ketchikan, in Alaska. So important would be the event that Sharp-Teeth and his tribe convoked more people than were ever brought together on the North Pacific coast to be witnesses of the joint victory of the Eagles, the Wolves, and the Kanhaades over the ancient Killer-Whales. The guests already were landing near the village, but the carving was not yet quite complete, and the hosts were much worried. Oyai called in more assistants, while the elders fretted at the delay. On the eve of the first ceremonies, the work at last was finished, with more than thirteen figures carved from the top to the bottom.

To raise from the ground a tree of this size and plant it in a hole three fathoms deep was a problem never before encountered by the assembled nations of the coast. Failure would bring humiliation and disgrace. Nothing was spared to make sure of success. Large crowds of helpers pulled on the stout cedar-bark ropes, or the nettle ropes made of old candlefish nets, tied at three places on the long shaft. A trench leading to the hole was dug, into which the butt of the pole sank slowly. Thick planks held in place the crumbling earth around the pit; supporting posts were planted here and there; and trestles, pushed under the rising shaft, made progress secure at every inch gained, while a huge crowd pulled at the ropes. Women sang haul-away songs and beat skin drums, to urge the workers at the ropes. Higher and higher went the pole, the fact of its carvings mounting toward the sky. Whenever any dirt fell into the pit, a chief of high standing, who was called forth, stepped down, cleaned it out with his hands, and was liberally compensated for his service.

Liberality was part of the grand show that made the name of a pole famous, and its commemoration remembered for many years in the land. Gifts changed hands on all sides, the hosts showing their wealth by their lavishness, thus adding to their prestige. Oyai, the carver, was paid ten white and two black trade blankets, two moose skins, a musket, and other goods, for his work. Twenty new guns of the old type were cast into the pit under the pole, with other valuables—blankets, coats, and kettles—to honor the deceased uncle in whose memory the pole was to stand. The guests and workers were fed, entertained, and compensated. This the Eagles and the Wolves could afford, for they were becoming the ruling clan of the whole river and of the Alaskan border, northward to the Stikine and southward to the Skeena. Both together, invaders from the north as they were, they had proved great hunters and fisherfolk, and the keenest traders on the coast. When it came to warfare, they were bold and unscrupulous, and their power was growing every day. They terrified their enemies into consternation. Among them Sharp-Teeth and his nephew, Mountain, not to mention their adopted kinsmen, Laderh, were foremost on the Nass. Their power was still rising, as only recently they had annexed to their ranks not a few Tsetsaut hunters, nomads of the northern mountains.

For two days the crowds pulled at the fiber ropes. Then a half-breed trader, Mattheson, arrived at Gyeetiks in his sloop and saluted them with a gunshot. He would assist them with his tackle—ropes and other machinery recently acquired from white seamen. It was the first time that ropes of this kind, which seemed much stronger than their own, were used in this country. Haul-away songs instilled fresh vigor into the workers, the drums beat still louder, and the pole soon stood nearly straight up. But it was only at the close of the third day that the triumphant Eagle and Thunderbird reached their lofty destination in the sky.

Sharp-Teeth and his nephew, Mountain, came forward in full regalia, at the height of their glory. This was the greatest moment of their lives. Then they sang the sacred song of their ancestors: "The golden eagle of the mountains will spread his wings, as he sits above the chiefs on the hilltops." And Laderh, in his turn, intoned in Tlingit the dirge of Chief Lanemraet: "The glacier is safe for us all."

The Killer-Whales, the earliest Nass River occupants, now thrown back, had to accept their final defeat. They sat low and praised the Eagles with the rest, and cursed them under their breath. The Killer-Whales, that day, moved back from the front rank, and the Eagles and the Wolves stood close to shore, facing the sea, and speaking for all others behind them on the Nass, under the shadow of the huge Eagle totem at the village of Gyeetiks.

Further to humble his rivals the Eagle chief, Sharp-Teeth, that night stood in front of his new pole and, close to a blazing fire, related at full length the story of his tribal migrations from the Far North to the blessed land of Leesems.

RAVEN DRIVES SOUTH

THE KANHAADES alongside of the Na'as, after they had crossed Bering Sea, followed the trails which wild animals long had marked in the valley of the Yukon River, or the sea lanes along the Aleutian Islands. The immense stream of the Yukon, extending from the seacoast far into the Rockies, had thrown a door wide open before these Siberians, whom invaders had pushed off the steppes or who were drawn forward by barter with American neighbors—or who, perhaps, looked for new hunting grounds where caribou, being plentiful, were a facile prey in their seasonal migrations north and south.

For many, though not all, of these marauders the course of the Yukon River determined the path toward the sunrise or the south. Others, whose hereditary preferences were for the salt waters, followed the coast line to the south, or who, at least, did not journey far inland.

Of a different stock and a sea folk by heredity, the Eskimos everywhere hugged the coast and hunted caribou only a short distance inland. The majority proceeded eastward along the Arctic coast, and, in their advance by slow stages, they never stopped until they had reached the Labrador and the Gulf of St. Lawrence, or had crossed Baffin Bay into Greenland. At the end of the tenth century, the Eskimos encountered the Icelanders, who discovered them in Helluland—presumably Labrador—somewhere near the mouth of the St. Law-

rence. In later generations the Eskimos and the Icelanders, in southern Greenland, seem to have mingled
extensively.

Other Eskimos, at Bering Strait, turned in the oppo-
site direction and drifted south onto the chain of the
Aleutian Islands, where they encountered Asiatic and
American natives, mingled with them, and became the
Aleutians. Their features and language, in consequence,
were not pure Eskimo, but a blend of mixed elements.

The presence of the Eskimos along the coast north and
south of Bering Strait, in the past two thousand years or
so, did not bar nor lock the door to Siberian fugitives,
traders, and hunters, any more than it has kept the
Chukchees of Siberia from trading every year, virtually
to the present day, with the Alaskans across the narrows.
Never, in prehistoric or in historic times, have the
natives ceased to move back and forth across Bering Sea,
either at the Strait or along the Aleutian Islands. Of
this the early white navigators of the Pacific Ocean
since its discovery have furnished ample evidence. For
them the theory of Asiatic origins is everywhere at the
forefront, and the conclusion is uniform: the bulk of
the Alaskan population was obviously Asiatic.

As soon as the nomads of the old world had become
Americans, they looked for new habitats of the type
familiar to them but less densely occupied—the canoe
folk along the seacoasts, the fishers along the rivers, and
the caribou hunters on the open barrens—and they began to roam over immense territories, which they made
their own as they went forth. Accustomed as were the
tundra tribes to feed upon the domesticated reindeer and
to use its skin for clothes, they did not mind the difference when they passed from the reindeer to its North

The young fisherman appeared soon after, in careless attire and seemingly unaware of his lapse from convention PAGE 148.

American equivalent, the caribou, an improved substitute, as it was easy to capture and more plentiful.

The nomads whose chosen course was the Yukon had no choice but to move up its central stream, or turn aside along one of its several tributaries. Their fan-wise expansion over a large part of our continent depended upon their orientation at this turning point of their existence. Wherever they went, after ascending the Yukon or one of its tributaries and passing out of it, they never failed to adapt themselves promptly to a new environment. This faculty was the secret of their amazing success as invaders, raiders, plunderers, hunters of slaves, rapers, murderers, and sometimes valuable allies.

Just as this huge river spreads its branches in the shape of a hand into a mountainous country, so did the nomads following its arteries disperse far and wide.[1] Some of them went up the main river nearly two thousand miles inside the continent until they stood within measurable distance of the foothills, the swamps, and the northern prairies to the east. Others adopted the northeastern tributary, the Porcupine River (whose name, in the Déné language, was Beaver River) until they reached its headwaters and crossed the divide to the Peel River, flowing into the Mackenzie River. These northerners— Yellow-Knives, Dog-Ribs, Loucheux—trekked eastward, and their pioneers reached a long way toward Hudson Bay, where they encountered the Eskimos and the Crees. All along their wild pathways close to the Arctic coast they often trespassed upon the preserves of the Eskimos, for whom they entertained no friendly feelings.

[1] Rev. F. A. G. Morice, in "The Great Déné Race," *Anthropos*, II (1907), describes "Their receptiveness" (p. 24), "Their cruelty" (p. 25), "Their shrewdness" (p. 23), and their other traits.

Southbound Alaskan elements of the same stock ventured almost due south while ascending the Tanana
River, a tributary of the Yukon, and crossed the divide
over to the Copper River flowing south into the Pacific
Ocean. These nomads were the Tananas and the Copper
River bands, whose lake, river, and seacoast representatives became the northernmost Tlingits.

The caribou hunters, the northernmost Dénés, retained ancient habits of the tundra country all the way
within their unchanged type of habitat, whereas the
southward-bound branch, whose chief pursuit was salmon fishing on the rivers, remained a fisherfolk. Morice
has furnished an instance to the point:

> The semi-sedentary Carriers, whose staple food is salmon, have
> to borrow from the vocabulary of the nomadic Sékanais several of
> their terms to designate the various stages in the growth of caribou,
> while their dialect is exceedingly rich in words denotive of salmon
> under all possible aspects.[2]

Preferring the Lewes River, an important tributary
of the mighty Yukon River, other bands journeyed onto
the plateaus and into the northwestern spurs of the
Rockies, where they are still represented. It is mostly
to this element that the Wolf, Raven, and Killer-Whale
clans of the North Pacific coast and rivers trace back
their ancestry and traditions.[3]

As the Killer-Whales and the Eagles were primarily a

---

[2] *Ibid.*, V. (1910), 113.

[3] *Ibid.*, IV (1909), 585. Morice accurately describes their type of nomadism in
the following terms: "These natives generally move within a given perimeter,
which represents their ancestral territory, instead of constantly changing their
habitat (which they occasionally do)....The Tartars and Mongols may certainly
be taken for typical nomads; yet each of their bands has well defined boundaries,
which it respects." Bergeron, in *Relation de Voyages* (quoted by Morice), wrote:
"The Tartars have no permanent abodes and never know where they may be the
next day, though every chief of a horde knows the bounds of his pasture grounds."

canoe people, their route southwards must have hugged
the seacoast. Their traditions and pursuits are also
mostly of the sea. With the likely exception of the
northernmost part at the start, they covered much of the
distance in skin boats and in dugouts, until they had
reached their destination. But their progress was not
hidebound. They stayed wherever they found a living,
or as long as they could. When pushing on, they usually
left behind some of their kin, to whom they occasionally
returned or had recourse, if pressed by urgent need.

The Kanhaades (our subject here) did not always
claim the Raven as a name or an emblem, nor did they
exist under the banner of the Raven (Yaehl or Kaq),
who was a semi-divine creator in the new world, not
only of themselves but of all the other tribes in the
Northwest. Although the Raven as a myth is almost as
well known in Siberia as it is in Alaska and farther south,
it was not at first the emblem of any clansmen anywhere.

The northwestern clans of the Dénés under the aegis
of the Raven still bear the names of Kanhaade, Larhsail,
Koala, which are old enough to have lost their meaning
through mutations. As applied to them the badge or
name of the Raven is quite recent.[4]

The Kanhaades from time immemorial had been one
of the exogamic moieties or halves in a social order
brought over from Siberia by the remote ancestors. One
half or moiety intermarried with the other. The opposite
moiety, devoid of a general name in Alaska, lately assumed, among the Tsimsyans alone, that of the Wolf,

---

[4] James Teit, in "Tahltan Tales" (Mss., National Museum of Canada), says:
"Raven ordained that people should be borne and die. He then divided the people
into exogamic phratries. He put half of the people on one side and called them
Katcede, and the others, on the other side, and called them Tāxtlowĕde. He said
that the right-hand people (Raven) should always marry the left-hand people
(Wolves). It would not be well to marry otherwise."

The terrifying voice of the supernatural Raven broke forth.... This was the first appearance of the secret spirits of the narhnoks PAGE 153.

or Larh-Kibu ("On-the-Wolf"). To this day the Tlingits never have systematized its name or crest, nor have
the Haidas at any time admitted into their own ranks the
Wolf as a clan emblem. If the two main moieties in
Alaska, the Yukon, and northern British Columbia have
become known to us as Ravens and Wolves, it is merely
due to cultural changes under the influence of the white
man.

The Wolves, as we have seen, split up into halves or
moieties—one of them, the Wolves proper, and the
other, the Eagles, in imitation of the Russian imperial
crest. The Eagle moiety or phratry, at the height of the
fur trade with the Russians and the British, rose to the
first rank among the Tsimsyans, the Haidas, and the
southern Tlingits. But their Tlingit originators, on the
whole, maintained their former allegiance to the older
dual moieties of the Ravens and the Wolves. And the
Eagles have tended to remain the allies of their former
sires, the Wolves.

The Kanhaades or Ravens, no less than the Wolves
and the Eagles, were still, in the last century, on their
way south along the seacoast. Of this there is no more
vivid proof than the fantastic adventures of their notorious leader, Copper-Shield (Haimas), who at one
time was a match for the famous Stone-Cliff (Legyarh).

These two extraordinary leaders and contemporaries,
Copper-Shield and Stone-Cliff, stand close comparison
in the limelight of a turbulent century. Their backgrounds did not sensibly differ, nor the span of their
existence; their forebears in the North were Tlingit,
yet with a southern admixture of Kwakiutl blood; and
their adopted nation and field of action were Tsimsyan.

The name "Legyarh" in Kwakiutl signifies "Stone-Cliff," and that of "Haimas" in the same language seems to have meant "Southwest-Gale" or "Southwest-Rain." However, "Haimas" might mean, in Tsimsyan, "bark sheath for copper shield," or "copper-shield case."[5]

When mere children, they both were taken from the Kwakiutl country of their birth to that of older relatives among the coast Tsimsyans, and very soon they rose to the front rank in their adopted nation. Because of their mixed ancestry, they introduced new ways and devices into their tribe and soon found themselves at odds with the older elements, whom they challenged and overcame by force of personality and courage.

Let us now hear a little of the traditional story of Copper-Shield, the Kanhaade or Raven leader, born Kwakiutl, bred Tsimsyan, and self-made outlaw on the outskirts of the Tlingit country! His lifelong ambition was to subdue the Tsimsyans, dominate his elder rival, Stone-Cliff, and conquer the Stikine River to the north.

A Tlingit chief named Kakae—in an episode anterior to the birth of Copper-Shield, about a hunded and fifty years ago—drove down the coast with his folk in several canoes and established a village on the southern side of the wide arm of the sea, now called Portland Canal. But he soon realized that for the security of his own Raven people he was still much too near his enemies, the Wolves of the Stikine. By killing two Wolf chiefs, in retaliation for mortal injury, he had aroused the wrath of their powerful clan. They would not fail at their first opportunity to retaliate. For greater safety, he resumed his canoe journey and sought, farther away,

---

[5] *Hayaetsk,* "copper shield" (here abbreviated); *mass* "bag" (or "sheath") of yellow cedar bark for a copper shield.

the friendship of the Gitlaen tribe on the lower Skeena River.

Chief Sea-Lion of the Gitlaens extended a cordial welcome to him and offered to take him permanently into his own household. He knew Kakae to be of the same Kanhaade crest as himself, and of very high rank among the Tlingits, his people.

This Tlingit exile was determined, if he could help it, not to die without issue—that is, a nephew by birth or adoption—for the souls in a family were bound up, in their reincarnation, with hereditary names. These names could pass down only from uncle to nephew, or from a sister to her own son. Names and souls otherwise would become extinct, to the everlasting shame of their living owner. But, to Kakae's poignant sorrow, his only sister died soon after his arrival at Gitlaen, and he grieved bitterly, for in her he had lost the one of his own blood whom he depended upon for a nephew who would be his presumptive heir.

Kakae, to relieve his sorrow, took a flying trip south to the Wudstae tribe (in the neighborhood of Vancouver Island), where he might establish his permanent abode, for he had heard that, among those southern people, a son—not a nephew as in the North—succeeded in direct line to a father.

In the house of a friendly host in Wudstae, he was amazed to see a young woman, a niece of the chief, looking so much like his deceased sister that he felt moved to say to his Tsimsyan escorts:

"Here is my sister! She has died and come back to life for our sake. I will ask the chief to let me take her back with me to Gitlaen."

His host at first was not willing to suffer the loss of

his niece, even at the hands of an ally of high rank from the North. Her young son, he objected, issued from a highborn Kanhaade father, was himself by blood a noble, and would become a chief. No one should be expected to make such a sacrifice out of mere good will.

Kakae, whose hope was no less than his pride, agreed, and said: "Like my own sister's son he shall be my heir, of a rank on a par with the highest chiefs of the Tsimsyans."

And he received the reply:

"If you promise to have him, in due time, installed as your successor, then he may be yours. Let his name then be that of Haimas, the peerless Copper-Shield!"

As nothing stood in the way of their solemn pledge, the young mother and her child were seated in the center of Kakae's war canoe, and gifts in dowry from their kin were piled high about them. Among these gifts, the most precious was the mysterious spirit secreted in a large painted chest, together with the dancing insignia of high chieftainship. And, satisfied, they departed on their long journey northward to the village where the Gitlaen tribe of the Tsimsyans now abode, near the mouth of the Skeena River.

The exiled chief of the Tlingits, who had not yet learned the language of his adopted Tsimsyan tribe, did not hesitate to give a big feast and introduce his young nephew and successor, no less than the Wudstae mother, whom he considered his reborn sister. After this gala event, both mother and child enjoyed the status of native chiefs of noble blood, whose will is the law of the land.

As young Copper-Shield had been trained in fishing crabs, clams, and other shellfish, an important pursuit of the southern coast tribes, he spent much of his time tending traps and fireweed nets and taking in a good catch. Young as he was, he already showed his pluck and unflagging industry. His Kanhaade uncle was proud of him, and the Wolf relatives of his Wudstae father already watched over his welfare in the hope that perhaps he might some day be of sufficient caliber to check the mighty Stone-Cliff of the Eagles, whom they feared no less than they resented him.

A Killer-Whale leader of the Mosquito tribe, giving a feast called *yaok* one winter, invited to his feast house all the chiefs of the lower Skeena; and foremost among them was the mighty Stone-Cliff of the canyon, who claimed the front rank everywhere. But he may have overlooked young Copper-Shield, who was busy as usual at his crab fishing in the coves.

After all the chiefs, attired in their regalia, had arrived and had been acclaimed at their entrance into the house, Stone-Cliff of the haughty Eagles walked in, last of all, as became his dignity as head chief in the country. Yet young Copper-Shield of the Ravens, who already had been raised to the second rank next to him, had failed so far to appear, much to the discomfort of the Killer-Whale host and Eagle guests alike. As if to make his mistake less pardonable, the young fisherman appeared soon after, in careless attire and seemingly unaware of his lapse from convention.

Stone-Cliff, who was never inclined to gloss over any oversight concerning his prestige, leaned over the boy as soon as he had sat down next to him, and said tartly:

"Young man, where have you been, and what were you doing? You have held up this *yaok* and kept it from getting under way."

"I was out spearing crabs," candidly answered the young fisherman, still unaware of his lapse from the high path of chiefly etiquette.

"If I were you," sneered Stone-Cliff, loudly enough to be heard by all, "I would, some time, invite my nation to a crab feast."

When the *yaok* was over, the uncles of the young chief, gathering around him, inquired anxiously, "What did the head chief say to you because of your being late in appearing beside him?"

"Young man," he answered, "invite my nation to a crab feast!"

From the mouth of a haughty leader like Stone-Cliff, this remark was no less than a challenge, flung at his youthful neighbor and, over his head, at the leaders of the Raven clan who were upholding him as a symbol of their stubborn resistance to his encroachments; not at the Ravens alone, who stood for his mother's folk, but at the Wolves as well. The influential Laranows represented his Wolf father. Both Ravens and Wolves smarted under the sting from the pursed lips of their impetuous tribal leader. Very soon afterward they held in secret a joint council, to figure out how to counteract the taunt and meet the challenge.

Laranows, the one leader marked for the initiative, now declared:

"All right, he will have his crab feast, and we must shame him who meant to shame us, you and me! Let us bring out, as is our right, the Tall-Hat with ten disks, our most valuable heirloom from the days when our forebears owned the high prairies at the headwaters of the Stikine. Let us show him the headpiece called 'He-Walks-Toward-His-Hat,' which is our glorious family

crest! Once long ago a child, our ancestor, was trying
to keep up with his elders, and he would stumble and
cut his face on the sharp blades of the tall grass of the
prairie. . . . "

And everyone was left to himself to remember the rest
of the traditional story of how, to protect his head, his
fond mother had fashioned for him a hat with a wide
rim all around, shielding his eyes and cheeks. This hat
after a time was considered a mark of high rank. And
now it was the most precious of all clan possessions.

"Stone-Cliff wants to appropriate Tall-Hat, but our
chance now is too good for us to miss. Let us openly
reclaim the right to its ownership. Here is a lad who is
fit to uphold it, like our child ancestor who first wore it
amid the tall grasses of the upper Stikine!"

In their plan to give a crab feast at Knemas, the Nass
River fishing station of the young man's foster father,
Kakae, the chief resolved to build a new house wherein
to gamble their all for a high stake against the Eagles.

The house, meant to be Copper-Shield's own, was
made large and different from the ordinary. It belonged
to the *da'q* type—semi-underground, with step-like
grades down to the center, where the fireplace was situated under a wide opening in the roof. Laranows, the
Wolf head chief of the Gitlaen tribe, himself took
charge of cutting the heavy house posts and roof beams;
he was known as an expert builder and wood carver.

As the time approached for the event, Nass River
hunters of the Wolf clan climbed the high mountains at
the head of Observatory Inlet and along the Skeena,
hunted the mountain goat and brought back large quantities of kidney fat and meat, a specialty of the upriver
tribes and a great delicacy when coupled with dog

"Let the mink break wind! Let the mink blow gales!" PAGE 164.

salmon cured in the sun and dried over smoking embers.
Berry pickers, the autumn before, had been engaged to
gather, dry, and smoke wild berries, relished by everyone,
crab apples from the marshlands, soapberries and huckleberries from the mountainsides.

As it was now Kakae's intention to show in public the
mysterious spirit of the painted chest given by the
Wudstae chief to the child, his henchmen secretly at-
tended to all preparations for its production at a fair
distance up the Knemas River in the mountain, where
nobody could spy upon them. There they brought the
Raven spirit out of the box and became experts in the
trickery of handling as a mask its large wooden head—
that of the Raven—with hinged parts moved by hidden
strings.

The wearer of the mask and feathered costume im-
personated the Raven and imitated its motions in a dramatic pantomime, while ghostly cawing from large
cedar calls screened behind the walls conjured the under-
world into a loud outburst.

As soon as the split or box calls and whistles—with
one, two, or three pipes—were completed, they were
tested in the open, yet far from indiscreet ears. The
voice blowers, giving vent to their stout lungs, awakened
wild echoes; they were themselves moved into fear and
real ecstacy. One of the voice makers crossed the river
into the brush on the other side, and did his make-believe
cawing. Another, in a thicket on this side, replied in
kind, and both went on chattering like true ravens for
a long time, until they were both masters of their sacred
instruments. And this secret spot ever since has been
called Place-of-Echoes (Lukul'ait).

A little before the opening of the candlefish season,

the Tsimsyan tribes, who had all been invited beforehand, arrived at Knemas in their dugout canoes, set foot
ashore, and made ready for the celebration. Donning
their regalia, the chiefs proceeded one by one to the *yaok*
and were cordially greeted in by their names.

From the outset they were astonished at the sight of
the reddish glow within the graded house, a strange
ghostly light never seen before. It was secretly produced by rotten wood pulverized into dust and scattered over the floor. Some of it, mixed with candlefish
grease, cast by ladlefuls into the fire, was burning with
a sizzling noise. From this the new structure, Copper-
Shield's own, became known under the name of Inside-
the-Red-House-of-Marvels.

On the heels of this development, the terrifying voice
of the supernatural Raven broke forth in the forest out-
doors; then similar voices, much nearer, responded from
outside the walls, from the roof top, even seemingly
from underground, and from all sides. This was the first
appearance in this northern country of the secret spirits
of the *narhnoks*.

This memorable event, so often repeated thereafter,
never has been forgotten on Portland Canal to this day.

Truly, Copper-Shield, the young host, who commanded the nether world so plainly, could not be dismissed as
a mere upstart, not even by a tower of strength like
Stone-Cliff himself. This Eagle leader, whose origin also
went back to the south, had an inkling as to how to ignite
a reddish light and how to make the supernatural Raven
caw his blatant worst. Yet nothing could be done now
but accept the inevitable. His young rival, Copper-
Shield, had stolen a march on him. Let the young buck
have his fling, but not for very long!

Before the brooding Eagle leader had time to recover his wits, a handful of young men stepped in, and Kakae, the host, bade them:

"My nephews, go out and spear the crab! For this is Copper-Shield's crab feast to all the tribes of the Tsimsyans."

While they were out, supposedly spearing crabs in the cove, messengers laden with delicacies faced the guests and laid before them piles of dried salmon and candlefish grease from the river, wild crab apples from the marshes, huckleberries and soapberries in dried and smoked rolls, and, last of all, heaps of kidney and fat of the mountain goat, which was such a rare tidbit.

Very soon the crab hunters returned with many short-pronged spears, stood in front of the chiefs, pretended to spear the goat fat and the kidneys in the dishes as if they were drawn out of the sea, and offered the catch to the astonished beholders, saying, "Here is crab meat from the salt waters!"

Chief Kakae, speaking in Tlingit to his Tsimsyan hosts as he always did, asked repeatedly: "My nephew, Copper-Shield, what have you caught in the sea that might satisfy the hearts of our guests?"

One of his nephews walked in from the rear, a large dish of fat and mountain-goat kidneys in his hands, and deposited it near the red fire which made everybody look ghostly. With a short-pronged spear the host lifted a large piece of fat, roasted it over the fire, and tendered it to his guest of honor, Stone-Cliff, who had to take it with his hands and burn himself severely.

"This is a crab from the cove," explained the host with a touch of sarcasm, "the cove wherein my nephew spends his time without remembering his engagements.

Never to my knowledge has there been such a crab fisher in the country."

Then, while the much humiliated head chief was forced to swallow his pride with the hot morsels, the host went around the feast house, clamoring, "You, Chief Trakaks, here is your spear, here is your crab! You, Chief Skagwait, of the canyon, here is your spear, and here is a crab! And you, Chief Rpeelek of the Eagles. . . ."

All the other chiefs of the allied clans were served with crab meat in turn, the crab meat which, in the hands of a careless but lavish young man like Copper-Shield, turned into the choicest meats and fruits of the river, the lowlands, and the mountain peaks.

Copper-Shield, before the close of the ceremony, appeared for the first time in his robes of high chieftainship, which came from Bella Bella to the south, and wearing on his head the Tall-Hat on ten desks, the Tall-Hat from the northern prairies of long ago. After this display of liberality and power, no guest here present could withhold his approval. The host, therefore, stood silently awaiting his due. A clamor of recognition broke forth from every side, yet it was far from spontaneous, for resentment already rankled in many hearts. While he blew the soft white down of the eagle as a symbol of peace all round, he was conceded only as much as he had bargained for. As for the rest, the future only would tell.

From this memorable night on, Copper-Shield ranked high among the leaders of the nation, second only to the imperious Stone-Cliff, whose authority he might challenge some day. And Kakae, at this moment, was anxious to add his own last contribution to the meteoric ascent of his chosen nephew. He said:

"Until today, I, Kakae, have owned and held in the face of all, Tlingits and Tsimsyans alike, the mouth of this river. Moreover, the Gitlaen tribe of the Tsimsyans of the Skeena have made of me their head chief, and, as a result, the tongue of my northern nation now is spoken or understood along the coast as far south as the Oxtall River, if not farther. All of this coast now is Tlingit-speaking. Even the noble Stone-Cliff, here present, is part Tlingit and knows the vernacular. But my power is spent, my life is almost over. Copper-Shield, my favorite nephew, stands in my place. Knemas and the Nass River I bestow upon him. There he is bound to uphold the prestige of the Kanhaades. And who knows but he may rise even higher—he, the new man who now wears the Tall-Hat on his victorious head!

From this day on, Copper-Shield boldly entered upon a career which has, long since, become the central theme of semi-epic narratives of the Homeric type.

Inspired by his old uncle, Kakae, he led a raid in force, with forty canoes, on the Stikine and Sitka tribes to the north, because there was still an old score to settle with them. Victorious, Copper-Shield took back home the Tsimsyans whom his enemies had enslaved.

While he was away on his expedition, a band of Tlingits from Klawaq besieged his own new village at Kundaw on the Nass and burned it down to cinders. But he was not of a breed to be disheartened by a mere reverse in which the scales, on the whole, tilted in his favor.

Still early in his life, as head chief of his Tsimsyan tribe, he crushed a vanguard of Tlingit invaders who, at the time, occupied Kton—now Work Channel, between the mouths of the Skeena and Nass Rivers close to the seacoast. And he made Kton his own, thus reinforcing in the face of Stone-Cliff of the Eagles his hold upon the estuaries of both these rivers. On this occasion he captured from the defeated some copper tools which he prized highly because they gratified his partiality for native copper. He made the well-known myth of Haloos and Tsawde his own. It explains how copper shields and tools once were made and bartered by legendary ancestors in the Far North; and he claimed them as his own forebears.

At the height of his power he launched headlong into a deadly fight with the canyon tribe under the leadership of his born rival, Stone-Cliff. The stakes at this juncture were so high on both sides that the defeat of either would leave the other in mastery for generations to come. No one as yet could tell who would win the day in a struggle dividing the nation asunder for a tribal showdown. Copper-Shield (or Southwest-Gale) showed his mettle in adversity no less than when he had the upper hand.

Pursued by his Tsimsyan enemies, who had banded themselves together to stamp him out, he was prudent enough to vanish into the wilderness for a time, lest they might pounce in the darkness upon his tribe. While in search of a hiding place among the islands and the fiords to the south, he and his followers chanced upon a small Killer-Whale band of Porcher Island Tsimsyans, and catching them off their guard they overpowered them and escaped with the booty southward into Grenville Channel, where the native occupants were few and elusive and the dangerous whirlpools at the entrance would keep off roving avengers from the north. There he es-

tablished his fortress upon a cliff across the bay, at what
is now Baker's Inlet.

A dreaded monster, besides, kept all timid folk away
from the inlet, but to Copper-Shield and his henchmen
the bugaboo served only as a tool in time of need, long
enough for them to prey upon the milder people to the
south, make captives or slaves, and replenish their ranks
and their stores.

Native foods aplenty here beckoned to them, as no
one had ever preyed with a heavy hand upon their
bounties—seals, crabs, and shellfish in the salt sea, deer
at the edge of the forest, and berries of all kinds on the
mountains. But the only salmon stream was Salmon
River, close to their new fortress; here they could get
only the steelhead salmon trout, but it satisfied their
imperious need of fish fit to cure and dry.

After the outlaws had gathered and put up their supply of salmon trout, one early spring, they paddled their
many dugouts across open water outside the bay without
fear of being detected and pursued. For, at this time
every year, the coast Tsimsyan tribes of the
Porcher Islands were engaged in their candlefish work
on the Nass to the north.

Unknown to them, a Haida raiding party of the Queen
Charlotte Islands was then traveling back home along
Grenville Channel, after a successful attack upon Wudstae. A few canoeloads of these bloodthirsty warriors,
coming across the tail end of the homeward-bound fishermen, thought they had to deal here with the shy folk
of the hidden inlets, and would not miss such a fine opportunity to increase their booty.

As the entrance to Salmon River was high, rocky, and
devious, it hid the canoes and the fugitives, who tried to

dodge a fight with a force much superior to their own.

Copper-Shield and a few of his picked warriors, once he knew that the Haidas were hot on his track, sat on a cliff near the fortress, pretending to eat his dinner. While he was observing the cautiously approaching Haidas, a flying arrow struck him deep in the hip. Gritting his teeth, he quietly whispered to his men.

"A Haida sliver has touched me from behind. Do not get excited; only pretend that we have not seen anything. As soon as we are ready for the fray, let us spring up and give a good account of ourselves!"

His outlaws, always ready for a dog fight, at once bared their weapons and crept up to vantage points at the edge of the cliffs. The few who happened to be with their chief on the exposed bluff did not attempt to hide. This maneuver made the Haidas only the more self-confident. Without waiting for their full numbers to be assembled for an assault, they moved up quickly, neglecting the usual hide-and-seek precautions.

Copper-Shield and his men, having finished their feigned dinner, stood up and walked away, in spite of great torment as the arrow still lay embedded in his thigh. But he did not for a moment lose control of his wits.

Reckless, all of them, the attackers wanted openly to overtake the few retreating men who still seemed unaware of an intrusion upon their privacy. It was not worth while wasting valuable arrows upon them. A few blows from stone mauls would dispatch them in short order.

"Wai, wai! Well, now!" shouted Copper-Shield, in a sudden *volte-face*, "Now is our time to strike back!"

His warriors sprang forth, and with a few turns of

the hand killed or overpowered the Haidas, who had
been taken wholly by surprise. As this unforeseen en-
gagement came to a lucky end, the outlaws found
themselves enriched by a number of subdued captives,
and they appropriated a number of slaves from the
south who were being taken back to the islands. The
booty accruing to them was enough to cheer their
hearts. At this pace they would raise their heads again,
win over new allies, and soon boldly return to the
Skeena for a fresh stand in the struggle for supremacy.

The following generation of semi-outlaws of the Gitlaen tribe incessantly kept up its subversive activities
among the Tsimsyans, who were swayed by the power of
Stone-Cliff. This Eagle head chief, on his side, never
missed a chance to hound his opponents of the lower
Skeena and try to push them off into the sea. But the
underdogs of the Kanhaade breed would never let themselves be silenced or destroyed.

Better to hold their own in the face of vexations, they
organized the fraternity of the Secret Braves (Wudzen-
Alerh), and recruited its members from all clans and
tribes, whether Tsimsyan, Tlingit, or Wudstae. This
Fraternity formed a cross section of the younger generation with a leaning for rebellion, adventure, murder,
and whatever fanned their unruly spirits. Their sworn
aim was revenge upon the Eagles and, if possible, the
capture of supreme power from their mighty leader.

The numerous raids of the Secret Braves, carried out
singly or in small wolf-like packs, always occurred under
the cover of darkness. They defied all attempts at a
stand-up fight. The perpetrators were too elusive even
for a stab in the back for retaliation.

Conspiracies arose, such as were familiar in the past century and under the very eyes of the white traders, calling for countermoves and intrigues that often ended in ostentatious potlatches. Here the Ravens, in the long winter nights, cawed and trumpeted their ghostly mysteries accompanied by the dog-biting rituals of the dreaded Hamatsa—a secret society from the Kwakiutl country in the south, at the time spreading like wildfire all over the North and undermining the moiety system of the totems.

Stone-Cliff, the supreme leader, a partisan of action, always prompt at quelling insurrection by means of counterblows, conjured up similar trickery. Indeed, he outdid all others by perpetrating the awe-inspiring performance of his own (pretended) death, incineration, and resurrection. For a while after this event, the Secret Braves of Copper-Shield had to content themselves with the pursuits of organized knaves whose misdeeds were carried out in secrecy. Yet they never for a moment renounced their aim, which was to overrun a land that the missionaries, after their arrival in the mid 1850's, branded as the playground of Satan on an infernal rampage.

An episode from the dawn of historic times on the coast will bear this out.

One of the few notorious chiefs bearing the name of Copper-Shield in the succession of individuals directing the activities of the Secret Braves, was the son of Big-Shaiks, who was the Grizzly-Bear head of the Mosquito tribe of Tsimsyans.

As a lad, after a hereditary pattern, young Copper-Shield played with the boys of his age in his father's tribe; he preferred them to his own maternal cousins in

the Gitlaen village. The rules of maternal descent, unchallenged among the northern nations, were at times
overlooked by the older groups of Kanhaade iconoclasts,
who claimed that their local ancestors used to intermarry without regard to a moiety system. In other
words, they had indulged in incest without being aware
of it. The new clan practice of exogamy had been imposed upon the older occupants by the Eagles and the
Wolves from the North, who brooked no contradiction.

Young Copper-Shield trained a little band of juvenile
outlaws who were fast getting out of hand and worrying
their uncles. For the older generation was bound hand
and foot to the prevailing order; and this order, they
were willing to admit, was far from barren of fruit.
The chosen leaders usually worked hand in hand with
Stone-Cliff, who knew how to keep them responsive to
his will.

One day young Copper-Shield walked up to his
paternal uncle, Grizzly-Bear, and asked him for the
loan of his best dugout canoe, a fine piece from the hands
of a master canoe builder. This canoe had been carefully
adzed inside, and two Grizzly-Bear totems had been
painted in red, black, and yellow ochers inside, at the
bow and prow. The uncle curtly refused the loan. A
ceremonial canoe of this type never is handled as a toy
in the hands of uncautious boys, particularly when they
are sons rather than nephews.

Affronted and indignant, the young Secret Brave
crept into the bush at the edge of the sea, where the
canoe was kept covered with logs and wet moss, and
knocked a big hole in its bottom by using a sharp-edged
boulder. Thus ruined, the canoe was discovered by its
owner, who wanted instantly to retaliate. Yielding to

anger, he cracked Big-Shaik's main canoe and rendered it useless. This was the only fit way to get even for the offense at the hands of the chief's incorrigible son. The time had come to send this unruly boy to his mother's kinfolk; they might curb his foul instincts.

Big-Shaiks, informed of the truth, was much upset. At first he wanted to atone for the damage caused by the boy; but when he discovered that his own fine canoe had been ruined in retaliation, he grew angry and threatened reprisals.

The outcome was the dismissal of the young wrong-doer. Henceforth he was branded a renegade—the Kanhaade renegade. But the curb upon his rashness had come too late. As a Secret Brave supported by his own accomplices, he withdrew to the hills and lived off the country and the surrounding people by plunder, until he reached maturity. Without a pang of remorse he robbed the food caches of the various clans, stole their tools and weapons when a chance offered, and kept the whole neighborhood in a state of nervous tension at a time when foreign enemies only too often appeared on the threshhold or at the back door.

After he had grown up into a strong and resourceful man, Copper-Shield returned at last from the hills to his mother's tribe, the Gitlaens, and he was welcomed. For, in the rising generation, he stood in line for the post of head chief, and his tribe just then felt the need of a courageous leader at the helm in tribal affairs. The Tlingit invaders were more troublesome than ever; the Haidas of the islands remained dangerous; the Tsimsyan tribes of the canyon and their Nass River relatives were still to be feared, no less than the bloodthirsty foreigners.

Copper-Shield once more became their man of destiny. They raised him to the pinnacle, without a word of protest from his former allies, or even from his distrustful opponents.

Just as his great-granduncle had been fond of the sister whom he lost in death, to his grief; so had the young chief of Gitlaen become interested in the welfare of his own elder sister. She was the most beautiful of all the maidens of her generation, and sought for by not a few suitors of high rank.

She was too haughty and discriminating for the nephews of ordinary chiefs, and the one finally to win her was no other than High-Cliff (Gusraen), a chief in line for the headchieftainship in the Wolf clan on the lower Stikine. Her wedding, an incident of some interest in inter-tribal relations, took place after the establishment of Redoute Saint Dionys in the 1830's, since it took her to the recently established Russian post at Wrangell. There she helped to uphold the prestige of her husband's household in the company of his senior wives. All the chiefs in those days were polygamists.

But the other mates of High-Cliff resented their chief's philandering outside the borders of their own Tlingit nation; and one of them at least belonged to an Eagle clan that opposed all ties with the Copper-Shield faction.

Ere long, the jealous wives had a tête-à-tête with a Chilkat sorcerer, who espoused their cause and devised a means to humiliate the newcomer and make her ridiculous in the eyes of the tribe. Cutting out the rectum of a mink, he boiled it with the seal meat which she was to eat, while he chanted over the dish an incantation with the words, "Let the mink break wind! Let the mink blow gales!"

From that day on the striking beauty of the Tsimsyans, whose misfortune was to have become the youngest wife of a Wrangell chief, could not help causing merriment among the folk wherever she happened to be and bringing embarrassment to her proud husband. Strange noises issued from under her when she squatted down, or followed behind her as she walked by herself.

High-Cliff led her at night into the seclusion of a forlorn camp and summoned medicine men to treat her by means of potent songs and resonant drum beats. But their power was no match to that of the reputed Sitkan necromancer, and they were forced to retreat before the growing threats of the mink.

The young woman, of her own accord, asked her master to take her back to her brother, who had always been devoted to her. He would welcome her home and be willing to suffer her adversity. But, at this moment, she failed to remember how proud her brother was and how fiery on occasions he could be.

Much humbled, High-Cliff, the Tlingit, landed at night from his dugout on the beach facing the house of Copper-Shield, his precarious brother-in-law at Fort Simpson, and, unseen or unheard by anyone, imparted to the Tsimsyan chief the reason for his unusual errand. The Tsimsyan welcomed his sister, but kept her hidden at the rear of his large house.

The local Eagles, secretly informed of it, spread the news, expecting to confront the young woman face to face and find out for themselves the cause of her disgrace.

On a silent night of midsummer, while the people of the Wolf and Eagle clans gathered cockles down the beach, they spoke in jest to each other, and their voices carried a long way through the stillness of the air.

As he stood in front of his doorway, Copper-Shield heard gay sounds of laughter from afar, and listened intently. Cockle diggers, compressing the air within their inflated cheeks, would then release it with a cracking noise, and burst out, "Oh! there you are, Tsat-Kurh!" This was the name of the young woman now in her hiding place not so far out of hearing. The opposite group on the beach would answer back, "She reminds me of the mink!"

Profoundly upset, Copper-Shield re-entered his house, brought his beautiful sister forth into the fireplace, dressed her in her choicest finery, put the halait crown of chieftainship on her head, and seated her on a wide board on which the black Raven, his emblem, was painted. Then he walked out, leaving her alone to her thoughts.

Outside, he called up his nephews, and, on the open beach, they built a pile of pitch firewood in the manner of a funeral pyre. And he burned her alive, chanting a dirge: "High-Cliff's poisonous wives shall be satisfied. But for their villany they shall pay dearly."

Before the first flicker of dawn he summoned his Secret Braves and started with them for the Nass River. On the site of what is now the mission village of Kincolith on Portland Canal, just north of the estuary of the Nass, he built a new house, a feast house large enough to shelter his band of renegades and outlaws.

The house no sooner was erected than Copper-Shield dispatched messengers to the tribes of the Tsimsyans, inviting the chiefs and their helpers to a housewarming party the following spring, when they would be on their way to the candlefish spawning grounds. The messengers, before they left, were impressed with one reservation: "Do not invite He-whose-Buttocks-Are-Haida-like"—(that is, whose broad posterior is like those of Haida sea folk, their lives being spent squatting in canoes). As this chief of the mid-Skeena had always proved a staunch friend to him, he wanted to spare him the trouble of a voyage which somehow might turn into a disaster.

The Skeena River guests in the early spring began to arrive in family groups, the chief accompanied by his headmen and nephews. Even before landing from their canoes, they heard songs and loud drums beating within the new house, which looked different from the ordinary. The ceremonial entrance was of an antique type—the guests, one after the other, having to climb a few steps on a notched ladder, and then to go through a small oval doorway headfirst.

As soon as a head appeared inside, a stone club hammered it in before a sound was uttered, and the body, deftly hauled in, was tumbled into a large pit, while the herald within clamored the appropriate name and the singers sang only praise.

When Copper-Shield's uninvited friend appeared in the doorway, the host wondered. He asked: "Who called your name, Kawm of the canyon, my ill-advised friend?"

Kawm, smarting because of what he had mistaken for a slight or an oversight, had come without an invitation, and here he was to pay with his life for his mistake. At this stage no exception could be allowed. Else the secret might leak out and the well-planned slaughter of the Eagle chiefs and their henchmen be frustrated before it had reached its bitter end.

When the heads of the oncoming guests had all been smashed, their scalps taken off, and their bodies dumped into the pit, the hymns of welcome gave way to exultant war songs.

Thus was the foul injury to Copper-Shield's beautiful sister avenged for all time, and the name of Kincolith, or Place-of-Scalps-on-Sticks, retained ever after by the tribal village on this spot, which not long afterward became a missionary center of the Church of England.

For a brief period after this event the Secret Braves of Copper-Shield resorted part of the year to their fortress of Kundaw on Portland Canal, and associated by preference with the southern Tlingits of Larhsail in Russian territory. When it became clear that the Eagles of the Skeena were not bent upon revenge—which was due to the influence over them of the Hudson's Bay Company traders at Port Simpson—the outlaws once more began to drift back to the estuary of the Skeena; and step by step they resumed their former drive southward along the seacoast.

While Copper-Shield still spoke Tlingit as his habitual tongue, he secretly assassinated the old Tsimsyan head chief of the Salmon-Weir tribe, who was his own clan uncle. His purpose was to succeed him. During the course of a memorable potlatch he was raised to his position, the better to resume hostilities against his ancient foes the Eagles of the canyon. But there was, at the time, little fight left in the Eagles, who were adopting more and more the ways of the white man. And the fierce Stone-Cliff himself was soon to become a Christian at the mission town of Metlakatla.

Remaining to the bitter end a conspirator and a man with a shady past, the chief of the Secret Braves had the courage to expose on a large copper shield the remains of his Salmon-Weir uncle, whom he had murdered in cold blood, and to wait for paid mourners and invited guests to come in for the funeral. But the memory of the Place-of-Scalps affair was still too fresh. Very few outsiders ventured within, only to hear their host cast aspersions upon the Tlingits whom he blamed for the crime, and sing without shame dirge songs which he was making his own without a trace of remorse.

Laranows, the Wolf leader whose wife was the niece of the dead chief, threatened retaliation, but did not dare to put his threat into action.

As a conspiracy against Copper-Shield was brewing— he was to be shot when stepping into his dugout—he decided once more to go into a safe retreat, this time at Red Bluffs near Fishery Bay on the lower Nass.

His fortified village at Red Bluffs was attacked in force by the canyon Eagles and the island Eagles jointly. And this last fight of a dark age, replete with treachery, ruse, and trickery, ended in the killing of many assailants and, last of all, in the destruction of Copper-Shield himself, who was hit from behind in his own house, to the utter relief of the whole population.

With his timely passing the subversive activities of the outlaws came to an end, and the way at last was opened for a new age, the age of the practical traders and the men of the Gospel.

ALL TREK FORWARD

WHEN sailing from Vancouver to Ketchikan, twenty-nine years ago, I was greatly surprised when I saw for the first time the North Pacific coast and its natives. Being an Easterner, that was not the country I was accustomed to; those were not the Indians I had met near home. The farther north toward Alaska we advanced, the more exotic were the geographic features. There was something decidedly un-American in the North Pacific coast: a balmy breeze from the South Seas and an incisive tang of Asia.

Here, along the coast, was a jungle not very different from that described in the tales of Conrad. Here one came across haunting reminiscenes of the Orient, of Asia. Fleecy clouds cut across mountain peaks that were tipped with snow, just as they are painted in Nipponese water colors. We had come much nearer Japan, as we could see on the map. The currents and the winds across the Pacific brought over the balmy air from Polynesia, as they at times drag uprooted trees for thousands of miles from the South Pacific and beach them on our receptive western shores. The dark-green drapery of the forests, rich with moisture, looked semitropical, along island channels that reflect, like a mirror, trees, high cliffs, and mountains.

At Alert Bay, the smell of the salt weeds and mud flats pinched the nostrils. In the Indian village we had the first impact of things quite novel to an outsider. Indian women squatted on platforms facing the sea in front of their village, wrapped in shawls draped around them and over their heads. They were sullen and motionless, like stone idols before a Chinese temple. Behind them plank lodges, low and squat, stood in a row, and children in the doorways peeped at us with slanting, mysterious eyes.

The faces of the Alert Bay natives were broad and heavy-jawed; their noses were flat, and their eyes, like their hair, were jet black. They were short and broad in stature. Those we could see standing were bowlegged, presumably from a racial habit of squatting in canoes. Their physiognomy, quite different from that of the prairie nomads, was Mongolian. Our fellow-visitors would say, "These people are not American Indians— they are Asiatics."

The northwestern Indians truly do not belong to the America we know best; they are of a different type. There is no such thing as a unified race of American Indians, red of skin, whose origin may be traced back to the same Garden-of-Eden-like cradle. The North Pacific coast and Alaskan tribes stand by themselves, apart from the rest of America, a challenge to the wholesale uniformity of the native races. At least three or four distinct types of Redskins, so-called, including the Eskimos, exist more or less side by side on this North American continent alone. These types surely go back to different waves of migrations that arrived here in turn and followed their own uncharted path onward.

The discovery of the Mongolian spot among North American natives—bluish patches on the lower part of the back, in infants—has brought out a specific similarity between the children of both contiguous continents, America and Asia. Beforehand, the Mongolian

eye was known, on both sides of Bering Sea. Sixty per
cent of native American children in the Northwest have
the Mongolian spot, according to a fairly recent compilation, and this may represent the proportion of native
to European blood in their veins, many of them being
"breeds."

Whoever has observed the natives for thousands of
miles on both sides of the northern Pacific, fails to find
a hard-and-fast racial frontier anywhere. Our northwestern Indians are Asiatic-like; or, to put it otherwise,
the eastern Siberian tribes are strikingly American. Some
ethnographers for this reason have suggested that the
northeastern corner of Asia might have been peopled
from America—a theory which cannot find much support. Whatever direction was taken by the migrants,
they have left behind them no fixed racial boundary, no
break between the continents. Nor is there an absolute
barrier anywhere.

After the fur traders of the Hudson's Bay Company,
in 1832, had established a fort at a point named Graveyard Point, at the mouth of the Nass River, an open
battle soon broke out between the Haidas of the Queen
Charlotte Islands and the local Tsimsyan villagers. To
uphold the professed right to "free trade" with all their
customers at large, the Hudson's Bay traders were forced
to fire their guns at them. They did not realize that this
was the last outbreak of a feud the beginning of which
went back to prehistory.

The natives from far and wide, particularly of the
frozen North, for countless generations had always tried
to gain a foothold on the salmon rivers and on the seacoast, to share in the bounties that made life easy. This

*During this highly creative period—1840 to 1890—the totems of
the North Pacific coast rushed into existence* PAGE 244.

likewise was true on the prairies, where the buffalo herds had drawn scattered bands from around the periphery. There was a difference, however. The whole coast southward was equally inviting to the newcomers, whereas the winters in the buffalo country were cold everywhere, and the northern interior was as bleak and barren as the tundra and muskeg steppes of the Far North.

The mouth of the Nass, where the Hudson's Bay Company first established its post, was exactly as bounteous an estuary as the northern tribes were apt to consider Leesems, the promised land. Particularly for its runs of *ulaken* or candlefish, salmon, and halibut, it attracted many people from long distances, and held them close together in the spring of the year at Fishery Bay within tidal waters.

The candlefish provided in huge quantities the fat that was one of the staple foods of the Indian population, in the interior no less than on the coast.

It was a trade article, along the many "grease trails," in great and sustained demand. So much so that several thousand fishers within measurable distance migrated yearly for the spring run at the mouth of the Nass, and put up a large quantity of fish oil in wooden containers. For miles on both shores stood the camps of five contiguous nations—the Niskae, the Tsimsyan, the Gitksan, of the Skeena and the Nass Rivers, the Haida of the Queen Charlotte Islands, and the Tlingit of southern Alaska.

During the salmon run up the rivers in the summer, the coast people ascended the streams to set their weirs close to waterfalls, some of them to canyons, others as far as the headwaters. There they often encountered the nomads of the interior and engaged in feuds with them over disputed grounds, just as their kinsmen, along the coast, forged their way south. The stories of warfare among them, if fully recorded, would fill a bookcase.

The Hudson's Bay Company was right in considering the Nass a thoroughfare of Indian life and a great trade center. But it soon realized that the unsettled scores of the past between tribes of several nations made access perilous most of the year, unless the trading parties came in great force. The Nass, besides, was the home of vindictive Wolf clans, whose quarrels with the Kanhaade or Raven clans were as bitter as they were ancient.

Dr. Kennedy, the chief Hudson's Bay Company trader, married Stone-Cliffs' niece, about 1831, and then moved down to the preserves of this powerful chief of the Eagle clans on the coast, to what later became Port Simpson. Under the aegis of Stone-Cliff, the removal of the trading post happened in 1833.

The story of Stone-Cliff and his ancestors is an epic of the last hundred years or so. The first Stone-Cliff, whose identity is remembered under another name, was forced by a victorious Wolf clan to leave Naha Bay, Alaska, with his clan, and the members of his clan settled in three foreign nations to the south, who welcomed them because they were reputed warriors and traders, and belonged to the native aristocracy. Their wealth and prestige, no doubt, was derived from their earlier contacts with the early Russian traders from Russia.

Stone-Cliff, who had won the confidence of Dr. Kennedy and the Hudson's Bay Company, was a famed trader and warrior. With his kinsmen, he monopolized much of the northern coast trade, amassed wealth, and terrified his enemies and his potential victims. His Eagle followers were the only internationalists of the seacoast, as, through their kinsmen and representatives, they belonged to three or four Indian nations. They had risen in the ranks to the first place, during the consecutive lives of three or four Eagle leaders of the name of Legyarh in the course of as many generations. Their clan meanwhile had spread to many tribes through a series of effective alliances based upon intermarriage.

The rise of the Stone-Cliff faction, in the first part of the last century, worried the older local tribes, who were fast losing their privileges to one whom they considered an unscrupulous parvenu. But he had relatives among six or seven northern nations, and he could travel and be received in security wherever he pleased for his barter —a privilege not enjoyed by most others. As he was bold, ambitious, and powerful, the white traders were shrewd enough to pick him out for an ally and to use him to their own ends.

His rivals once decided in secret assembly to check his rise by defeat and humiliation. They pooled their currency—large copper shields with engraved emblems— and challenged him in a contest of wealth, an event unique in native annals.

Stone-Cliff got wind of the affair in good time, as he had a finger in every pie. Through his nieces and nephews in other tribes—women are apt to whisper and gossip, and he had his ear close to the underground channels—he heard of the plot and secretly organized his kinsmen everywhere, as far as he had time to reach out, for a fight and for the defeat of his rivals once and for all. To the amazement of his rivals, whose means of getting information and gathering wealth did not measure up to his, he came out victorious in the course of a memorable contest which made history. His wealth, defiantly

exhibited in the presence of his nation, consisted of fourteen coppers, whereas his opponents, who had challenged
him, could exhibit only thirteen in all.

Too canny not to exploit his victory to the utmost,
Stone-Cliff hired a Haida kinsman from the neighboring
islands, who was a great carver, and elaborated a unique
plan with him. He brought him to a high cliff in a narrow channel, near the mouth of the Nass, where every
tribe coming for candlefish from the islands, Alaska,
and the coast to the south, had to pass every spring.
There they contrived a device, with the help of long
poles, to which were attached ropes cut out of the hide
of killer whales, whereby the artist was let down the
face of the cliff from above, to engrave a man's radiant
face surrounded by fourteen coppers, all of them painted
red.

This painted engraving commemorated the victory of
Legyarh and the Eagles over the combined Ravens,
Wolves, and Killer-Whales of the three Tsimsyan nations, a victory that was to be the last. It symbolized the
southward drift to a migrant clan and its rise to power
over the indigenous occupants of the land and the coast.
Previous, though similar, invasions from the north, for
untold ages, are likely to have occurred in successive
waves along the same coast channels and the same trails.

Such, in a nutshell, is the history of the North Pacific
coast tribes in so far as it can be unraveled. The fight
that broke out in 1850 in front of the fort of the Hudson's Bay Company at Port Simpson, was a belated echo
of an old quarrel between the Eagle clan of Port Simpson
and some Haidas of the Queen Charlotte Islands as to
whether the Haidas had a right to set foot on coastal
territory other than their own. But Stone-Cliff, who

opposed their claim for a foothold in his preserves, was himself an intruder from the north, whose title after all was no more valid than theirs, since it went back barely a few generations.

In all the native traditions and reminiscences, the drift of northern nomads toward a warmer climate and the natural bounties of the coast is as uniform as it is impressive, and the movement forward was rapid. Every step in this advance can be proved with materials recorded in the past thirty years or so for the National Museum of Canada, map and statistics in hand. The struggle for the possession of fishing stations and hunting grounds was renewed not only at every generation, but more than once in a generation. And the invaders always came from the same sides—the northern coast and the interior.

Within the last two centuries or less, a complete change in population and culture happened at every spot. Even within the brief historical period since the Russians apeared on the coast, there were at first no heraldic emblems, no totemic clans, no totem-pole memorials, in the very districts where these features are now typical and world-famous. Tlingit elements, influenced by the Russians and moving south in continued dribblings, are responsible for these novelties, which reflect the deep influence of newcomers on receptive Indians.

While the people using the various coastal languages were fast moving south, some being pushed, others wanting to come in, the languages themselves maintained fairly steadily their footholds on the same rivers, the same islands, and the same territories, although there was a time when the Tlingit idiom threatened to dislodge the

This painted engraving commemorated the victory of Legyarh and the Eagles over the combined 'Ravens, Wolves, and Killer-Whales of the three Tsimsyan nations PAGE 177.

others as far south as Vancouver Island. The languages
did not bodily drift south with the individual emigrants
using them. New families and more clans seeped into
the framework of a nation, took up the prevailing language as a garment for themselves or the next generation, then stepped out to new homes of their choice, or
forced upon them by necessity, and had no objection to
changing their tongue as often as convenient.

A language under such a strain, with new elements
breaking in on every side, must have changed sensibly
and speedily. New blood and varied habits forced the
old molds into new shapes, without smashing them altogether. But their framework at times trembled in the
balance, as was true, at the dawn of historical times, of
Tlingit, Tsimsyan, and Tsetsaut. The three dialects of
the single Tsimsyan language came into existence, distinct from each other, within only a few recent generations.

Scattered families from three different northern nations—Tlingit, Tsetsaut, Sekani — poured in at such
a rate at times that they almost submerged some of the
local tribes, in particular the Gitwinlkul on the Grease
Trail from the Nass to the Skeena rivers, and two Tsimsyan tribes of the estuary of the Skeena River. The new
and the old elements could ask themselves what language
was actually holding its own or was being dislodged by
the other. The older Tsimsyan language, called *see-
algyarh* ("real language"), did not require long to become diversified into three dialects as a result of foreign
infusion, and this infusion was much hastened by the
arrival of the Slavs in Alaska.

The same must have been true of the Aleutian language. This northern idiom is quite divergent from any

other—the only one of its kind—and it seems to have
come into existence not so long ago, through similar
circumstances.

Under the external pressure of incessant migrations
and shifts of important elements, a new language and
culture was bound to grow at a rapid pace, even within
the span of a century. That is exactly what happened to
the Aleutians, the Tlingits, the Haidas, the Tsimsyans,
and other nations down the seacoast and within measurable distance inland.

The recent history of the Tsimsyans is full of significance in so far as it is typical. It has a bearing on that of
other northwestern tribes far and wide. Wherever natives were found in the Alaskan peninsula or in the
northern Rockies, the same cultural processes were
steadily at work.

As soon as the northern prowlers scented a quarry,
they usually stumbled upon other natives that had preceded them and did their best to hold on to their privilege of early occupants. If at first repelled, the raiders
would soon come back. They were only a handful—the
sub-Arctic regions could not feed an army nor even a
full-fledged band—and had to fall back upon ingenuity
to drive in a wedge before them. This they did instinc-
tively, and the process is strikingly the same everywhere.
In times of starvation, they fell upon their opponents
before dawn, when they were alseep. The next day they
owned new food stores, new hunting and fishing preserves. These were always farther to the south, nearer
to what they called Leesems, the mystic concept of
plenty.

As many comers chanced upon the same preserves,
there happened, within a small space on the map, re-

peated invasions, incessant warfare, the growth of population, the ramification of languages into dialects, sundry ambitions, and strong incentive for progress. All these are dominant features in North Pacific coast ethnology, a good deal of it in historical times, within the living memory of the elders.

CHANTING BUDDHIST DIRGES

THE GRANDIOSE strangeness of nature in the northern Rockies might be oppressive if it remained silent. But it soon finds a voice. The songs of the Indians trickle down the mountain slopes, from sheltered huts and hidden trails. They are lofty and aerial, and they seem to belong to humanity at large, not only to the native clans of the Wolves, the Bears, and the Eagles.

Women and children sing more than men in the open, and their voices are clear and silvery. There is a sense of freedom about them, and a lyric inspiration that spells enchantment. How beautiful those voices, how entrancing those tunes! These chants are often called "mountain songs" or "love songs" by the white settlers who happen to hear them, though they may be neither to the singers themselves, who find in them an outlet for their changing moods: lonesomeness, vacuity, longing. To us here, they mean a great deal more, for they open wide vistas upon the historical past.

In the summer of 1920 and in subsequent years, I engaged a number of natives at various places in turn to sing for me. The result eventually was a collection of about three hundred songs, recorded on a small Standard Edison. These songs are now preserved, with the large collections of Indian songs from elsewhere, in the National Museum of Canada.

The so-called "mountain" or "love song" that first arrested my attention was not a melody with a single form as I had surmised, but several tunes after the same pattern, with words varying almost at pleasure. It seemed as if I could not capture any variant that was quite as beautiful as the ones I casually heard in the distance, made as it were of passing whims, of luminous air, and of the scent of alpine flowers. Yet some of them were akin to the living song that somehow could not be trapped for love or money.

Here is one of them in inept black and white, without its slow descending glides, its remarkable diminuendos, its ethereal glow, and shorn of the Alaskan voice quality that colored it with longing and Oriental fatalism.

This lyric song was a vehicle for the singer's feelings, whatever they chanced to be. It holds no word, only meaningless syllables. It was sung by Ada Quok, a young woman of the Tahltans, a band of Siberian-like nomads at Telegraph Creek on the Yukon frontier. But it closely resembles many others already familiar throughout the northern Rockies. It is one of a type— perhaps the most familiar in that semiboreal country that blossoms under the breath of the warm Pacific currents, in the summer moons.

When the Carrier and Gitksan Indians of the interior plateau still assemble in the canyons of the upper Skeena River to fish salmon and celebrate the return of plenty, they begin to beat their skin drums and to sing songs that soon permeate the air. A great voice at times falls from the cliffs down upon the swift stream where fishermen spear the spring salmon or the sockeye. No one who has ever heard those songs of midsummer and swayed to the rhythm of their drumbeats can forget them. Remote as they are in a way, they come near to the heart of all alike, white man or Indian, for they are broad, melodious, and deeply stirring. If their words are lost on all but the natives, they are uttered with such lyrical feelings that they awaken response tender and urgent. The white people know them under the name of "mountain songs" or "love songs," and gladly listen to them. Somehow they are the living embodiment of summer and harvest in the far Northwest, on the border lands of America and the Orient.

A Japanese tune on a phonograph arrested my attention, as, in 1927, I was studying the Niskae tribes at the Arrandale cannery on the shores of Portland Canal near the mouth of the Nass River. And, to my surprise, it resembled the "mountain" or "love songs" of the Yukon and northern British Columbia, which I had been recording among the natives.

The Japanese tune scaled a high curve, at the beginning, and touched a top note, then cascaded down to the bottom, where it droned leisurely, just as do the tunes of a number of typical Indian songs. Like them, its scale was pentatonic—that is, of only five notes, a few of them separated from the others by wide intervals. The melodic resemblance between the Japanese and Indian songs reminded me of the nearness of Alaska to Japan, especially when the Aleutian route is considered; of the Mongolian features of both natives and Japanese; the fanlike migrations of the Indians away from Bering Sea; and the cultural stamp of the Mongolian culture noticeable on the whole North Pacific coast.

Unbroken contacts tended to reunite the related peoples on both sides of Bering Sea, long after they had parted, and those on our continent had strayed away to farther districts. The American and Asiatic natives kept in touch with each other for barter. Two trade routes, since prehistoric times, extended across Bering Sea, and branched off as far as Hudson Bay, and in other directions. No sea nor mountain barrier ever kept apart those widely scattered people, who sought each other seasonally for the exchange of commodities essential to life. Customs and culture passed back and forth also, slowly but surely.

As ancient traditions accompanied the early migrants in their trek eastward into the Alaskan tundras, it may be surmised that, together with other things, some of the ancient songs survived at least in type or melodic pattern. Newer songs also spread from one end to another along the trade routes. Traders were wont to sing before the barter as a pledge of peaceful intentions, and during the affair, to impress would-be buyers with the excellence of their wares. Asia had much to furnish. She was like a large container overflowing with riches into a still uncultivated and hungry America. The little Japanese song I heard on the phonograph at the Arrandale cannery of the Nass was enough to remind one of all this.

Some years later, after having transcribed for publication nearly a hundred of those songs from the northern Rockies, I showed about twenty of them to Professor Kiang Kang-hu, an eminent Chinese authority then lecturing at some universities in the United States and Canada. The results of our contact far exceeded my expectation, particularly when it came to dirges or funeral songs, of which there were a number.

The dirge of Raven-Drum instantly drew Professor Kiang's attention, as though it were an old friend. This Indian song was the exclusive family property of

The Indian songs of Alaska and the northern Rockies are typical of the country to which they belong. Medicine men sing incantations over their patients PAGE 197.

Kweenu, a Raven chief of the Gitwinlkul tribe on the
Grease Trail between the Skeena and the Nass rivers in
northern British Columbia, and the ancestors of this
family not so long ago had migrated down from Alaska.
Their traditional dirges, of which the following is one,
were used only at the death of chiefs, and during the
cremation of the body on a pyre. Its words are:

> The Raven drum now has come back. We can hear nothing but
> its large voice, its large voice. It is like a great brightness.
> The great voice of the Raven, the cawing Raven all covered
> with pearls, is ahead of me. We can hear nothing but
> its large voice. . . .

This native song, to Professor Kiang, seemed similar to
a Buddhist chant for funeral services, used among the
nomads of Mongolia. And he had not been told at the
moment that this was a funeral song of a family of
Indians whose home stands in the northern Rockies of
America.

His statement led me to look for other similarities
between the mortuary rituals and songs of Asia and of
the North Pacific coast. How startling a turn my studies
would take if the resemblance were to change to identity
in such things as ritual forms (in the use, for instance,
of similar drums to mark the rhythm), or the appearance of Asiatic words—perhaps Chinese words—in the
songs! Buddhism, though in eastern Asia typically Chinese, has traveled far to the north, among the primitive
Siberian tribes. It is familiar among the present Kam-
chatkas close to Bering Sea. Who knows but it might
have been there, ready to cross the waters with the ancestors of the present coast natives of the North!

The next dirge we examined belonged exclusively to

a branch of the Eagle clan of the Rabbit tribe (Kitwanga), on the middle Skeena River. Those Eagles had come from the coast to this district a little over a hundred years ago. Here are the melody and the texts of the dirges of the Eagles (Geetanraet). The words of the first are:

> Daylight came down early from the east, as I looked up to the sky.

This funeral chant reminded Professor Kiang "very much" of a Chinese ceremonial song he had heard coffin carriers sing in the streets of Pekin. So, from Mongolia we had gone a step farther into China to find further similarities with Indian songs.

The next song brought us a greater surprise still. The refrain was the very same as that used in Chinese funeral songs. The second dirge of the Geetanraet Eagles is:

> Alas! Alas! Alas! Alas! Hayu, hayu! The chiefs mourn the last survivors of Geetanraet. Alas! Alas!
> Now that the great chief has died, it is as if the sun were eclipsed. Alas! Alas!
> My heart overflows with grief, because the burial boxes of the other chiefs (unlike ours) are quite empty. Alas! Alas! Alas!

The words of the main section of this song were in a familiar dialect, and it referred to a fairly recent tribal event. But the refrain, *hayu, hayu, hayu,* was unintelligible, meaningless to the singer.

Not so to Professor Kiang, who was amazed. In Chinese, *Hayu!* means "Alas!" and it is exactly what dirge singers in his country are accustomed to exclaim in frequent repetition. It forms a habitual part of familiar

Buddhist rituals. So the Indians here were, all unaware, singing a Chinese mournful refrain to one of their own burial songs. This was a startling discovery.

Looking over a number of other songs recorded on the phonograph for our museum collections, I find that the refrain *Hayu!* ("Alas!"), wherever it appears, is used with the right context—that is, in songs of mourning over the death of a relative. In every instance, it is employed by members of the Eagle and the Wolf clans, both of whom were fairly recent newcomers from the North along the seacoast.

The singsong-like way of moaning which usually breaks out at the death of a dear relative suggested to Professor Kiang other striking resemblances in Chinese mortuary customs. While I was at the Arrandale cannery, during the fishing season of 1928, a tragedy brought grief to the natives stationed there, as several of their people, after eating decayed salmon roe, died of poisoning. Dirges commenced early one morning, and throughout the following days women kept moaning in the woods.

At the first news of the misfortune in the summer village, old women began to wail pitifully. Crouching on the ground in front of their houses, they tore their hair and beat the ground with their foreheads. They cast restraint to the winds and gave vent to grief. Professional mourners, like those of ancient Greece, rent the air with laments, and sprinkled ashes on their heads.

"Just as it would happen in China," Professor Kiang said, after I described the occurrence to him. "There also mourners pound the ground with their foreheads, and they are paid for it. Quite typical!"

From these dirges Professor Kiang and I passed on to

*The Garuda bronze figurine, discovered close to the Alaskan border,
suggests the presence of Buddhism and ancient Chinese mortuary
customs* PAGE 200.

others. One of the most striking, because of its strange melody was *Hano!* the funeral song of Skateen, the Wolf head chief of a Nass River tribe.

For impressiveness nothing approached this dirge. The lament of the mourners rose plaintively and fell in descending curves, like the wind in a storm. It was the voice of nature crying out. For modernity it went beyond the moderns. The intervals sounded strange, at times like quarter-tones.

The syllables *Hano* are meaningless. The only words of significance are: "He used to be the head chief!"

Somehow this dirge seemed familiar to Professor Kiang. "It sounds very much like a Buddhist chant in a funeral service," he declared. "Yes, I know now! It comes from Hindu music." This is another link in the long chain of origins: From Alaska we pass on to Siberia, to China, to India.

Another Indian dirge of northern British Columbia, that of Small-Raven of Kitwanga, "sounds like a night-watchman's song in Pekin," said Professor Kiang. "The watchman goes out and shouts: 'Be careful of your fire and your doors! Beware of thieves!' Drumbeats accompany the night calls." The rhythm of the Indian dirge also is marked by drumbeats.

Other native songs from the northern Rockies likewise resemble Asiatic songs. To Professor Kiang the lyric tune of "Honekone," a love song, was "like a harvest song of China. Girls sing it while working in the fields and picking tea leaves." Another, a lullaby of Nampks on the Nass River, "resembles a Chinese shepherd song. It is very much like it."

A peace song of the Haidas and the Nass people, the words of which are in a foreign language not understood by the singers, is reminiscent of "a Chinese sacrificial song." It was learned by a Nass River Indian, the old singer's father, from Haida Indians of the Queen Charlotte and Prince of Wales Island. The Nass people had fought the Haidas long before, and peace had been restored after prolonged enmity. Nine canoes of the Nass tribes went to Klawaq, on Prince of Wales Island, and a feast was held. The Haida chief sang the peace song during the ceremony. The guests from the coast of the mainland stayed there for three weeks and learned some of the songs of their hosts. After that time the Haidas and Nass people intermarried. The learning of the peace song by the singer's father shows how songs often travel from tribe to tribe. Many Nass River songs are in foreign languages, mostly those of northern tribes— the Tlingit of the southern Alaskan coast and the Tahltans and the Sekanais of the Yukon, in the interior.

A lyric melody of the uplands, the Fireweed song of the Skeena headwaters, resembles a "Chinese street tune." Its first part certainly sounds exotic, almost Russian-like, if heard among other Indian songs. The words of the Fireweed song are:

> The Fireweed people will drink fermented juice with the Wolf and the Raven tribes. Why think you that we know not how to brew it? We walk about proudly, because we have made it for a long time.

Another song, a lullaby, reminded Professor Kiang of a lullaby to the accompaniment of which Japanese mothers sway the children wrapped upon their shoulders, as Indian mothers are wont to do, in the northern Rockies.

A lyric song of a type very widely diffused in Alaska

and northern British Columbia and recorded by James
Teit among the Tahltans of the Yukon, was characterized by Professor Kiang as much like "the lyric song
of Blue-Chamber." The Professor and I recognized a
similar tune in two Chinese phonograph records.

The use of the drum in the Indian songs is an important element to consider in tracing their origin. The
Indian drum of Alaska and the far Northwest consists
of a smoke-tanned skin dried and stretched over one side
only of a closed circular band of wood. It is exactly
similar to the instrument which the Koriak tribes of
northeastern Siberia use in funeral rituals. Siberian
drums, according to Jochelson (*The Jesup North Pacific
Expedition*, IV), are "covered on both sides with hide,
like those found among the American Indians. . . . Together with drums covered on but one side," they "are
used in Siberia only by the Buddhists" in "their divine
services." Even in size the Siberian and Alaskan skin
drums are much alike. In northwestern America the
drums were used not only in "divine services" but also
in rituals of cremation; for dead bodies, as in Siberia,
were burned on a pyre surrounded by dirge singers and
mourners.

Over a hundred wax records of Siberian songs recorded for the Jesup North Pacific Expedition to the
North Pacific coast and Siberia have been preserved,
unpublished, for about forty years at the American Museum of Natural History, New York. These were recently transferred to Columbia University. Their use-
fulness in the present investigation can hardly be exaggerated, as I realized upon first hearing them in 1923,
for they incorporate definite evidence of historical re-

lations between the two cultural groups on either side of Bering Sea, such as were hardly anticipated. For instance, surprising similarity in several types of songs and peculiar ways of singing is clearly noticeable among the Chukchee of northeastern Siberia and the Salish of southern British Columbia. Yet the gap between them on the map is considerable, and other native nations now stand between them. Their songs and mannerisms are quite alike, yet different from those of the intervening people. It seems, on that score, that the two nations must have lived some time in close proximity, if they were not actually related.

The Siberian songs recorded on the phonograph for the American Museum of Natural History constitute valuable evidence of the Asiatic origin of the Athapascan, Salish, and other native northwestern American stocks in their neighborhood.

The conclusion has now been reached, at least tentatively, that the songs of the Siberian natives represented in this collection—the Chukchee, the Koriak, and the Yukaghir—are of three main types, according to their source: purely native, Mongolian or Chinese, and Tartar or Slavonic. The last, on the upper levels, may be fairly recent. The Mongolian influence is much older, and presumably belongs to several periods. The residuum, with a much wider diffusion extending into North America, is undoubtedly ancient.

This last native type is predominant in many songs, particularly those of the Chukchee. Yet these Siberians often sing in the Chinese style, even with a Chinese string instrument; they are also well acquainted with the Russian style, and they use Slav songs in the diatonic scales (major and minor). Even the Siberian Eskimos have adopted, in some of their songs, the intricate way of singing and the artificial falsetto-like voice.

The same types of songs and style of singing also prevail among the Déné, Salish, and Tsimsyan tribes of Alaska and British Columbia. There can be no mistake about it. The evidence is overwhelming and the more secure from error because of its highly complex nature and its abundance, save perhaps in Siberia.

An important type of Yukon and northern British Columbia song is distinctly Tartar or Slavonic. It consists of swaying melodies with wide intervals, definitely pentatonic, covering a wide range. These tunes may have been introduced by the Russians in Alaska or influenced by them, or else they traveled orally with the natives from Siberia into America. Quite possibly they filtered in, a few centuries ago, at the time of the migration of those nomads into America.

The Mongolian way of singing, highly artificial and complex, is strongly in evidence in Alaska, the Yukon, and British Columbia, among the Salish no less than among the natives farther north: tremolo-like pectoral vibrations, "throat rattling." Siberian quavering on high notes, ventriloquistic effects, "spirit noises," coyote howling, animal-like calls, laments, exclamations such as *Huy!* often interrupting the flow of the melody, diminuendo descending curves, high-pitched singing, words adapted to the tunes and sometimes half-improvised, intricate tunes and rhythms, and the identical use of the skin drum.

In my preliminary survey of these Siberian records, I was impressed by the close resemblance between many Chukchee and Salish (Thompson and Fraser rivers) songs. These are the same in type and style; they belong together somehow. Even an expert might at times mistake one for the other.

The Salish of southern British Columbia and the state of Washington, on these if on no other grounds, must be related to the Chukchees of northeastern Siberia. This link may be racial, or simply due to contiguity and borrowing at a time not too far distant. The Mongolian and native strains in both are closely interwoven.

Naturally, these three types of Siberian songs and singing have merged to a varying extent in most of the songs, although the isolated original types definitely stand out in a limited number of songs, wherever they are found, in Siberia or in northwestern America.

The best recorded instances of quasi-identity are found in a series of medicine men's incantations of the Thompson River Salish, in southern British Columbia. A Chukchee song (130) was almost identical with the "Prairie-Chicken" dance tune recorded at the National Museum of Canada by a Thompson river singer named Tetlanitsa. The intricate Salish song, "Blue Jay," in which the singer imitates the chirping of the bird, is remarkably similar to a Kukaghir song of Siberia recorded by Bogoras. The throat rattling, spirit noises, trills, voice quaver, and drooping in curves are much the same in both songs. The words are interspersed with meaningless syllables throughout the song, the singers' voices are quite similar, and the drumbeats are irregular though spirited.

The Indian songs of Alaska and the northern Rockies are typical of the country to which they belong. Like the totem poles they express the soul of a bold and restless people whose ethnic affinities are Asiatic rather than American. They mean joy or sorrow to the people, as they usually conjure up tribal recollections or arouse emotions seated deep in the singers.

The hunters sang incantations over the bears and the mountain goats they killed, to appease the spirits. The medicine men clamored their chants and loudly beat their drums. The warriors on their way home intoned hymns of victory or chanted their grief. Peace was sealed to the tune of a Haida *kawagyanee* or treaty song. The chiefs in the feast house boasted of their prestige. Whenever they gathered for duty, business, or pleasure, the people resorted to song rather than to the spoken word, since it brought them together more readily and stirred up response into a common audible voice. Singing was far more habitual to those semi-nomads than it is to us in our modern surroundings. It was raised by necessity and custom to the rank of language—a language expressive and self-sustained, that reached out for greater things and larger spaces. It was the outcry of transient emotions in terms of power and permanence. Hence its importance and diversity.

The songs of these northwestern Indians differ on the whole markedly from the dance tunes of the nation east of the Rockies. Vastly more varied and interesting, they are not confined like them to the function of accompanying monotonous dance steps. Their scales are different, more exotic to our ear; their melodic range more extensive and colorful; their themes much richer. The northerners' custom of singing to words rather than to meaningless syllables—as other Indians are wont to do —opens wide vistas of historical and literary interest. Their songs are valuable for their texts no less than their melodies. They belong to a world rather apart in America, a world that is reminiscent of Asia and the Pacific.

Should it be finally established that an early derivative form of Buddhism once prevailed in the mortuary rituals of the North Pacific coast, the new evidence now under observation would assume historical authenticity. For Buddhism and the Chinese mortuary customs are not essential to human nature; they are a cultural growth, largely accidental, which has taken place in time and in a limited geographical area. Whenever they are found elsewhere, they can at least theoretically be traced back to their source, and it matters little whether or not some of the links in the chain of transmission are irretrievably lost.

Primitive Buddhism in Alaska and British Columbia, asuming that it has existed, prompts us to look for clues as to its agents of diffusion across Bering Sea. And the discovery of a Garuda bronze figurine, close to the Alaskan border, at once draws our attention, as it illustrates the type of archaeological evidence which may eventually become significant. Besides it, other finds of the same kind,[1] west of the Rockies, have from time to

---

[1] Babirussa tusks from an Indian Grave in British Columbia, *Science*, IV (July 11, 1884), 34. "Many curious and unlooked-for objects are frequently found in Indian graves, and not least among these is a pair of the tusks of the Babirussa. They were extracted in August of last year by Mr. James S. Swan from the grave of an old Indian doctor at Kah-te-lay-juk-te-wos Point, near the north-western end of Graham Island, one of the Queen Charlotte Islands, off the coast of British Columbia. The Babirussa, as every one knows, is an animal of the hog tribe, inhabiting only Celebes and the adjacent islands. The question then arises, How did these teeth come into the possession of the Indian doctor, who died some fifty years since at an advanced age?

"Mr. Swan suggests an ingenious and plausible solution of the problem. In his letter of the 4th of January to Professor Baird, he writes as follows: 'Lieut. Bolles, of the U.S. surveying schooner *Ernest*, tells me that the Siamese junks make regular trading voyages to the coast of Africa, even as far as the Cape of Good Hope, running down with the north-east monsoons, and returning when the favorable monsoon blows. They bring products of every kind, and trade with Japan and China. He thinks that some of these junks may have been wrecked, and carried by the Japanese current to the American side, and perhaps cast ashore on the west coast of the Queen Charlotte Islands, where quantities of drift-stuff of every kind is to be found. . . .' "

time been made—for instance, of ancient Chinese pottery and of coins dating back several centuries, all of
which tend to prove repeated contacts, in late prehistory,
between Asia and the New World.

The Garuda bronze figurine dug up in a potato patch
at or near Kincolith (Place-of-Scalps), at the mouth of
the Nass River, has been described by Dr. Franz Boas.
Here I abbreviate his statement:

In 1894, while visiting the village of Kincolith, my attention was
called to an interesting bronze figure in the possession of the Rev.
W. H. Collison. The figure was evidently cast, showing a distinct
seam. The method of manufacture as well as the form of the figure
suggested at once a foreign origin. According to the testimony of
Mr. Collison, which was borne out by remarks of Indians who had
seen the object, this figurine was found in digging over a potato-
patch at a place which had formerly been covered with heavy timber.
It does not seem at all likely that the specimen should have got into
this position recently.

I submitted a cast and photographs of the figure to Prof. Albert
Grünwedel of Berlin, to whom I am indebted for the following
statement. "A comparison with a number of bells in the Royal
Ethnological Museum in Berlin . . . proves that the object in question
must be considered as the handle of a *ghanta*—a bell used by the
Brahmana in the Puja ceremony. The small flattened projection seen
under the beaded column which forms the handle was originally
riveted into the bell. The specimen is most easily identified by this
beaded column. All the bells mentioned before came from Bengal,
Orissa, and Nepaul. The kneeling winged figure on top of the
column is undoubtedly Garuda, characterized by the wings attached
to its upper arms, the beak-like nose, the somewhat degenerate headdress, and the drapery hanging down from the waist.

"None among the very modern bells in the Berlin Museum is identical with the present specimen. The nearest approach is No. 2501, on
which Garuda is represented kneeling on the top of the handle. This
piece comes from Asika (Asca), Orissa. Two others, from Orissa
and Bengal, show the kneeling Garuda at the side of Hanuman. A
very small bell from Nepaul, and another one from Calcutta, have
a standing figure of Garuda, the forms of which resemble closely
those of the kneeling figure of the present specimen.

"It is not possible to determine definitely the age of this Garuda un-
earthed in Northern British Columbia. It may be a hundred years old
or a little older. It is not more recent, although the workmanship
is very crude." [This was published in 1901.]

According to Prof. Otis T. Mason, an American authority then
consulted: "There is not the slightest embarrassment in the way of
this bronze image having been transported [via Spanish vessels crossing the Pacific Ocean between Mexico and the Malay Archipelago]
from Manila to British Columbia at any time between 1570 and
1770."[2]

Whatever may be the truth about this Garuda figure
introduced among the natives of the North Pacific coast
—whether a hundred and fifty to four or five hundred
years old—it undoubtedly is southern Asiatic and brings
back to mind the Tsimsyan dirge of *Hano!* which Professor Kiang identified as being "like a Buddhist chant in
a funeral service, coming from Hindu music," or the
dirge of the Gitanraet Eagles, the refrain from which is
Hayu ("Alas!") in Chinese, and a feature of Buddhist
mortuary rituals. Both of these bits of evidence point
to central Asia as a focus of diffusion of culture into
North America, in late prehistoric times.

Once this is generally taken into account, many other
so-called independent creations of ancient America are
bound to prove derivatives. Professor Kiang, impelled
by this new drift in research, at my suggestion prepared
a list of striking similarities between Mexican and Chinese civilizations and published them in a paper entitled
"Resemblances Seen between Maya Civilization and that
of the Chinese."[3] His brief outline further tends to
break down the cultural "insularity" of our continent.

In the light of these discoveries, a new field for fruit-

[2] *Bulletin American Museum of Natural History*, XIV (1901), 51-52 (illustrated).

[3] *Royal Society of Canada*, Section II (1933), pp. 75-85.

ful investigations lies open before us. Theorists for many years endeavored to explain the independent origin in America of cultural features known elsewhere. Primitive men, wherever they chanced to be, were supposed to find within themselves the faculty of re-creating the same conceptual processes over and over again. For lack of historical records it was impossible to check the application of this theory to features that refused to reveal their origin to scholars and were, accordingly, swamped under a deluge of vague or sentimental assumptions. But things are now taking another turn, with the native songs and traditions of the people on both sides of Bering Sea going back to a common Asiatic source.

COPPER WOMAN

IF SITKA JACK, the best Tlingit silversmith and goldsmith of his generation, often carved precious metals into fine brooches and bracelets for casual American customers, who were not very numerous in his day, his fine art for all that was not purely commercial. For the needs of his domestic clientele he did not mind falling back upon racial experience and twisting imported native copper or imported brass into bracelets, anklets, and nose rings in the older style. Other native craftsmen, his elders, before him had practiced the craft of the metal smiths in the manner of the Russians, their masters, established for many years in the Alaskan capital at Sitka, which at first was named New Archangel.

To whomever would listen, Sitka Jack or his wife, also a silversmith working alongside him in his little shop, could have retold the familiar legend of Copper Woman, once famous among all the northwestern tribes. This legend holds more than a grain of truth; it reflects the past history of Indian metalcrafts in Alaska and the Far North.

As recorded by the French missionary, Father Emile Petitot, in the 1860's, the story of Copper Woman is called the national legend of the Yellow-Knives (Couteaux-Jaunes), whose name was derived from their copper or yellow knives. All the Déné or Athapascan tribes of the North, also the Eskimos of their neighborhood, on the Kenai peninsula of Alaska, knew it from infancy; and Baron von Wrangell heard it, about 1840, among his Tlingit hunters of the North Pacific coast.[1]

This epic tale outlines, under symbolic terms, the origin of copper among the peninsular natives, and it points to Bering Strait and the Aleutian Islands as having been the center of its prehistoric diffusion.

After their arrival in the wild lands of America, the Siberian migrants are said to have received more than once, from the land of sunset, the visit of a strange woman, who was bringing metals to them from across the salt sea. Like the natives of Bering Strait and the Aleutians, she would cross the waters in a skin boat (umiak or bidarka), and once she escaped with her young son from the hands of the Innuits (Eskimos), who were trying to hold her as a captive. After she had landed on the Alaskan shores, she scaled a volcano, and saw red metal in its seething crater. In this new country unknown to her, as she advanced farther inland, she marked her path with boulders that would enable her to retrace her steps homeward.

Recognizing her as a compatriot, the Déné tribes received from her hands the copper which they had known in former times and still badly needed for their awls, their knives, and their spearheads. Upon her they bestowed gratefully the name of Woman-Coming-from-Heaven.

Many times she followed the trail of boulders and went back to the seashore, where she picked up metals— red copper and iron—for the use of her favorite people.

But as they lapsed into familiarity with her, they grew disrespectful, and one day they mortally wounded her

---

[1] The explorer, Samuel Hearne, was the first to record this Indian myth, in 1771, in the region of Coronation Gulf (in A Journey from Prince of Wales' Port in Hudsons Bay to the Northern Ocean [London, 1795], pp. 175-76).

pride. Resolved not to follow them any longer into their remote lands, she remained close to the sea, perhaps finally to go back to her homeland. As the winters went by, they almost forsook her because of long distances and numerous obstacles in their path.

Once in many years they would trek back to the salt sea, looking for her in their craving for metals, and they would encounter volcanic mountains belching flames. There they discovered her buried up to the hips in the lava, and they lamented their estrangement from her. As she still fondly remembered some of them, she yielded to them handfuls of red copper. In later years they came back, only to find her almost gone, and they secured very little from her. When again they looked for her remains, she had disappeared, but traces of her were left in the red nuggets picked up along some of the tributaries of the Yukon River. Because of her these people were called Copper-People.

This old legend, which Sitka Jack and his compatriots could have told the buyers of silver bracelets, is far from hiding the actual truth under the thin veil of its symbolism. For pure native copper, found in quantity along the Copper River and the White River, was extensively used by the natives at the time of discovery by the Russians. Even as late as the present day an old Tlingit coppersmith, near Dawson, still hammers down native copper picked up in his neighborhood into souvenirs for tourists. Copper and iron, besides, were steadily brought from Siberia in small quantities, along ancient trade routes over the Bering Sea, either through the Aleutians or across Bering Strait into the Alaskan interior, then down the Pacific coast, or to the frozen lands eastward to the mouth of the Mackenzie River, and far beyond.

In late prehistoric times the Alaskans were acquainted with the practical uses of copper and iron. This has been made clear in recent years by the digging of archaeologists into ancient camp sites along the migration and trade routes close to the Bering Sea. The American nomads of the northern peninsula, like their Siberian neighbors, the Kamchadales, the Chukchees, and the Koriaks, were still in the later stages of the Stone Age when discovered, and they belonged to the same linguistic stock as the Athapascans. This stock, one of the most widely scattered anywhere, ranges on two continents from New Mexico far into Asia, perhaps as far as Burma. Yet its Stone-Age culture, restricted to America, was only partial and far from uniform. It shaded off from the full possession of metals at its western end in Asia, near the cradle of the race in Mongolia, into mere dependency, at the opposite end in the new world, upon scanty supplies of metals from afar. The great cultural recession that came upon these nomads in the course of their incessant migrations has been pointed out by Father Petitot, the missionary. It is an unusual occurrence, well illustrated in the symbolism of Copper Woman.

Before the coming of the Russians in Siberia during the sixteenth century, iron and copper were obtained deviously from Mongolian sources of supply across the salt waters. The Tungus and the Yakuts, in northeastern Siberia, knew how to cast iron or work it in primitive fashion. The Koriaks, close to Bering Strait, hammered it out in a cold state, as the Alaskans did.

No real barrier stood in the path of the trade in metals and artifacts from Siberia to America. Captain Cook, in 1778-79, noted that there is no current in the Strait, which is less than sixty miles wide. The two continents are "usually joined together by ice" in the winter, and the natives travel swiftly from one to the other; in the summer they sail across in one day. In clear weather one can see, from East Cape in Siberia, Cape Prince of Wales on the opposite side, and more easily still the Diomede Islands midway.

Vitus Bering, upon reaching the Aleutian Islands in 1741, found their occupants in possession of "long iron knives, apparently of their own manufacture." Steller, accompanying him, stated that these knives were not of European workmanship. And a scientist, T. A. Rickard, has recently written:

> It is probable that before the Russian fur-traders came to Alaska, the natives obtained iron from the Chukchees of northeastern Siberia. The Chukchees met the Aleuts on the Diomede Islands, half-way across Bering Strait.

The American natives engaged in barter with the Chuckchees on Diomede Islands were either Eskimos or Dénés of the lower Yukon River, or both in turns. Whymper declared that the Indian trade at Port Clarence and at Kotzebue Sound was carried on, in 1868, between the Chukchees, who had crossed Bering Strait, and the Kaveaks and the Malemiuts—these last, although different, intermingling cordially. He added:

> Inter-tribal commerce goes on to such an extent that clothing worn hundreds of miles up the Yukon, and in other parts of the interior of Russian America, is of Tchuktchi origin, and is made up by the women of the coast tribes. . . . From the Yukon, in exchange, some fine skins go to the Tchuktchi and ultimately reach the Russians of the Anadyr River.

Whymper leaves us under the impression that "the coast natives of northern Alaska are but Americanized

Tchuktchis from Asia," and that "with little difficulty
a colony of wandering Tchuktchis might cross from
Asia and populate the northern coasts of America."

At an earlier date, in 1787, William Coxe, speaking of
the Russian discoveries, had written likewise:

> The Tschukshi carry on a trade of barter with the inhabitants of
> America; they employ six days in passing the strait which separates
> the two continents; they direct their course from island to island.
> The distance from one to the other is so small that they are able to
> pass every night ashore. More to the north, the two continents ap-
> proach still nearer to each other, with only two islands lying between
> them.

Another source of metal supplies for the natives of
the North Pacific coast has recently been indicated by
Dr. Rickard. He writes:

> We have good reason to infer that the indigenes made their first
> acquaintance with iron, as the South Sea Islanders did, by means of
> drift-wood, brought by the oceanic winds and currents, both moving
> persistently eastward from the Asiatic shore to the American main-
> land. Japanese and Russian vessels, wrecked on the Kamchatkan
> coast, would yield woodwork containing iron, that drifted north-
> eastward and then eastward toward the American coast, to be cast
> ashore on the Aleutian Islands, and southward along the mainland.
> We find many wrecks. . . . Hardwood and bamboo from Asia are
> washed ashore on the Queen Charlotte Islands. Many of the glass
> balls used by Japanese fishermen for buoying their nets, to-day, find
> their way overseas to the shores of Vancouver Island.

In the light of this, we easily understand why the sea
captains, at the end of the eighteenth century, discovered
metals widely in use on the whole North Pacific coast of
America. Captain George Dixon, in 1785-88, observed
that ornaments worn by the Alaskan natives "were undoubtedly introduced here by the Russians, who have
constantly traded with these people for many years

past." He added, "I have also taken notice of things most acceptable in barter. Copper is almost the only article in request at King George's Sound."

Drawing closer to the country of the Tlingit of southeastern Alaska, we find, in Captain George Vancouver's *Voyage of Discovery* ... (1790-95), that the spears of the Nass River tribes, on what is now Portland Canal, were "about sixteen feet long, pointed with iron wrought in simple forms, amongst which some were barbed. Each man was provided with an iron dagger, suspended from his neck in a leather sheath, seemingly intended to be used when in close action."

A few years earlier, in 1785-88, Captain George Dixon wrote: "There is little doubt of the variety of metals and minerals found here. We frequently saw large circular wreaths of copper both at Norfolk Sound and at Queen Charlotte Islands, which did not appear to be of foreign manufacture, but twisted into that shape by the natives themselves, to wear as an ornament about the neck."

Captain Etienne Marchand reported, in his *Voyage Round the World* (1790-92), that the native women of Norfolk Sound (southern Tlingit and Tsimsyan) were "adorned with a necklace, composed of copper wire interwoven, and this ornament does not appear to be of European manufacture; it might be taken for the work of their hands."

A thin plate made of virgin copper was found on the Copper River to the north of Sitka. It was three feet in length, twenty-two inches in breadth at one end, and eleven inches at the other, with varying figures painted on one side. This was seen by Baranov, according to Urey Lisianski, in his *Voyage* (1803-1806.) Such plates, in the form of conventional copper shields, later became

the most valuable form of property all over the North
Pacific coast; they symbolized native wealth. Even at
that early date they were, according to Lisianski: "possessed only by the rich, who give for one of them from
twenty to thirty sea-otter skins. They are carried by
the servants before their master on different occasions
of ceremony, and are beaten upon so as to serve as a
musical instrument. The value of the plate depends, it
seems, on its being made of virgin copper; for the common copper ones do not bear a higher price than a single
skin.

The Sitka tribe, to which the Tlingit silversmith,
Sitka Jack, belonged, is reported by Lisianski, early in
the last century, to "have some skill both in sculpture
and painting. On seeing their masks, their different domestic utensils, which are painted and carved with various figures, and their boxes, the tops of which are curi-
ously inlaid with a shell resembling human teeth, one
might suppose their productions to be the work of a
people greatly advanced in civilization."

Several Eskimo girls at Kotzebue Sound were said by
F. W. Beechy, in his *Narrative of a Voyage* ... (1825-
28), to have worn massive iron bracelets. "One had a
curb chain for a necklace, and another a bell suspended
in front, in the manner described the preceding years at
Chores Peninsula."

Bracelets, necklets or collars, and earrings were in
favor many years before Beechy's visit on the coast. Dr.
Rickard points out that Friar Juan Crespi, with Jean
Pérez on the *Santiago,* in 1774 had observed that the
women were wearing "rings on their fingers and bracelets of iron and copper," and that "these were considered
of great value." In another Spanish expedition, in 1779,

Bodega and Artega, while exploring the Gulf of Alaska, also had seen on Prince of Wales Island in southeastern Alaska "the natives wearing bracelets of copper, iron, and whalebone on their wrists, and on their neck, sundry rows of beads made of bone, and necklaces of extremely fine copper; and in the ears, twisted wires of the same metal." About the same time John Ledyard and others had recorded similar observations. For instance, Ledyard had written: "We found [at Nootka] a few copper bracelets and three or four wrought knives with coarse wooden hafts."

The first copper ornaments used by the Haidas, according to Alfred Adams, of Massett, were anklets or rings worn just above the ankles. Some anklets recently were found in old coffins on the west coast of the Queen Charlotte Islands. The Tlingits to the north, according to Adams, had introduced the fashion of wearing metal ornaments, and this was due to their overlords, the Russians, who had arrived early among them. Adams added: "The Tlingit had learned lots of things from the Russians." Yet the term among the Sitkas for large copper shields or plates was *tinnah*, from the name of the people along the Copper River to the northeast who provided them with nuggets of native copper. Farther down the coast the copper shields were not at first made by the Haidas of Kyusta, as they were later, but were imported ready-made from the Chilkat country north of Sitka.

Silver and gold in jewelry were introduced among the natives much later than copper and iron. The most valuable gifts from the Russians to the Tlingits were of copper until rather late—for instance, "the imperial arms on a copper plate" presented by Baranov to a Kenaitze chief, which were to be shown by him to foreign shipmates as a protection against harm. And the coat-of-arms of the Romanovs buried at the foot of a tree near Sitka, as a mark of imperial possession, was also of copper.

It was after 1843, when Victoria was founded by the Hudson's Bay Company, that silver and gold were circulated as currency on the North Pacific Coast and used by the Indian craftsmen in their derivative handicrafts. The earliest silver item so far noted down is included in "The Report of the Chief Manager of the Russian American Company for 1828." It consisted of a silver badge engraved "Allies of Russia," presented to a Tlingit chief named Quatka, in recognition of his releasing from captivity and certain death a "Kolosh" boy slave.

The first silver bracelet mentioned in historical records is the one which Robert Campbell in 1838, received at Terror Bridge, near the headwaters of the Stikine River, as a gift from a Nahannie chieftainess. "On parting," he relates in his journal, "I gave her my handkerchief and all the loose nicknacks I had about me, and received in return her silver bracelet." And that is a little over a hundred years ago.

It is true that, for many years, the Tlingits had been able to admire fine church plate, jewelry, and ikons in the Russian Cathedral at Sitka. Perhaps they had tried very early to imitate this form of intrusive art, for a picture of the Immaculate Conception was described by Captain Etienne Marchand, about 1790, as being "the production of the fine arts of the North West Americans."

At that early date, there must have been other manifestations of native talent and aptitude for plastic and pictorial art, as Marchand observed: "What is most astonishing is to see paintings and sculpture everywhere, among a nation of hunters." European tools and utensils, sheets of copper, large pieces of bar iron, "the whole of English manufacture," are found at random, mixed with indigenous work.

The greatest stimulus to the Tlingits undoubtedly came from the Russians established at Sitka very early in the last century, for, at that time, Sitka was one of the main focuses of handicrafts on this continent. Von Langsdorff, in his *Voyages and Travels* (1803-1807), vividly acquaints us with its cultural activities. He wrote:

Among the Russians established here are handicraft workers of almost every kind, who have each their workshop allotted to them. Numbers of these men were persons who, for some stroke of genius, were banished to Siberia; they were tempted to seek their fortune under the wings of the Russian-American Company in this remote corner of the globe. It is therefore not surprising that some very excellent workmen, such as watch-makers, gold and silver workers, shoemakers, taylors, smiths, etc., should be found among them. . . .

Langsdorff concludes with the statement that all kinds of industries were introduced in the Indian villages, including those of spinning and weaving. Out of this craft of weaving may have issued, at least indirectly, the world-famous Chilkat blanket.

This initial art impetus was later commented upon by Ivan Petroff in his *Report . . .* (1882) to the American government. He stated:

The shipyard at Sitka was as complete as any similar establishment in the Russian Empire. It provided all kinds of workshops and magazines, even having brass- and iron-factories, machine shops, and nautical instrument makers. Experiments were made in the manufacture of bricks, wooden ware, and even woolen stuffs of materials imported from California. Skilled labour was imported from Russia at great expense. And many workshops were maintained at Sitka, among them the manufacture of agricultural implements for the ignorant and indolent ranchers of California, and thousands of primitive ploughshares in use in that country. These were made at Sitka for the Californian and Mexican markets. Axes, adzes, spades, hoes were turned out by industrious workmen of the Sitka ship-yard, while the foundry was for some time engaged in casting bells for the Catholic missions on the Pacific Coast, many of these bells still being in existence. . . . The discovery of gold in California, in 1845, provided a ready sale of shop-worn goods from Alaska, and many Aleutian fishermen went, as labourers, to the California mines.

The Hudson's Bay Company, whose headquarters in the 1830's were at Fort Vancouver in the mouth of the Columbia River, exchanged with Sitka its agricultural and garden surplus for Russian tools and agricultural machinery.

Hector Chevigny, in *Lord of Alaska,* published in 1942, may not be far from the truth when he writes that Aleut women had something to do with the preparation, and the decoration with bead work, of the church vestments in the Cathedral of St. Michael at Sitka, and that the Eucharist vessels were made of Spanish silver by the local blacksmiths.

In these cultural surroundings, the natives must have worked under wages as helping hands with Russian masters. Some of them may have branched off into derivative activities of their own. The evolution of their crafts was a result of fruitful contacts and prolonged training. This transfusion came to the end of its course only recently, after having brought into existence the unique art expressions of the totem pole, of the smaller carvings in wood, stone, ivory, and argillite, of decorative painting on house fronts, leather, engraved boxes, of silver and gold work, and of the fine Chilcat

Sitka, very early in the last century, became one of the main focuses of handicrafts on this continent PAGE 213.

robes for chiefs, which are creative imitations of church copes and chasubles in use at the Cathedral of St. Michael at Sitka.

When Major General O. O. Howard visited Alaska in 1875, he stopped over at Sitka, then in an advanced state of decadence because of the departure of the Russians after the American purchase, and he was greatly impressed by the ceremonies in the Sitka cathedral. Yet he noted: "I wish I could report that the morality of the priest and the people was equal to their devotion. He was frequently reported for drunkenness."

The Aleutians farther north still remember without malice this foible of their Greek Orthodox pastor, when, according to what Langdon Kihn recently heard, they imitate in their own Christmas ceremonies the divine service at the altar, with the priest tottering from side to side on his feet.

At the time of Howard's visit, Sitka Jack was away from home, but his absence could not be overlooked, because "he controlled at least one half of the households. Annahootz, the chief who governed the rest, spoke at the meeting for the whole tribe." From the context, it may be inferred that Sitka Jack was the focal head of Eagle clan, whereas Annahootz (whose name meant Grizzly Bear) was the Chief of the Ravens.

Two years later, in 1877, after the withdrawal of the American troops from Alaska, Sitka Jack was responsible for an outbreak which called for the dispatch of a gunboat to quell the agitation. The only record left in the Washington reports bearing on his political activities is: "Considerable excitement was occasioned by the threats of a chief known as Sitka Jack." Many outbreaks," adds the official commentator, "have been threatened by this tribe, arising mainly through the influence of liquor and the natural viciousness of some influential man with the idea of bettering his condition."

Eleven years later Sitka Jack appeared as a silversmith catering to strangers, in an amusing incident anonymously reported in *Harper's Weekly*, September 8, 1888:

Sitka Jack and his wife Susie are silversmiths, who take your dollars and half-dollars and transform them into bracelets of varied shapes, adorned with Indian conceptions of whales, bears, eagles, and such other animals or fish as belong to their history and religion. Jack made me a pair of bracelets. When I expostulated with him on the price, he replied—appreciating his own value and the frenzy of tourists—, "You no take? All light! You pay no seven toller? All light! You go 'way. Man come, next boat. Him pay eight. Vely good!" I took the bracelets.

The same observer reported that Marshall Atkins had shown him "a charm on his watch chain in the form of a horseshoe, made out of Alaska gold by a native, who had never seen either horse or horseshoe, but closely followed a drawing." And he added the typical detail: "You will come across women in dirt and rags, or blankets, wearing gold and silver ornaments made by their own people. The ornaments are most excellently engraved."

The large section of Sitka "controlled" by Sitka Jack consisted of a number of Tlingit households. In the long list of these houses, recorded in 1904 by J. R. Swanton, the partiality of their inmates for metals is revealed. Among their names stand: Copper-Plate house, its owner, Naxana bearing a Russian name; Steel-House, so-called because its head, once in a fight with the Russians, had captured a piece of steel and placed it in front of his dwelling; and Iron-House, on account of the first nails seen in the country having been obtained by its chief long ago.

The arts were more or less hereditary among the northern coast tribes,[2] and Sitka Jack undoubtedly belonged to a privileged clan, presumably of the Eagles. The Eagles, among the three northern nations, were born leaders in the fur trade, in warfare, and in all the crafts, especially in metalwork. A closed shop or clan system with extensive privileges was in evidence everywhere, even in the early stages of coppersmithing. A good reason for this was that the work required training and practice. We find a hint of this in Lieutenant W. R. Abercrombie's *Report of an Expedition into the Copper River Valley* (Alaska) in 1884, as he stated that "Years ago, coffee bowls, often of immense size, beaten out of native copper, and knives from the same source, highly valued, were in use among the Yakutats and the Chilcats, but have since been superseded by those of other material." Such bowls were the handiwork of experts.

Petroff, in his well-known Report wrote:

Long before the first meeting of the Tlinket with the Europeans, they possessed the art of forging copper, which they obtained from the inhabitants of the Copper River region. A tradition exists to the effect that an old woman of Chilkat invented the art of forging [this is another allusion to the Copper Woman legend], and that she was worshipped as a benefactress of her kind. For long years this art was a hereditary secret with certain families.

Several silversmiths in Sitka, which at first was the center for their calling, have left us their names and numerous examples of their splendid workmanship, which is nowhere else surpassed. In beauty and perfec-

---

[2] In "Paleosiberian Languages" (*American Anthropologist*, Oct., 1942, p. 609), Roman Jakobson writes: "Pictography has a rather well-rooted tradition among the Eastern Paleosiberians (cf. a high degree of graphic art characteristic of all the Paleosiberian people)."

tion their work is only equalled among the later Haida engravers of Massett farther south. These Haidas, it must be acknowledged, had derived their silver and gold technique directly from the Sitkan craftsmen, with whom their own Eagle clans were related.

After copper and brass had lost much of their former value, with the American purchase of Alaska in the 1860's, silver and gold gained the ascendancy as precious metals, and, as they were eminently suitable for jewelry, they lent themselves to the same traditional patterns and decorations. Some of the early copper bracelets were so beautifully shaped, engraved, and ornamented with insertions of haliotis shells that they served as models. A specimen of this type was mentioned by Alexander Mackenzie in his *Descriptive Notes* ... (1891):

This is very old, and it is the only copper armlet in the Haida nation. It has been preserved in the same family for several generations and worn by the chief's wife.... Since they have had the opportunity of obtaining silver from the whites, all bracelets, bangles, and other ornaments are made of white metal. Copper is now considered too base a metal for such use, although it used to be esteemed of high value, next to iron.

Fine copper bracelets are occasionally claimed to be very old—in particular that of Mrs. Lott at Wrangell (now in Walter E. Waters' possession). Being over eighty years old herself, she declared that her heirloom had belonged to her great-grandmother.

Nowhere can a clearer insight be gained into the secrets of the Sitka silversmiths and goldsmiths than in the museum collections—in particular those which were made, in the early 1880's, for the National Museum in Washington and by Lieutenant T. Emmons for the American Museum of Natural History in New York.

These two collections contain many of the finest samples of Sitka Jack's work, as well as those of his wife and contemporaries in Sitka, at Wrangell, and elsewhere. The recorded names of Tlingit and Haida smiths of Alaska—which do not include the long list of smiths farther south on the coast—are: Sitka Charley, Kasank, Yukas, the elder, and Charlie Gunwack, all three of Wrangell; Haida Charlie, a former Eagle chief of Howkan, who resided at Sitka; Gunahltu, goldsmith at Klawock, who specialized in bracelets and complicated earrings; Haida John and Sanarhot, both of Kasan, who made silver and gold bracelets; Karh-tsirhkut, of Tongas; and not a few others.

The European custom of marking the work with a dye or a punch, containing the maker's initials, never prevailed on the North Pacific coast. Yet the craftsmen occasionally engraved on it the name of their town, and sometimes even the date. Gold earrings of the drop-pendant variety, in Mr. Waters' possession at Wrangell, bear the inscription: "Tlingit made in Sitka 1869." Another pair in the same lot, going back to about 1880, is marked: "Tlingit Indian earrings, made at Sitka." Two spoons out of a set of ten, made in the winter of 1891, are engraved, carefully and decoratively, with the name of SITKA in the bowl. Other spoons, at the Museum of the American Indian, in New York, are similarly engraved in the bowl. Presumably all these went back to the same hands.

The predominance of the Sitka silversmiths and goldsmiths, and the rare quality of their work, in the oldest collections at the National Museum at Washington and at the American Museum of Natural History in New York, is almost unchallenged; and their style is on the

The current stylization of heraldic figures on totem poles did not exclude the carving of mystic animals in bone or ivory charms used by medicine men PAGE 231.

whole less native-like than that of their imitators farther
away from their foreign masters and models.

Only a few samples of their work can be described
here, for they have come down to us in considerable
numbers.

A pair of ornate and complicated silver earrings, in
parts joined together by rings, in Mr. Waters' collection
at Wrangell, and labeled "Made at Sitka, 1865 and
1869," are not Indian-like. A number of old earrings,
fairly large and rather flat, were made at Hoona, near
Sitka, in the form of triangular shark teeth, with ser-
rated edges. And Lieutenant Emmons found at Wrangell
(now conserved at the Museum of the American Indian) some "ear-bobs," apparently made there by a
member of the "Stikine tribe."

A set of ten spoons at the American Museum of
Natural History (Nos. 2435-2445) is accompanied by
the following significant label, presumably by Lieutenant Emmons:

This set of silver spoons was made out of coin silver by a Tlingit
silversmith at Sitka, Alaska, in the winter of 1891. Each spoon
was made out of half a dollar piece. The coin was heated by placing
it in a small stove among the coals. After remaining for some minutes, it was removed, placed on an anvil and beaten with a hammer,
then reheated and rebeaten until formed into a bar which was then
ready to be hammered into shape. . . . The bowl of the spoon was
formed by being beaten out into a mould of wood. Metal or horn
thus took the shape of the bed piece. When shaped, the spoon was
rubbed down with fine sand paper and pumice stone. In primitive
times, and even yet, it is not uncommon to see dog-fish skins sub-
stituted for sand paper. The pumice stone was found floating along
the seashore. The ornamentation was done with knives made from
old files or razor blades, which were sharpened at a broad angle; and,
often times, the handle was loaded to give weight. In the case of this
set of spoons, the original designs were executed without drawings,
just as they were thought and worked out.

Another label, in the same collection, contains additional details on the process of ronde-bosse, which was distinctly foreign (E/2117):

The silver bar ... was beaten out into a small spoon in rough. The bowl was shaped by placing it over a spoon-shaped cavity in a hard-wood or bone rest, and a convex plug of exact shape was placed over the silver, and by beating and further hammering was wedged into the designed pattern.

The remarkable set of tools belonging to Sitka silversmiths in the 1880's, collected by Lieutenant Emmons and now kept at the American Museum of Natural History, throws a vivid light upon the origins of silver and gold craft among the Tlingit, and the available information on these is far too extensive to be utilized here in full. For instance: among the tools, from a Sitka shop, for forcing silver and gold into shape are three wood carvings serving as forms or cores. Two of these (2115 and 2017) are pieces of hard wood called *kainugai* tapering to a rounded point for shaping the head of a bracelet, the bowl of a spoon, or the parts of earrings. A thin, flattened plate or band of silver or gold was laid on a cavity in a bed plate or base block of the same wood corresponding to the first piece. Then the soft metal in between was slowly pressed into the required form by means of repeated tapping with a wooden mallet. A third piece of wood in the shape of a dish (2112) was meant as a rest for small bracelets that were fitted on it for rubbing down, polishing, and to provide the required rigidity for carving.

A silversmith's anvil of iron, called *donai eoch* (2106), fitted on a block of wood, was used to beat out small pieces of gold, silver (mostly coins), or copper.

An old Russian hammer, called *tukle* (2111), with an iron head ornamentally carved, served in beating out fine metals into bracelets, spoons, and ornaments.

A small silver bar ready to be fashioned into a narrow bracelet or a spoon had been drawn from a half dollar piece, or from a dollar cut in halves. During its preparation it had been repeatedly heated to soften it, then hammered a little at a time until the desired shape had been attained.

As soldering was called for in a number of cases—in brooches with a pin, and in complicated headdresses or crowns of silver—a tool required was a soldering iron (2016) consisting of a "piece of copper secured by means of iron wire to a handle of strap iron. . . . " Another tool for this purpose, called *kui-qwur* (2109), was a "piece of hoop iron used to soften silver ore by placing it among hot coals; the handle was wrapped in cedar bark as a nonconductor to save the hand holding it from contact with the heated metal."

Casting was also resorted to, whenever necessary. So a wooden crucible or mold called *kai-qwut-lae* (2110), consisting of a few combined parts, was fitted out by a native Sitka jeweler, to receive the melted filings and pieces that were cut or chiseled out of the bar metal and retrieved for use. Casting was also needed in making large bracelets and ornaments for which more than dollar coins were required.

Two silversmith's retorts (2012-13) attached to iron handles, *denai-ki-ya* . . . , were made of Russian brick, and lined with borax. The label explaining them reads: "The scrapings and fillings in silver and gold working are melted in this vessel, turned into a wooden mould, and run into a bar for future use."

Carving tools in this representative collection from Sitka are a *kletae* or *ketai* of iron or steel (2107-08), a double knife made from an old file. This was used in carving ornamentation on gold, silver, or copper. The head of at least one of these two *ketais* "is loaded with lead to give steadiness to the hand in working."

Pumice stone, called *geeft* (2101-13), was found in the tool box of every native jeweler, for use in rubbing down metal work before it was finished, and also for cleaning it. The stone was picked up in a natural state on the shore in several localities. After using pumice stone, the skin of the dogfish served for polishing.

A dogfish tail, called *toon* (2102), picked up in a work box at Sitka, is described as having been utilized "as a rubbing down or polishing medium in metal, bone, and ivory carving."

The native jewelers at Sitka and elsewhere in southern Alaska were equipped for their work with tools they had fashioned in the manner of their Russian masters. Besides, they had under their eyes fine jewelry and vessels which inspired them into free imitations or creations of their own. In the same Emmons collection we find two samples of such foreign handiwork that must have been highly appreciated by the local craftsmen.

One of these is a brass hat (2308):

... made after the pattern of the native spruce root dancing hat [which went back to a Mongolian source]. This is an historical piece carrying the stamp of the Russian factory, and it was made by the order of Baranoff, the first Russian commander, who established forts and trading posts in southeastern Alaska, and was presented to the head-chief Michael of the Sitka kwan, early in the century, in satisfaction of a treaty of peace between the Russians and the natives about Sitka. ...

An intriguing specimen of foreign craftsmanship, long possessed in the country, that possibly fostered imitations was an

. . . ivory snuff box, called *to-war-ku* [2399], from Kluck-kwan or Chilkat, ornamented in cuts and lines which would indicate that it had been procured in trade from the interior tribes and possibly had come from the Bering Sea by way of the Yukon River, to carry native snuff in. . . .

A "fire case [2299] found in the possession of an old woman of the Sitka kwan at Sitka" calls for further speculation as to the early foreign influences at play in Alaska. It consists of a small container.

. . . of a type found in Thibet. It was likely brought to America by some early Russian employee of the fur company from Siberia or China, and had fallen into the possession of the natives. The owner could give no account of it beyond the fact that it had been in the family for many years. It consists of a small leather case ornamented with brass and carrying a slightly rounded or curved steel at the lower end, while the pocket enclosed the flint. It was used to produce fire by friction. . . .

The Tlingit and Haida jewelers preferred gold and silver coins to other fine metals for their work. Among the Eagles of Massett, on the Queen Charlotte Islands in the 1880's, Edensaw is said to have used coins, mostly dollar coins, "and the American were the best. Some Mexican dollars were brought up to him once, and they were splendid; but the supply was very limited, and it was not replenished."

The natives also obtained much gold from the Klondike, and the salmon canneries at one time used to pay in gold. This, according to Alfred Adams, one of their elders, was a great inducement for the use of home jewelry—rings for nose, ears, fingers, and bands for the arms. These ornaments, being marks of rank and distinction, were in great demand among the tribesmen themselves. And they were sold in large numbers to outsiders, who were fond of souvenirs and totems.

Silversmiths also flourished because of the difficulty experienced in safeguarding gold and silver coins in open houses or in the wilderness by Indians who often were paid for their furs or services in specie. It was found expedient, for instance, to have twenty and ten dollar gold pieces hammered out into bracelets, which the engraved crests made recognizable to everyone at sight. Thus not a few old women, until recently, would treasure their savings in the form of bracelets and brooches, which they proudly donned on ceremonial occasions, to the envy of their less thrifty children and grandchildren.

Tlingit and Haida jewelry, abundantly represented in the museums of America and Europe and in private collections, is far from being all of one type or tendency. Much of its production candidly discloses the source of its foreign inspiration—mainly Russian, sometimes Chinese. A great deal more of it has decidedly taken to byways that are part of their backgrounds. Here we find the native craftsmen at their impressive best. By introducing their own totems or fancies into their decoration, they changed the face of their art so entirely that we are apt to think that it is wholly original, without any debt to outsiders. Because of this, the world at large, no less than most of the anthropologists, have been misled unawares into believing that heraldic or illustrative symbols had come down straight from prehistory. The vast majority of them all really do not antedate 1860. A conclusive proof of this lies in their absence in archaeology and in the early museum collections—in particular, the Scouler Haida specimens in the Trocadero Museum in Paris, going back to 1825, and the Wilkes collection at the National Museum in Washington, going back to the late 1830's.

The splendid silverwork collected after 1875 by J. G. Swan for the National Museum at Washington plainly reveals the dual tendency, at that time, of silver craft among the Tlingit and the Haida jewelers. The one adheres to the foreign models, and the other, once the impetus was given, boldly branches off toward independent self-expression. This aptitude for untrammeled individualism in North Pacific coast art is the more in evidence the farther southward one gets away from Sitka, which was the seat of Russian art in America.

The handicap experienced by the native workers who could not forget the sources and constantly remained under Slavonic tuition explains why the Sitkans and the northern Tlingits did not create the stately totem pole, nor even adopt it as their own. Yet they had contributed more than any other to their devious inception. Nor did the jewelers of Sitka, in spite of their superior tools and equipment, and even their superior manual technique, show as much individuality in their silver and gold work as did, a bit later, the Haidas of Massett or Skidegate.

The Sitkans were too often content to make crowns of silver that look too delicate and pretentious, or elaborate combs in the *Senorita* fashion, or daggers too fine for any practical use. Even their bracelets and brooches often carry conventional decorations consisting of acanthus leaves, scrolls and foliated lines in the Greek manner, lotus flowers, fret borders, crosses, and cross-

*The engraved surface decoration of silver and gold on the Queen
Charlotte Islands is quite remarkable* PAGE 230.

hatching. The Russian or the American eagle is a favorite theme, and angels or figureheads with chesty sirens make an appearance. In an exceptional bracelet, we find an American coin with an anchor reproduced in a smooth engraving, down to the lettering around it: "Half dol." and "States of America" (National Museum, No. 19533, collected at Sitka by J. G. Swan in 1875).

It is only while silver craft marched southward from Sitka that it truly adapted itself to natural surroundings, as it did among the northern Haida silversmiths.

The metalwork of the northern Haidas, from 1870 onward, far more than that of the Tlingits, forms a group by itself and gives an illusion of unity and authenticity; it seems unrelated to similar crafts in other countries. The engraved surface decoration of silver and gold on the Queen Charlotte Islands is quite remarkable —indeed it is unique. Its features conform with those of other crafts among the same people, as in the carving of masks and totem poles, the painting of flat or rounded surfaces, and the making of large coppers and of fine blades and tools embellished with the owner's animal crests. It is this latest development in the art that is nowhere surpassed for creative stylization and utter individuality.

Most of the native silversmiths whose work is represented in the museums were Haida; but other skillful craftsmen on the adjacent main coast, in particular among the Tsimsyans proper and the Bella Bellas, also contributed a fair quota of their own. Among the Tsimsyans, the jewelry collected was usually attributed to Haida makers, which shows that silver work, quite restricted in its distribution, spread everywhere through direct contacts from the same centers — that is, first from among the Tlingits, and then among the Haidas, to a few of their neighbors.

Since native metal work for many years was directed to the making of bracelets and brooches, only a little embossing was required in hammering out gold and silver coinage into narrow and thin convex bands, which were highly polished and to which a pin attachment was soldered. As the engraving of a pattern on the outer surface was customary, it called for great skill in the engraver, and it drew upon the resources of other pictorial arts. It absorbed with slight transformation the current stylization of totemic or heraldic figures on totem poles, in house-front paintings, and in all sorts of domestic and ceremonial objects. In this it is wholly derivative yet aboriginal.

The most familiar engravings on silver now are the eagle, the raven, the grizzly bear, the killer whale, the beaver, the shark, and the frog, and their variations. These are the crests of the makers or of the owners—though at the time of their making the crest system was not strictly enforced. A very few of the patterns never were heraldic, or even native; they were borrowed from the white people (for instance, the American eagle, floral scrolls, and common fret designs).

The North Pacific coast art at its best, among the Tlingits, the Haidas, the Tsimsyans, and their neighbors to the south, is highly original and stylistic. Among the Haidas it reached the peak of its stylization, whereas among the coast Tsimsyans it retained, as in wood carving, more of its inspiration from the animal world. In the few specimens from outlying districts, it is clear that the Gitksans of the upper Skeena were naïvely naturistic, and that the Bella Bellas of the coast north of Van-

couver Island remembered the fantastic but firm outlines familiar in their ancient house-front paintings.

The decoration of the silver work among the Tlingits,
the Haidas, and the coast Tsimsyans conforms to standards that are consistently carried out, as the engravers
used a stock of conventional patterns and symbols into
which they injected new life and incessant variations—
no two pieces ever being quite alike. The first require-
ment was that the whole outer polished surface must be
filled to the edge with the design; in other words, that
the animal or figure must be made to fit within the small
and rigid space available. The features and the limbs of
the totemic animals must be either enlarged in proportion to the rest, boldly reduced, or torn apart. Thus the
head and face of the grizzly bear may occupy one third
of the space, one side of the whole body another third,
and the other side the remaining third; or, elsewhere, the
head of the raven may form one end of a narrow bracelet, two tail feathers the other end, and the body between
them may be represented by slender twin rows of conventional feathers and hourglass-like sections of the
backbone. Sometimes the head in the center is twice
shown, back to back or face to face, and the two split
halves of the body are almost always spread out in opposite directions, on each side of the head or the repeated
heads.

The limbs or the parts of the body are usually symbolized or suggested rather than actually outlined. Thus
the legs or the feet are represented only by claws, and
the body by a few ribs for a quadruped, a fin or two
for a fish, and some feathers for a bird. The stylized
heads for the bear, the wolf, the beaver, the whale, and
the shark being almost alike, they are differentiated by

means of a characteristic feature or two: the two large incisors and the checkered tail for the beaver; the huge mouth with even-pointed teeth and the four paws for the grizzly bear; the wide mouth with two pointed front teeth, and the curled-up tail, for the wolf; the large face with zigzag teeth, and three crescent-like gills for the shark.

Interesting conventions, besides, help in the decorative treatment of limbs or in filling empty spaces. The joints are represented by eyelike patterns; that is why eyes or ovals stand for the elbows, the legs, or join the claws or the wing feathers together at the top. Conventionalized ears, nostrils, teeth, fins, claws, ribs, tails, feathers, backbone rings—some of them doubled up—are adroitly disposed wherever space filling requires them; and, in some instances, the whole field is given up to such symbols now torn away from their natural associations and thereby stripped of any meaning.

Technical devices, together with the tools, were everywhere borrowed from the white craftsmen in the North who had helped in the first stages of the native craft. For instance, fine hatching and checkered lines diagonally intercrossing, to form a shaded background; incised or slightly depressed small surfaces and wide lines, and some floral and scroll-like ornaments of exotic appearance. The pictorial engravings in a few pieces of silver from the Skeena River are enclosed as it were in a frame of hatched lines within long borders.

TOTEMS

THE FAMOUS rows of totems that once conferred glamor upon coastal towns now belong to the past; they almost disappeared from their vantage posts, after these were deserted by the decimated occupants. The majority have fallen and decayed in a new forest growth engulfing them; or they have been burned up as firewood. Not a few were purchased in the nick of time from demoralized owners, who had lost interest in them, and they were planted elsewhere, in public parks. Some of these, painted in fresh and gaudy colors, and shamefaced as it were, can be seen in modern surroundings at Sitka, Ketchikan, Prince Rupert, Vancouver, and Victoria. A tall one, with a notorious record, is paraded in a public square at Seattle; another gazes with blackened eyes upon the passing trains of the Canadian National Railways in Jasper Park. Two more were recently transplanted from the volcanic canyon of the middle Nass to Bronx Park in New York. Others decorate the rotundas and the halls of museums in the main cities in America and Europe; they are treasured there as a tribute to prehistoric art and culture.

At the beginning, these enigmatic carvings went back to smaller and obscure prototypes that have since virtually ceased to exist. These prototypes were graveyard figures of people or animals, which the early explorers observed along the coast from the mouth of the Fraser River northward to Bering Strait, and also in adjacent

Siberia and Japan; or they were akin to "grotesque" house posts with figures of the type recorded by Captain Cook at Nootka Sound, west of Vancouver Island; or, again, they followed the earlier style of miniature carvings of stone, ivory, and wood, occasionally found on the same coast, that seem somewhat older. In these latter we notice traits possibly derived from Asiatic sources. But, in their present form, the totems themselves are not by any means prehistoric or even a hundred years old.

The Russians in Alaska failed to leave a record of any such totems among the Tlingit tribes. These decorated columns made their earliest appearance at the southeastern tip of the Alaskan peninsula and farther down the coast, among the Haidas and the Tsimsyans who were their true originators. The white seamen that first explored this country after 1780 noticed in one or two northern towns of the Queen Charlotte Islands a very few carved house frontals in the form of posts through which a round mouth-like entrance had been cut. This type of house embellishment also contributed to the later inception of the detached memorial posts standing in front of the principal dwellings in the old centers.

It is only between 1860 and 1880 that true totem poles became the fashion among the Niskaes of the Nass River, among the Haidas of Queen Charlotte and Prince of Wales islands, and among the southern Tlingits below Wrangell. The outlying Gitksan tribes of the upper Skeena adopted the custom of carving memorials rather late, certainly after 1850, and observed it until after 1900. A few indifferent poles were erected there as late as 1944, although the dead as a whole are no longer honored in this old-fashioned way. The younger genera-

tion of Indians everywhere looks down upon these
monuments as worthless reminders of a past which it is
doing nothing to preserve.

Wherever these impressive memorials still raise their
bold and wild profiles against the sky, on the sites of
abandoned dwellings, they are a cause of wonder to
visitors unaccustomed to them. But their meaning remains obscure, when it is not entirely lost. The information volunteered on the spot is often groundless and
misleading, and undue antiquity—hundreds of years—is
ascribed to them. The reason for this shortcoming on
the part of the guides is that our published literature has
fallen far short of the mark.

That totem poles are not really ancient, or that they
belong only to the historical period, very near us, will be
shown here by a few typical examples bearing on the
Russians since their occupation of Alaska, on the early
white seamen in Pacific coast waters, and on the early
fur traders of the North West Company and the Hudson's Bay Company in northern British Columbia and
the Yukon.

The splendid pole of "Chief Skowl," recently transplanted from Kasan into the park at Ketchikan, shows
three Russian priests, one above the other, figuring impressively with round staring eyes, curly hair, drooping
mustaches, short twisted chin beards, and ample church
robes. The arms of one of them, in the center, are
crossed piously on his chest. The hands of the two
others are raised. One, at the base, is giving a blessing;
another, near the top, points with one hand to the sky
for a warning, whereas the other hand, wide open, rests
upon his heart. He is no doubt preaching a sermon. In
lighter attire than his fellows, he wears wide sailor

*The splendid pole of "Chief Skowl" at Ketchikan shows three
Russian priests ... PAGE 236.*

trousers split at the ankles over his leather boots with raised heels.

The imperial or American eagles sit, the larger one looking sideways, with wings widespread, on the covered head of the clergyman at the base of the column; and the other, whose wings are half-open, faces forward, on the head of the preacher at the top. A cherub with a human face, staring eyes, and composite wings covered with feathers, rests upon a foliated scroll above the priest in the center. And classical fretwork decorates the edges up and down the large red cedar tree.

This superb monument, perhaps the finest in Alaska, was erected about seventy years ago, at Kasan on Prince of Wales Island, for an Indian named Young, of the Raven phratry. This Haida-Kaiganee was noted in his day for his liberality in large feasts and for boasting of his knowledge of the Greek Orthodox church at Sitka to the north.

Another Kasan pole with scroll fretwork was said by an old Indian woman to have been carved by her uncle, who wanted to display on it a Greek Catholic church certificate in his possession, of which he was unusually proud.

On a number of other totem poles, white men and Indian notables occupy the foreground. One of the carvings, now in the park at Ketchikan, is supposed to stand for Captain Cook, who made landfalls on the North Pacific coast in 1778-79. Other poles are surmounted by carvings representing white men in overcoats, top hats, and long trousers, one of these being a sailor at a steering wheel. Native chiefs in paraphernalia and conical hats, standing or sitting on Haida chests, are too numerous to count.

The native memorial to Captain Cook challenges attention only because of its historical portent, for in itself it is not an important piece of craftsmanship. Small and merely affixed to a thick-set mast, it consists of the upper half of a human figure facing forward and resting on a boat placed sideways and dotted with portholes. The accuracy of this local ascription to Captain Cook is questionable, as the carving lacks authenticity, and as Captain Cook never touched the Alaskan seacoast except in the Eskimo area within the Bering Sea, far to the north. And the figure itself is decidedly that of a woman, whose delicate hands are clasped in front. The close-fitting bodice is buttoned in the middle; it ends at the neck with a collar and at the wrists with narrow cuffs and trimmings. The long hair is parted near the center and smoothly combed sideways.

No Tlingit ever saw Captain Cook, or possibly any other British seaman, before the coming of Captain George Vancouver. While making a careful survey of the coast, in 1793, Vancouver sailed with his ship within the wide inland waters now known under the name of Portland Canal. There he brushed past the estuary of the Nass River and encountered a party of Tsimsyans who had not seen any white man before. While on his way from the Nass northward through the islands and canals to the present site of Wrangell, where he missed the mouth of the Stikine, he probably came across the southern Tlingits, who do not seem to have remembered his passage, as the Niskaes do, in a tradition among them which I have recorded. All told, there is no more reason to ascribe the memorial now at Ketchikan to Cook than to Vancouver.

This intriguing carving has a better chance of por-

traying Captain Swanson's Tlingit wife, about whom old
Mrs. Tamery, of Wrangell, had the following story to
tell:

"The first white sailor ever seen ['remembered' would
be a better word] in this country landed at Tongas, on
the present sea-coast border between Alaska and British
Columbia. There he took to wife a young woman of the
Ganarhadee tribe, who bore a child by him. Yet he soon
went away without her. Afterwards she married Hah-
skap, a chief, who adopted her girl child as his own.

"This daughter of the white sailor grew up and became a beautiful young woman, whose complexion was
like that of her father's people. After her mother died,
one day Captain Swanson anchored his ship in front of
the village and came ashore. As soon as he saw her
he wanted to take her aboard, just as the earlier white
man had taken her mother. The adopted father refused
at first to give her away, because he still remembered how
her mother had been forsaken. To gain her, Captain
Swanson promised to bring her to Victoria and marry
her there, as a white man would. This was enough for
him to win her, and she went away with him. This
foreigner was different from the first, for he treated her
as a grand lady. She always traveled with him on board
ship, and everybody knew her as Mrs. Swanson. She
came back to this country with her husband and her
two children, a son and a daughter. As she was famous,
I often heard of her, and once when I was young I met
her, at Metlakatla, Alaska. She looked like a very old
woman, quite small, but still graceful, and the people
said that she was nearly a hundred years of age. For a
time she lived abroad with her daughter, but was far
from happy there, because she always longed to return

to her tribe at Ketchikan, and one day, after she had become feeble-minded, she came back to die with her mother's people."

In this light the feminine figure on the Ketchikan pole lends itself to re-interpretation. It may have been meant to commemorate the passing of Mrs. Swanson, who, unlike the dusky "pillow mates" of sailors, was not forsaken by her white husband, who remained fond of her to the end of his career at sea.

The white men whose likeness is preserved on other memorial columns can no longer be identified. At Tongas, one of them stands at the top of a stout mast, a tall beaver hat on his head, and wearing a Prince Albert. His thick beard is trimmed square around his strong jaws and large face, and his right hand rests resolutely on his hip. He undoubtedly was a man of power and authority, perhaps a historical personage like Baron Wrangell, of the 1840's, or else Governor Douglas, former head of the Hudson's Bay Company in Rupert Land. On a similar vantage post, in front of him, an Indian chief sits with high "skil" or ceremonial hat, on a Haida box, with his knees raised to his chest.

At Kasan another white dignitary, also wearing a tall hat and a Prince Albert, occupies the summit of a totem pole, which, below him, bears the Raven and the powerful Soo'san, a hero of Kaiganee mythology. Different from the other, this white man is beardless, and his hair, on the forehead and over his ears, is curly. The face of the man on the next pole, a smaller one, also looks strongly European, with an aquiline nose and a mustache.

This bent of the natives to march with the times and portray actuality in their carvings is well illustrated in a few poles of the Gitksan tribes on the upper Skeena, showing, in the guise of so-called totems, a white man's dog, a palisade, a wagon road, and cedar shingles on a roof.

The Sea-Gull tribe of the Gitksans had its village near the mouth of the Babine River, a tributary of the Skeena, about 225 miles from salt water. And it was not far removed from Fort St. James, the earliest fur-trading post of the North West Company, established in 1808 in the northern Rockies. The company had at some time built a subsidiary post at Bear Lake, under the direction of a Mr. Ross, and soon after a Tsetsaut party unexpectedly came upon it. The Tsetsaut warriors attacked the village of Kisgagas (Sea-Gull) while most of the hunters were away, killed two men with the flintlock musket in their possession—the first gun seen in the country—and returned home with a female captive, the niece of the head chief whom they had killed. The young woman was rescued by the white people at Bear Lake, and some time later was sent back home.

A retaliation party, under her guidance, went to the Tsetsaut country, but on the way decided to visit the white man's fort, of which they had heard. Here, to their amazement, they had their first opportunity to see the white man and to marvel at his possessions and strange ways. What impressed them most, in what to them was a supernatural experience, was the white man's dog, the palisade or fortification and the house, and the wagon road so different from their faint forest trails. All three of these novelties in the country they decided, after they had reached home, to adopt as their own crests or emblems. Waiget, the head of one family, took for himself the white man's dog (or Mr. Ross's dog—called Masselaws); Malulek, another chief, made the palisade his own; and other participants shared similar crests. Representatives of other Gitksan tribes far and wide were invited as guests to feasts in the next two years, in which the chiefs of the Sea-Gull tribe exhibited with pride their new totems, which eventually were carved on their totem poles or built—the palisade in the form of a small fence—around them for all to behold to the present day.

Another family, at Kispayaks (or Hiding-Place) on the upper Skeena, that of Harhu, similarly acquired the shingle crest from the white man's roofing device of that name. And this Shingle emblem on a Kispayaks totem pole is still seen in the form of parallel lines sloping down on both sides of a central ridge cut deep in the cedar.

If these memorials look to us like novelties, their production was not a whit more recent than that of others which we might mistake for much older and more authentic, like the figures of wild animals, because they belong to the country. A proof of this may be found in the argillite or black-slate work of the Haidas. In the specimens collected in the 1820's and 1830's—that is, earlier than the erection of the totem poles known to us—by Scouler and Wilkes, we fail to discover true totems, such as were in evidence on totem poles in the 1870's.

The themes that are familiar in the earlier argillite repertory consist of white sailors with tight-fitting clothing, traders wearing swallow-tailed coats, Russian dancers in neat boots, ballerinas in hoopskirts, white men's dogs with drooping ears and tied to a post, fanciful horses drawn from imagination (as the horse had not yet been introduced in the country), even elephants from southern Asia (which the carvers had seen only in pictures or carvings on board ship), Siberian sleighs, blockhouses, cabins with windows in the European style, and wooden sailing ships. In a word, the native artists from the first reveled in newness from abroad. During a century of intense fur trading along their seacoast, they found their inspiration in contacts with foreigners from Europe, Asia, and the South Seas.

It is only after the craftsmen had trained their hand with the help of steel tools that they developed the skill and the impetus to carve large figures in the individual style on the totems that were to become world famous.

The period extending from 1840 to 1890 brought about feverish social activities among the coast natives —winter potlatches or festivals were given yearly in every tribe; chiefs vied with each other in the display of goods and liberality; and every tribe did its best to outdo its neighbors. A crop of totem poles, particularly after 1860, rose from the ground among the Haidas and Kaiganees of the Queen Charlotte and Prince of Wales islands, on the Nass River, and in southern Alaska. The carvers of totems in several villages often were the very same. Those engaged to put up the carved posts at Kasan or Klukwan on Prince of Wales Island were engaged at Kyusta or Yan on the Queen Charlotte Islands, or the reverse. The makers of several Tongas poles—perhaps the majority—were Niskaes of the lower Nass.

During this highly creative period of eighty years or less, the totems of the North Pacific coast rushed into existence. They blazoned the front of the Haida, Tsim-syan, and southern Tlingit villages, brought about a recrudescence of native lore and mythology, and produced glorious illustrations of tales and stories by local artists whose names have been recovered.

These craftsmen or artists, trained by their elders in the customary way, were gifted with talent, sometimes genius, and they were aware of the creative beauty of their art. As the majority of those who carved the large totems died in the 1890's, 1900's, or as late as the 1920's, they were the contemporaries of the impressionnists in Europe, or of Gauguin, Van Gogh, and Cézanne. They could have exhibited their smaller carvings at the fashionable salons of sculpture in Paris and London.

Once the illusion about the antiquity of the totems on the North Pacific coast is dispelled, it is much easier to proceed to their study with understanding, and even with greater interest, since they almost belong to our time.

After the Indian craftsmen had passed out of a tentative period of imitativeness, they went ahead full-fledged into the pictorial or plastic interpretation of their own traditional tales, their everyday experiences, and the personalities whom they wanted to portray. As the wild animals which they hunted were best of all known to them, they conferred upon them a knowledge and a feeling that is unique and wonderful. Their creative accomplishments in this field was nowhere else surpassed, not even equaled. And totems galore came out of their hands, as easily as stately portraits of grandees, long before, had come out of the hands of the great Venetian and Spanish painters.

The animals most commonly represented on the poles of the Tlingits, the Tsimsyans, and the Haidas are much the same. They are the eagle, raven, frog, finback whale or blackfish, grizzly bear, wolf, and thunderbird. Others, less frequently used, are the owl, salmon, woodpecker, beaver, shark, starfish, mountain goat, and puma.

The moon, stars, and rainbow also figure in some areas. In the last report, these symbols became property marks on the houses and household effects and ceremonial trappings of the owners—that is, of those who had paid the craftsmen to make them. They were not pagan gods nor demons, as they are often supposed to be, but they are to a certain extent comparable to the stylized figures in our heraldry. They usually illustrated myths or tribal traditions, and were never worshiped. If they were held scared, it is only because of their implications, and they were like tombstones. Some of the same crests, in the past fifty years or so, have been carved out of stone or marble at Port Simpson, Vancouver, and possibly Sitka, by white craftsmen for the new graveyards of the Indians. Modern tombstones have replaced totem poles.

The legendary origin of many of these totems was explained in traditional narratives sometimes recited in the winter festivals or potlatches. In spite of the decay of tribal customs, they are still remembered by the older generation. Survivors of the past tell how the ancestors long ago met with tribulations and adventures; how they were harassed or rescued by supernatural beings and monsters; how benevolent spirits appeared in visions and invested charms on their protégés; and how ancient warriors conquered their enemies in raids. The carved illustrations of these stories served a definite purpose, besides those of commemoration and ownership, for they made familiar to all in tribal life the legends and recollections of the past.

Soon after the death of a chief, his family appointed to his post a leading nephew, whose induction took place during elaborate festivals in the presence of a large number of invited guests. The name of the uncle passed on

The native craftsmen or artists were gifted with talent, sometimes genius, and they were aware of the creative beauty of their art
PAGE 245.

to his nephew, while the erection of a totem pole crowned
the event. Groups of related families mustered all the resources available to make the event memorable, as their
standing and influence depended exactly on their resources thus advantageously displayed. If power and
wealth were the ruling factors in the life of the North
Pacific coast people, it is obvious that these were modern
among them; they issued from continued and stimulat-
ing contacts with white seamen and traders, from the
greed for trade goods, and from a keenness and industry
inborn among these natives, whose recent origin was
Siberian or Mongolian.

The remarkable development of native technique and
style in totem-pole carving is largely confined to the
period subsequent to 1830. It hinged upon the steel ax,
the adze, and the curved knife, which were made at
Sitka by the Russians or imported by the sea traders and
bartered off in large numbers to the natives from the
days of the early circumnavigators, that is, after 1778.
The lack of suitable tools, wealth, and leisure in the prehistoric period had precluded the elaboration of ambitious structures and displays. The benefits accrued from
the fur trade at once gave rise to local ambitions; they
stirred up jealousies and rivalries, and incited incredible
efforts for higher prestige and leadership. The only desire
everywhere was to outdo the others in ingenuity, wealth,
and the display of power. The totem pole more than
anything else gratified these ambitions. It became the
best way of showing one's own identity in terms of the
illustrious dead, the decoration of imposing houses, and
the implications of ancient imagery. The size of the pole
and the beauty of its figures published abroad the fame of
those it represented.

Feuds over the size of totem poles as a result broke out among the leaders within a Nass River village, after the Hudson's Bay Company had established its trading post on the lower Nass in 1831 and transferred it to Fort Simpson in 1833, and had founded Victoria in 1843. The Hudson's Bay Company, at that time, was bent on challenging the might of the Russian Bear in Alaska.

There is no evidence of real Haida totem poles ante-dating 1840 or 1850, though a few earlier and transitional ones—mostly portals and graveyard posts—had served to introduce the fashion, and it is a common saying that the fine row of poles in one of their best-known towns on the Queen Charlotte Islands had risen from the proceeds of an inglorious type of barter in Victoria.

All the totem poles of the northern islands were of the same advanced type, from the hands of contemporaries imitating each other; and of the same period—1840-90. Their style and composition were influenced by miniature argillite or slate carvings that for many years had been made in large numbers for the early sailors, traders, and curio collectors. When, after 1890, the Haidas first became converts to Christianity and in consequence slowly gave up their customs, their totem poles were from ten to twenty years old. As a result of the change, some of the owners cut down these memorials or sold them to white people, and Dr. Franz Boas purchased the first ones for the Field Columbian Exhibition in Chicago.

If the expansion of native art and totem-pole carving on the coast goes back to the earliest days of the fur trade, it is a good deal later that real progress was achieved, chiefly after steady contacts and exchanges had been established between the natives and the Russian

American Company, the Hudson's Bay Company, and
the American traders. One of the earliest instances of
the direct influence of the white man has been quoted by
Judge F. W. Howay; namely, that of a seaman named
Jefferson who, as early as 1795, had lent some machinery
to the Haidas, together with sailors to assist, for the
erection of a carved post. Similar assistance was at least
once given to the natives of the lower Nass by a captain
on a sailing ship. The trench method itself for beginning
the erection of a tall pole, by sinking the lower end into
a hole, is identical with that of the South Sea Islanders—
Kanakas, Hawaiians, or Sandwich Islanders—who were
fairly numerous on the coast, as a result of their early
arrival in this country, in the service of seamen and the
fur-trading companies.

The circumstances accompanying the carving of a
totem pole never were quite duplicated; they varied
with the times and the persons involved. Occasionally
they were sensational. For instance, about seventy years
ago, a domestic quarrel led an estranged couple to challenge in songs and gifts, and to the erection of a totem
pole at the village of Angeedae near the mouth of the
Nass.

The head chief of an Eagle clan, named Sarau'wan
(Sharp-Teeth), was deeply wounded in his pride by his
wife's desertion. Quite attractive, and perhaps ambitious
or merely fickle, the young woman had forsaken native
rank for the favors of Captain McNeill, a Hudson's Bay
Company official who often visited Portland Canal to
further the interests of his company in its contest for
pelts with the Russian American Company. She had
gone to live with the fur trader down the coast at
Victoria.

A crop of totem poles rose from the ground, after 1860 PAGE 244.

To wipe off his shame in good style among his people,
Sharp-Teeth, at the first opportunity in a tribal feast,
held up in his hand ten beautiful marten skins, and began
to sing to an old tune a new challenge which he had
composed to cast ridicule on the deserter. He sang with
sarcasm:

> Wait and see what a chief can do! Wait, O sweetheart,
> that you may learn how, after my humiliation because of
> you, I have again raised my head! Wait, O flighty one,
> before you send me word of how you have failed in your
> foolish escapade and pine once more for my love!
>
> Time is now ripe, O woman who would belong to the
> bleached Victoria tribe, for you to send me a bottle of Old
> Tom. For my part I now dispatch to you this small hand-
> ful of mere beaver skins.

Actually there was more than a "small handful," and
the skins were even more valuable than beaver. They
were picked marten, such as an indignant and wealthy
chief could sacrifice to heap ridicule upon a woman un-
worthy of him and surely unable—after her desertion—
to reciprocate in kind. The only way now for her to
redeem her reputation, according to native standards,
was to return a gift of still greater value. She would
certainly fail and be covered with shame to the end of
her life. But, unexpectedly, she did not.

The gift which she had her brother Niskinwaetk of
the same village fling to her former husband's face was a
Haida canoe carved out of a huge cedar tree. Thus, with
the help of her white mate, she had changed the bottle of
Old Tom demanded by her dusky husband, Sharp-Teeth,
into a trade canoe, decorated at the prow with the Bear,
her own heraldic emblem. As the canoe was actually
given in a feast to the challenger, "she went over big"

and had the best of him. Sharp-Teeth had wanted to discredit her in the eyes of her people, because he was proud and she had shamed him. Now once more she had heaped new humiliation upon him, and the tribe was not sure that he had the wit and the means to retaliate.

He had. After all his wealth in pelts, copper shields, blankets, and trade goods, was gathered, he invited the neighboring tribes and made it known that he was about to cast off his unfaithful wife in a way that would brand her forever as worthless. While he lavished presents upon his guests in the feast, particularly those who had laughed at him, he sang a song composed for the occasion—a taunting song:

> Hush! stop your idle chatter! Why do you mind my own affairs!

And the people had to repeat the refrain in chorus, after he had sung:

> Why do you gossip about me? Why do you point your finger at me when your own hand is unclean? I speak to you, women of the Salmon-Weirs!

The chorus:

> Hush! stop your idle chatter! ...

Sharp-Teeth:

> Why do you single me out as the only black sheep? For this alone must I admit that I am lost like the rest? Oh: stop your idle chatter! I speak to you, women of the Place-of-Scalps!

The chorus:

> Hush, stop your idle chatter! ...

Sharp-Teeth:

> You waste your breath over my love affairs. Why
> should I mind you when my heart pines away? I have
> not seen my own sweetheart for a full moon—the Hutsinee
> beauty that has made a Christian of me!

The chorus:

> Hush, stop your idle chatter! Why do you mind my
> own affairs!

Captain McNeill's native partner now smarted under
the insult, far away though she lived from the scene of
her disgrace. She made up her mind to fight it out to
the end with her former overlord.

As her brother Niskinwaetk, with whom she shared
the leadership of a high Wolf clan, had recently died,
she decided to erect a totem pole in his memory and,
without the help of Sharp-Teeth, assume the leadership
of her clan. She would raise a fine totem, and enhance
her prestige and wipe off the shame of her dismissal by
her husband.

As the best carver of totems on the Nass was Oyai,
of the Canyon tribe on mid-river, she secured his services
for about a year, during which he carved a pole for her.

When the carving was ready, she came in person to
the Nass, bringing much property with her, and had
the totem erected to the memory of her brother, in the
midst of a great celebration. On this memorable occasion, she assumed the name and high rank of Niskinwaetk, and she stood on a par with her estranged husband,
who had lost his power over her. She had become a
leader among the Wolves, as he was among the Eagles—
their respective clans being the Wolf and the Eagle.

Her totem pole, indeed, was a fine memorial, at the head of a splendid row of totems. After the lapse of about seventy years since its erection, I discovered it, surrounded by a thick growth of wild crab-apple trees, still standing vindictively in memory of the Wolf chief who would not be downed by an Eagle. Its heraldic figures carved out of red cedar were weather-beaten, yet most original and expressive. It was evident that Oyai, its carver, deserved his reputation as the best totem carver of his generation on the Nass or anywhere.

This pole, a medium-sized one, has since been purchased from its owner by the Canadian National Railways and presented to the Trocadero Museum in Paris.

Its figures, admirably disposed on the wide shaft, are not those of Indian divinities—for which such figures often have been mistaken. They are simply heraldic symbols, somewhat like the coats-of-arms of noble families in Europe. Here the large figures, at the base and the top of the pole, are of grizzly bears, not the common grizzlies, but of semihuman grizzlies of the past about whom a myth or tale of origin is told, and of their offspring, semihuman like themselves. One of these has a human face and human limbs, while another is shown with animal features. This peculiarity illustrates how some ancestors of this Wolf family, one day, had chanced upon a spiritual experience that had led to the adoption of the grizzly as their heraldic symbol.

Mrs. McNeill's promotion to the rank of a high chief on the Nass, after the futile efforts of her deserted husband to shame her, was not accepted by him as the final episode in their quarrel. It only added fuel to the flames. And there was nothing which the outsiders—they were the majority—enjoyed better than a good

fight between their leaders. As they were the benefici-
aries of the lavishness of their hosts in the feasts, they
always stood on the side of the winner in the feuds and
rivalries between the Eagles, the Wolves, and the Ravens
in their southward trek from the Far North.

THE SALMON RUN

THE SALMON run, as it is called, forms part of an ageless pageant of wild life on the North Pacific coast. It has dwindled in size and impressiveness since the discovery and exploration of the western shores of our hemisphere. In the past hundred and fifty years the people, native, white, or yellow, never have ceased to prey upon fish, mammal, and fowl, without thought for the morrow. The huge salmon runs of former days in the Columbia and the Fraser rivers have been vastly reduced, although they persist in the face of encroachments. But the rivers farther north—the Skeena, the Nass, the Stikine, the Chilkat, the Karluk, the Yukon and others—still glitter in season with numberless fish bound upstream in one of nature's primeval missions.

Myriads of salmon, every spring, rise from the depths of the Pacific Ocean, move in shallow waters along the seacoast, and then swim up the rivers in schools. For weeks and months, while the sun shines on the snow-capped mountains and the glaciers and fills the streams to overflowing, the swollen waters are alive with salmon steadily on their way to the spawning beds in the glacial lakes or in the headwaters far away.

More than anything else on the Alaska side of Bering Strait, the salmon run has always been a powerful lure to the ever hungry nomads of the northern steppes after their landing in the New World. No sooner had they crossed the low divide between the coast and the lower

Yukon River than they came upon the salmon. As it was plentiful, in the spring of the year, they fished it, smoked it or dried it in the sun for a supply; and in time they followed it to its widely scattered spawning beds away up the immense river and its tributaries east and south. The pursuit of fish thus accounts for their dispersal over empty territories far inland, into the northern Rockies and over the plateaus to the head-waters of other rivers flowing southwestward to the Pacific coast.

No other phenomenon of underseas life in the northern hemisphere is as impressive as the salmon run. It is the most striking feature of the whole North Pacific coast, extending from the Bering Sea—even beyond it into the Arctic Ocean—to the Sacramento River and Monte-rey, in California. When, in the early days, the white seamen anchored their sailing ships in the coves and the estuaries of rivers, they marveled at the numberless fish and sea mammals that almost crowded each other out of the water: the whales chased the seals, and the seals pounced upon the salmon and devoured them. Schools of salmon, herring, and candlefish hugged the shore, and predatory sea gulls and eagles flocked over them all with wild clamor. The newly arrived Siberians must have been thrilled at this unexpected bounty, which was ever after to play such an important role in their lives.

After the salmon schools enter the estuaries of the rivers to which they belong, they drift up and down with the tides for two or three weeks, inactive and seem-ingly unable for a time to bestir themselves. At this stage, nowadays, the cannery fisherfolk prey upon them and scoop up in their nets and their traps as many as they can for the world markets. The fish meanwhile undergo a change that will enable them to migrate from salt to fresh water. No sooner are they ready for the run than a spell revives them; a strange thing from within gives them an orientation and speeds them on their way.

The irresistible instinct that drives the salmon on to shallow streams, some of them mountainous and hundreds of miles inland—on the Yukon River the salmon reaches 2,250 miles inland—is a true predestination going back to the earliest stages of life on this planet. Why should this ancient fish seek remote headwaters or glacier lakes wherein to spawn, rather than the more easily accessible gravel beds of the main rivers? No final answer has yet been given to this puzzling question, and the problem begs a solution, in spite of continued research at biological stations. Even after countless fish have been marked or tagged for at least two decades— that is, caught when young, numbered by a brass tag attached to a fin, or otherwise marked, and released— many questions remain unanswered to this day. Until twenty years ago, the salmon of the North Pacific coast were believed to migrate north through Bering Strait into the Arctic Ocean, and then return after two or three years to the waters where they were born. But now, in the light of new information resulting from the capture of marked fish, it seems that the schools of salmon from the many west coast rivers feed at sea, during their varying span of life in salt waters. They travel fan-wise, some of them south, others north. Salmon tagged in British Columbia waters have been captured on the Siberian coast.

The features of the salmon run are far from simple

and uniform. They vary with the five species of Pacific salmon, and in this the steelhead, often misnamed salmon, is not included, as it is really a trout resembling the salmon. They can better be understood through similes, when compared with the yearly migration of birds from southern marshes to the Arctic tundras for the nesting season; or with that of broncos on the prairies, which are said to have gone back, when in danger, to the spot where they were born.

The very force and blindness of this homing instinct in salmon is awe-inspiring. It never dies down until the very end—that is, until the fish have spawned in pairs wherever the river bed suits them, and then perished from sheer exhaustion. As soon as an obstacle bars their path they try to rush it, and usually succeed. In deep water they travel out of sight and are lost to the observer, but where the current is swift or obstructed by boulders, they hug the shore and swim in shallow waters. Some of them, in their frenzied efforts to ascend the rapids, almost crawl out of the water on their sides. It is thrilling to watch them, and to reach out for them and at times lift them out with a hooked gaff. As soon as they become aware of interference, they are frightened and shoot off into midstream.

One has only to stand motionless at the edge of a salmon river, and soon a few salmon appear together, jerking their tails sideways and darting upward from one eddy to another. Should they encounter a waterfall, some of them—of the sockeye species—jump it outright. They spring up five or ten feet, or even farther, out of the water. If they fall back, they start over again with renewed vigor and splash. Never do they give up, as long as they have the power, in their efforts to pass the obstruction and proceed on their imperious errand.

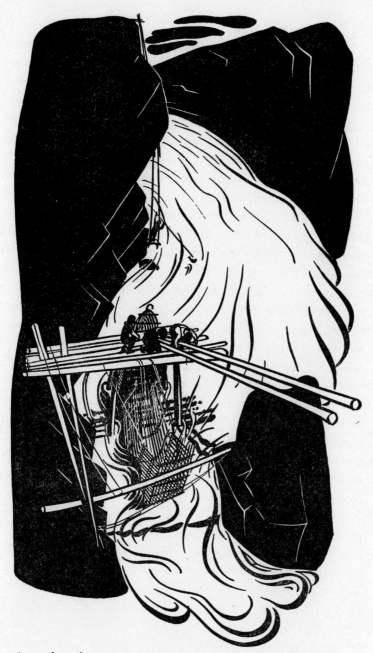

A wooden salmon trap erected in a nook of the Bulkley Canyon
PAGE 264.

The Bulkley Canyon, near Hazelton on the upper Skeena, the ribbon-like waterfalls within the town of Ketchikan, and the swift waters of the Naha River, are choice spots for entranced observation. At the spectacular Bulkley Canyon, on a bluff two hundred and fifty feet high, one can see Indian fishermen, on frail platforms suspended over eddies, spearing large fish, just as others do in the canyons of the Columbia and Fraser rivers to the south.

When, in 1920, I first stepped down a narrow path in the Bulkley Canyon at the Hagwelget Indian village, I encountered dusky girls and boys who drew aside to let me pass. They were "packing" salmon in cedar-bark bags on their backs. The smoke lodges where the fish were dried and preserved stood in a row on a terrace halfway up. And they are still there, in full operation, for the use of the neighboring natives. The descent down to the foaming waters seemed perilous; it made me dizzy. A slip of the foot might prove fatal—but the Indians never slip. In the most risky places, a pole to be used as a handrail is tied on to the rock or to dwarfed trees at the ends. A stranger naturally is overanxious for his safety, to the point of making the natives smile, especially when he steps for the first time down a notched tree trunk, in the Siberian fashion, serving as a ladder.

About fifteen feet above the water, in a broad crevice, two elderly Gitksan Indians were sitting down to a simple meal. They did not show any displeasure at my intrusion. Peter John, one of them, was known as the best fisherman of the canyon, who had no particular liking for the white man. His face was dark brown and he looked like a northern Tartar, a Siberian or even a Manchurian. I would have thought of a brigand, with hostile, inquisitive dark eyes, and a fearless attitude. Yet the canyon Indians as a whole are not unkind; they are only surly with strangers. And there is a marked difference between the occupants on the eastern side of the river, who are the Carriers, of a nomadic stock in the interior, and those of the western bank, who are of Tsimsyan or coast extraction. The first are mild, the second are of a brooding disposition. They were former enemies who for many years have buried the hatchet.

A pile of beautiful salmon, half covered with green foliage to keep them from drying in the sun, lay at the feet of the two Indians. Peter John brushed aside the foliage and let me see them, varying from ten to thirty pounds, with bright scales, some brownish, others pinkish and rather silvery. The fish were spring salmon, the first variety that appears in the Skeena and its tributary, the Bulkley, usually at the end of June each year.

Near the bottom of the trail, well above the water, was a smooth ledge of rock on which one could stand safely; then the path dipped down abruptly. An Indian fisherman stood on a suspended platform below, holding a long slender pole with a large detachable steel hook, with which he searched the eddy under him, seemingly ten or fifteen feet deep. With a strong and experienced hand, he held the pole down in the water until he suddenly gave a jerk upward. A fish had touched the end of the pole and it was caught on the hook. Then it swiftly emerged, fighting for its life. Drawn out of the water, the salmon was killed with a fish club carved in the shape of a sea lion; then it was cast off into an open rock crevice. There it lay with other salmon, under some foliage, awaiting the women or children who would "pack" it up the crags to the smokehouse. Many spring salmon continued their race up the canyon, and they would keep it up for two or three weeks, the exact period varying a little from year to year, according to the freshets.

The Indians, at the time, had been fishing this species of salmon for over a week, while the Bulkley still was high with the June freshets, as the warm sun melted the snow on the mountains. During this season, these fisher-folk had come to life again as it were, and gladly re-lapsed into a primitive existence long familiar to their forefathers. They kept busy in turns hooking the fish up, while the women above cut them up, cleaned them, and hung the meat on poles over smoldering fires in the smokehouses. For once the Indians were well-fed and happy, as they think they were before the coming of the white man.

Several times again that year, and on subsequent years, I went back to the Bulkley Canyon, and farther up to the Moricetown Canyon. Later on in the season—in July and August—the platforms were deserted and stood much higher than formerly above the eddies. The level of the river had fallen and rocks had emerged in midstream. The roar of the water had gradually died down.

Three new structures had been erected in the nooks of the canyon. They were wooden fish traps made of poles and clever basket work. The run of spring salmon was practically over, and had given way to that of the livelier sockeye, a second species, much smaller, with a smooth round body, darkish on the back, with a silver belly. This beautiful fish, whose flesh is red, seldom weighs less than five pounds or more than eight. As it leaped high out of the water in the rapids, several together at times, and often succeeded in landing above the rocks, I wanted to take snapshots, but was puzzled as to how—a salmon would spring up twenty feet away from the lens, others farther out, or nearer. Up they sprang and down they went, most of them thrown back into the fierce whirlpools. More kept coming. It had a strange fascination. I stepped down to the edge of the water, as near as I prudently could, and stood my tripod firmly on a ledge jutting out a few feet. As soon as the lens was focused at, say, ten feet, a fish leaped out at five feet, another at fifteen. It was like hunting—I had to wait. Soon, to my great elation, I caught a few at the right spot. Then I became aware of a risk, in my unwonted pursuit of flying sockeye. Swish! a salmon passed right over my head, to land flat on a rock. Another might slap my camera off its stand into the torrent; so I had better keep out of their path.

Other specimens of salmon, in July and August or even later, were not so spectacular in their behavior and in the handling of them by the fisherfolk. One of them, the humpback, began to appear at the canyon before the sockeye had finished going by. At this advanced stage of the run—180 miles from the sea—the body of the male is deformed. A large hump rises behind the head, and the sides are flat. Hence the name "humpback." The jaws are provided with crooked teeth for fighting.

The humpbacks are weaker than the other species. As they cannot jump over waterfalls, they crawl on their sides at the edge of the stream, at times almost out of the water. They spawn in vast numbers near the mouth of shallow creeks, where they die after days of incessant striving, struggle, and unbroken determination to face the current until death.

The later varieties that received scant attention at the
Bulkley Canyon, but were fished elsewhere with river
nets by the Indians on the upper Skeena River, were the
stubby and vigorous coho and the bulky dog salmon.
The dog salmon at this advanced stage of the run looked
like a bully, with curved jaws and vicious teeth.

Just as the five species of salmon differ in appearance,
so do their habits, in most ways. The spring salmon
(elsewhere called the king, tyee, chinook), in spite of
their large size, spawn in shallow creeks, as far up as
they can reach, at the very headwaters of the main rivers.
The sockeye take another course; they ascend branch
streams up to lakes that feed on glaciers—for instance,
Lake Gitwinlkul, on the Skeena to the north, and chiefly
Medziaden Lake, north of the Nass River close to the
Alaskan border. The humpback are spent earlier and
often are satisfied with smaller rivers near the seacoast;
or, when they ascend long rivers, they gather at the
mouth of creeks or pile on each other, until death, at
the foot of waterfalls. The dog salmon seek wide gravel
beds along the shore line, where they can be seen for
weeks. When you approach quietly, they do not notice
you and they can be photographed while they are
spawning in pairs. Boys often aim pebbles at them from
a distance. But they are not as easy a target as might
seem likely, because of the refraction of light rays by
the water.

Only one, two, or three species ascend certain tributaries of the rivers, not the others; and these are always
the same, on all rivers. Their habits are a law unto themselves, never at variance for countless milleniums.

The best place of all to observe the run and spawning
is far up the main salmon rivers, whenever they happen

to be, two or three hundred miles from the sea, particularly at the headwaters of the Skeena, the Nass, and the Stikine. Salmon formerly used to ascend the whole Columbia River, hundreds of miles to the heart of the Selkirks, not far north of the border between Canada and the United States. The shallow stream at the place named Salmon Beds, near Lake Windermere, in the autumn used to be choked with live and dead fish. Their bones, after they had decayed, covered the gravel and formed thick ridges that were still seen years after the salmon had been destroyed in that river and had ceased to reach the spawning grounds.

The distance in fresh water covered by the salmon is as short in some instances as it is immense in others. At Ketchikan the waterfall which bars the way to all but the most powerful fish, rises only a few hundred yards from salt water. In the Karluk River in western Alaska, one of the greatest salmon streams, the spawning lakes are sixteen miles from the coast; whereas on the Skeena the spring salmon travel about three hundred miles inland. Much greater distances were covered by the species formerly running up the Columbia River to Lake Windermere, by those ascending the Fraser River, and by the large numbers still reaching the upper Yukon River.

Spring salmon caught as far inland as Bear Lake and in the Clutantan Lakes at the headwaters of the Skeena are said to weigh from fifteen to eighty pounds. Salmon of from fifty to seventy-five pounds seem fairly common there. Some specimens elsewhere are said, by reliable authorities, to have exceeded a hundred pounds.

"In the Black River, at the head of the Nass, the salmon spawn in the shallow gravel bed of the river,"

Angus Beaton, a big-game hunter, said to me. "They swim through the first of three lakes, up a creek into a second, and then into Summit Lake. Queerly enough, this lake empties into two rivers: the Skeena on one side and the Nass on the other. It is like a marsh, very shallow in parts. A peculiar thing is that the Skeena River and Nass River salmon spawn about a hundred yards apart. Yet they are not able to meet because of the tall weeds and rushes in the center of the long lake. In half a day's work with pick and shovel, I could make the salmon run downstream into the Nass, or the other way about. A puzzle for the salmon—running downstream, instead of up!

"The salmon spawn in the Blackwater River at a spot where it is about forty feet wide and very shallow and clear. They can be seen for about a hundred feet up and downstream, and this is a sight never to forget. From thirty to fifty pairs of spring salmon keep on spawning busily from morning to night, and perhaps even at night.

"They push the gravel sideways with their bellies, using them like plows. This is what causes their bodies to become ragged, red-blotched, and covered with sores. The males plow a groove in the fine sand and gravel and the females follow along and, shivering, they shoot out the spawn. The males come back, follow the females and spread now and again their fertilizing milt on the eggs. Then in the same plow-like way, they cover the groove over with sand.

"Other salmon, freshly arrived, try to chase away the earlier occupants. But they have the worst of it, as the spawning fish dart openmouthed at their disturbers. The newcomers must rush by and find farther up whatever spawning beds are left.

A modern cannery is usually a big establishment, in a sheltered cove, and consists of several large buildings and sheds, and wharves for the fishing craft PAGES 285-86.

"The salmon are so thick at the headwaters that it is a wonder how they all manage to get up that far, and why they should want to spawn where there is almost no room, in such shallow creeks, and it is the same tale every year, from August until the river freezes up. A poor run, as is true of some years, makes little difference. In the June and July freshets, trees fall and block the creeks. There the oncoming salmon try to find a way through. When they fail, they keep piling hopelessly on top of each other for days and weeks, and they rot in heaps.

"Such waste is appalling. And this is true of most of the other salmon headwaters in the Rockies north and south. Preachers, when I was a boy, used to speak of Providence, and I have no doubt they still do. I did not question their wisdom until the sight of these fish, so entirely misguided by instinct, disturbed my peace of mind.

"After the fish have been spawning for over a month in the same gravel beds, a terrible stench spreads miles around. But this does not keep the coyotes and bears from feeding on spent and dead salmon until they fatten themselves for the winter."

A difference noticeable to sportsmen between the real salmon (*Salmo salar*) of the Atlantic Ocean and the so-called salmon of the northern Pacific—for they are said not to be real salmon—is that the first rise to the lure in fresh water. Fishermen every year enjoy casting a spirited fly at the salmon swimming up the rivers around the Gulf of St. Lawrence—the Moisie, the Cascapedia, and the Matapedia. But they would never think of wasting their time looking for the western salmon,

which differs in structure and habits from the eastern
owner of the name *Salmo*. Five Rocky Mountain and
Arctic species never rise to the fly or display qualities of
game fish, after they have passed out of salt water. Only
the spring salmon (king, chinook, or quinnat) and
the coho (or silver) will rise out of salt water, where they
still feed, for lures of various kinds, but not for a fly.

When some salmon-like fish, in the western rivers,
are caught on hooks baited with roe, they should not
be mistaken for typical salmon on the spawning migration. Only a few pounds in weight, they are the grilse
or the "jackfish." Some fishermen on the upper Skeena
thought that they were young spring salmon escorting
the adults in the rivers and poaching on their eggs. These
predatory fish are voracious, and it is great fun to lure
them on with salmon roe and catch them on ordinary
baited hooks. This is often done by white people on some
of the salmon rivers, particularly on the Skeena. According to the specialists, however, the grilse is an
undersized fish, of various salmon species, which has
matured prematurely and does not conform to the normal type.

A few of us, including the Kihns and two newspaper
friends from New York, were fishing at the foot of the
Hagwelget Canyon near the Skeena River one sunny
July afternoon in 1924, but without success. We were
marking time before an Indian feast about to begin in
the Carrier village above. I was ready to give up fishing,
due to lack of any success, when my rod was nearly
jerked out of my hands. The welcome surprise had
come from the first of several lively fish that were to
follow in less than twenty minutes. The half-dozen
salmon that rushed me were all grilse, and the seventh

went off with the tackle. Never in my life had I had
such an exciting time. As I did not want to spoil the
good impression, I would not again tempt my luck in
the next few days, but my friends in their turn were
quite as lucky.

Other poachers or spawn thieves, as they are called,
escort the salmon to the spawning beds and harass them
—the Dolly Varden (char or bull trout), and also the
rainbow trout. These poachers give the salmon constant
trouble. Sneaking behind the females or lying flat on
the bottom, they snap up the eggs, until the males notice
them and angrily chase them off. The fight is on from
morning to night, as the invaders are greedy and
numerous.

"When the water is not deep enough," Angus Beaton
explained, "the trout swim on their sides like the salmon,
and they keep on going ahead. I saw a large number of
trout as I stepped over a little bit of a creek one day. It
was easy to trap them by changing the course of the
stream, and that is what I did with a shovel in a few
minutes. While the bed of the creek was drying up,
the trout rushed for an escape with the water. But I
had placed an empty milk-tin box across their path.
Soon it was filled with lively little trout.

"In a deep hole left behind, five salmon splashed about,
as if they were worried. I was surprised to find them
there, so large. It is true that the Indians had told me
that salmon ran up this shallow creek, but I would not
believe them. Yet there they were. I couldn't say to
what species they belonged, as the salmon so far up
are spent and much deformed—hook-jawed, slab-sided,
humpbacked, and red-blotched.

"I cannot see how the salmon can ever get scarcer, if

Myriads of salmon, every spring, rise from the depths of the Pacific Ocean, then swim up the rivers in schools PAGE 257.

nothing interferes with the spawning beds and the fish manage to get there in sufficient numbers. Some Indians, I know, bar the creeks with their fish fences and, in their neglect or absence, the salmon fail to force their way through, and pile out of the water so thick that one could walk on them or hit them with a stick. But how can the law curb these poachers—the law officers and courthouses are two or three hundred miles away from the wilderness. When the authorities take the matter in hand, as they casually mean to, they would do well to direct their attention to the spawning grounds, and lessen the waste by removing log jams and building fish ladders from creeks into lakes, where waterfalls are the only obstacles."

This sums up one of the most urgent requirements for the safeguarding, and perhaps the expansion, of the salmon run. The important rivers for spawning should be under effective supervision, with constructive plans for improvement. If a few rocks were blasted in one canyon, and a fish ladder—a series of basins to one side where the fish can easily jump—were constructed elsewhere, numberless fish could proceed on their useful errand instead of being thrown back and bruised, perishing before they have spawned.

When, in northern British Columbia, the Babines were surveyed, the waterfall four miles below Babine Lake was measured and a fish ladder was planned. The salmon, unable to climb the falls, died there by the thousand. Yet the lake bottom immediately above would have been a splendid resort for spawning fish. These upriver improvements might be worth a great deal to the fishing industry along the seacoast. Gervais, an old Klondike miner, once remarked to me: "The people down there grumble that the salmon is going; that it is hard to earn a living. Yet, with more foresight, they could do a lot to improve their business, besides restricting the catch by various regulations. What are the government hatcheries, near the estuaries of rivers, compared with the big natural hatcheries that would be Lake Babine, or others like it, after a fish ladder is built."

From the prehistoric past to the present, the salmon run has provided a bounteous food supply to every tribe up and down the North Pacific coast and in the adjacent watersheds far into the interior. So important was salmon in the life of the natives, for countless generations, that it affected the whole pattern of their existence. It brought abundance to them, but in its trail it dragged in strife. Disputes and feuds as to who was entitled to the salmon streams, or the best of them, would frequently arise. Fishing stations and the sites for platforms along the canyons would forcibly change hands, and fish fences and wicker traps in shallow waters often had to be shared with intruders.

This natural bounty beckoned like fate to the famished nomads from the northern tundras. They envied the earlier occupants of the western or southern headwaters who caught salmon by the hundreds, cut them open, dried or smoked them, filled their "caches" with them, and thus had a good supply that lasted until the next run. At this juncture they could not very long curb their appetite. Weapons in hand, squatting in ambush and waiting for their chance, they leaped forward at dawn, while the fishermen and their families were fast asleep. They killed the men and sometimes spared the women and children, to make them their own. They held on to their new foothold and, when possible, enlarged it. They patched up a precarious peace with their next neighbors below, for fear of retaliation. And, egged on, they seldom failed to extend their stranglehold upon those ahead of them. Slowly they crept forward on their path of conquest, down the salmon rivers to the coast, and then southward.

This, in a nutshell, is the story of incessant shifts and invasions that have crowded the North Pacific coast with more native stocks of varied extractions, all of them from the North, than any other part of the American continent. More than anything else, the salmon was the lure that beckoned the Northerners. It would not have lost its power to the present day upon the natives had not the white people, by their greater might, put a stop to primitive law and progress.

The effect of the salmon run upon Indian life varied according to location and antecedents. The Niskae of the middle Nass River, close to Portland Canal, moved up for the fishing season to the upper canyons near the present Cranberry River, and later returned with ample provisions to their scattered winter villages. The Gitksan of the upper Skeena migrated likewise, in due season. But their kinsmen, the Tsimsyans farther down the same river, had their permanent homes close to their fishing stations. They moved down, for the winter only, to the mouth of the Skeena, where they held winter fairs. There ten or twelve tribes assembled at close quarters, and spent much of that season celebrating and attending to their business and social functions. This winter town, near the present Prince Rupert, is still called (old) Metlakatla. Its former name was Krado.

The Tlingit, now in southeastern Alaska, on the whole

are typically a seacoast people. But, according to their own traditions, many of their ancestors were not. Their origin can be traced back inland to the north. Their Wolf moiety, including an important section of the Eagle clans, were an inland folk, stationed for a time at the headwaters, but drawn forward to the seacoast by their inveterate craving for a better land. Once settled at the edge of the salt water, they reverted in the summer to the older pattern of existence long familiar to them. In the late spring they followed the salmon a long distance up their several rivers, preyed upon them for months, and reverted to bartering and quarreling with their nomadic neighbors in the interior.

Tlingit survivors of this former state of inland existence were left behind, in a few places. Some of these, to this day, can be found in a native village on the west side of Teslin Lake on the upper Yukon River (near the present Alcan Highway.) Others, mixed with Dénés, belong to the Champagne area, on Dezadeash Lake, west of Whitehorse.[1]

The description by Robert Campbell of a flying visit to the Tlingit fishing stations up the Stikine furnishes a vivid picture of this primitive frontier life. Robert Campbell was a pioneer trader of the Hudson's Bay Company, then encroaching upon the preserves of the Russian American Company in the Far Northwest. In his venturesome voyage away from the Mackenzie River and up the Liard River, he took his fate into his hands and boldly proceeded, in the summer of 1838, from Dease Lake to the headwaters of the Stikine River. There he was confronted with two Indian races, the Tlingit

---

[1] As reported, in 1943, by C. H. D. Clarke, of the National Parks Bureau of Canada.

and the Nahannies, brought together by the salmon run
and, at least momentarily, suffering each other for the
sake of mutual benefits. Robert Campbell wrote in his
unpublished journal, a copy of which is preserved at the
Public Archives of Canada in Ottawa:

As we were descending to Terror Bridge, we espied a thin line of
smoke issuing from a hut standing on a shelf of the opposite bank,
which showed the presence of Indians. Houle, a splendid hunter and
canoe maker, and most ingenious at all kinds of work, had no wish
to advance any further, as he feared the strange Indians. I told him
he had to go on. In a short time we came to the bridge, a rude
rickety structure of pine poles spliced together with withes and
stretched high above a foaming torrent; the ends of the poles were
loaded down with stones to prevent the bridge from collapsing. . . .
[After the bridge was crossed] we climbed the zig-zag path
leading up the steep rock to the hut, but on arriving there could
find no one. A bright fire was, however, burning, and around it to
our surprise were three metal pots, in one of which some salmon
was being cooked. Split salmon hung from the rafters drying. To
some of this we helped ourselves for supper, leaving in payment a
knife and some tobacco. We then recrossed the bridge. . . .

The next morning a small group of Indians arrived at
his camp,

. . . the chief holding out a pipe of peace, which was accordingly
smoked and passed around. While this was going on, some of the
young men took long poles, fastened on them large hooks (or
"cleeks" as they would be called in Scotland) and in no time had
some fine salmon lying on the bank. We presently had breakfast
on this delicious fish.
The Indians informed us that the tobacco we had left the previous
evening had the desired effect of letting the owner of the hut know
that we were friends and not enemies as he had supposed. During
the night he had run with the news to the main camp, but had
advised his own tribe only [the Nahannies] of our arrival. Hence
this early visit from the Nahany chief, who had left the main camp
secretly, fearing that the other Indians would come and kill us,
were they to know of our presence.

I told him I would go to the camp, while he did all he could to dissuade me from so doing, saying that the great chief "Shakes" from the sea was there and Indians from all parts without number, so that I was the first white man he had ever seen, that he had smoked and eaten with me, that consequently "he loved my blood and did not want to see it spilled," that his people had always been told that if they ever met White People from the East side of the mountains, to be sure to kill them, as they were enemies. So he begged of me not to go ahead. "Shakes will kill you, and though I and my band would be willing to protect you, we could not do so as Shakes' men are as numerous as the grains of sand on the beach." This he said, and as much more to that effect. But I was not to be moved.

The chief sent on two men, to let his tribe know, and we started on our way. After travelling for some time, parties of two or three began to meet us in close succession: They would push us and try to turn us back, always with the same cry, "If you persist, you will never return, Shakes will kill you." They suggested that they would take me to a spot where I could see the camp without being seen myself, and that the sight of such a multitude would convince me of the danger. But all their arguments were thrown away. I was determined to go on.

From the top of a hill we caught our first glimpse of the immense camp (about thirteen miles from the bridge) of which we had heard so much, and indeed the description given us was not exaggerated. Such a concourse of Indians I had never before seen assembled. They were gathered from all parts of the western slope of the Rockies and from along the Pacific Coast. These Indians camped here for weeks at a time, living on salmon which could be caught in thousands in the Stikine by gaffing or spearing, to aid them, in which they had a sort of dam built across the river. On the top of the hill I lost sight of my companions, including the Nahanay chief, and went down to the closely packed crowd awaiting us below, escorted by an Indian who called himself "Jack" and could speak a little broken English. Every word I said in reply to the numberless questions asked me was taken up and yelled by a hundred throats till the surrounding rocks and the valley re-echoed with the sound.

Presently a lane was cleared through the crowd for Shakes to come down and meet me. Shakes was a Coast Indian, tall and strongly built. I afterwards learned he was all powerful among the Indians on that side of the mountains. He ruled despotically over an immense band of Indians of different tribes, and came to the Stikine every year, with boats and goods, to the splendid rendezvous where I met him. Here he traded with the Indians of the interior for the Russians, who supplied him with goods at Fort Highfield at the mouth of the River. He shook hands with me and led me to a tent which had been put up for me. After entering and sitting down, he produced a bottle of whiskey and a cup. I merely tasted the liquor, but all the others in the tent had a drink. Meanwhile the din outside was something fearful.

I remained in the camp for some time, the object of much curiosity, till at length I got clear of Shakes and the crowd on the plain in safety. This was more than I expected when I first went among them. I found my small party also all right on the top of the hill, where I forthwith hoisted the H B C flag, and cut H B C and date on a tree, thus taking possession of the country for the Company.

Here I first met a remarkable woman, the chief woman of the Nahanis. The Nahany tribe, over which she and her father, a very old man, held sway, were then about five hundred strong, and like other tribes led a nomadic hunting life. Now and then a few of the leading men visited the coast at the mouth of the Stikine, but the Chieftainess said I was the first white man she ever saw. She commanded the respect not only of her own people, but of the tribes they had intercourse with. She was a fine looking woman, rather above the middle size and about thirty-five years old. In her actions and personal appearance she was more like the white than the pure Indian race. She had a pleasing face lit up with fine intelligent eyes which, when she was excited, flashed like fire. She was tidy and tasteful in her dress. To the kindness and influence of this Chieftainess we all probably more than once owed our lives.

This encounter of Robert Campbell with the Tlingits up the Stikine River conveys to us a picture of the primitive life of the northern Indians engaged in salmon fishing up the rivers, over a hundred years ago. Still at its peak because of the large size of the native population and the plentitude of the salmon run, this seasonal migration was bound gradually to decline, toward the end of the last century, because of the arrival of the white man. It virtually ceased at the time of the gold rush; the Tlingits, much reduced in numbers by then, turned to mining, cannery work, and modern pursuits.

Salmon fishing for the canneries, the salteries, and the refrigeration plants in Alaska and the North Pacific coast has for many years taken the whole stage to itself. The spearing and desultory capture of fish by the river Indians have almost passed out. In the light of changing outlook, salmon had become an essentially "commercial" fish. Even the sportsmen have dismissed it because of its lack of "game" qualities. Henceforth, it is to be merely a natural quarry—a rich one at that—for food, at the hands of business concerns for the world markets. The literature on salmon is no longer historical or romantic as it used to be in the days of the explorers or the early observers. It has become merely statistical and, occasionally, scientific. And it is, indeed, surprisingly painstaking and abundant.

The salteries blazed the trail for the business, the Hudson's Bay Company having been the first to buy salmon from the Indians and to pickle it in barrels for export to the South Sea Islands and China. Much later, the canneries put in an appearance. A small one was built, in 1877, at Iverness outside the mouth of the Skeena River. Soon after, in 1883, other canneries followed suit and, as the business slowly expanded, more canneries and salteries entered the field. Even the missionaries to the Indians—John Duncan, Green, and Robert Cunningham —contributed to their progress, the last two giving up gospel work to become cannery owners and traders.

The books and government reports, annual or otherwise, on the competitive salmon industry are quite numerous, and their interest is mostly transient. From their own point of view, a few are thorough and almost exhaustive, for instance *Pacific Salmon Fisheries*, by John N. Cobb (Department of Commerce, Washington, 1930), *North Pacific Fisheries,* by Homer E. Gregory and Kathleen Barnes (1939), *The Pacific Salmon,* by J. P. Babcock (The Province of British Columbia, 1931), *Statistical Review of the Alaskan Salmon Fisheries,* by W. H. Rich and E. M. Ball (1933), and *Report of the Provincial Fisheries Department, British Columbia* (1942).

These contributions and others of the same type, in the closed sphere of statistics and financial returns, leave little out of the reckoning. Only Babcock is satisfied with the scientific angle.

Cobb's *Pacific Salmon Fisheries* gives the full list of canneries, with names and dates, from the beginning. Others go into the classification of the various species of salmon, the marking of young fish, and the working methods of salmon conservation in the form of restrictive regulations, hatcheries, and fish ladders. But little is said of the backgrounds, and nothing of the summer life at the canneries—a picturesque byway of modern existence on the North Pacific coast.

The names of the five species of salmon are recorded there according to the districts. In brief, we find that the spring salmon is also called quinnat, chinook, tyee, and king; the sockeye is also the blueback or Alaska red; the coho is the silver or medium red; the humpback is the pink; the dog salmon, the chum or calico.

The spring or king salmon is larger than the others, averaging twenty-two pounds at maturity, and its run is the earliest, late in May or in June, in the North. Its colors are olive or dusky on the back, the head being darker than the rest of the body; silvery below; and bluish on the sides; with black spots on the fins, the tail, and back. Its flesh is usually red, yet in some it is pale (almost white). The sockeye or red—so named because its flesh is red—is the most valuable in the trade. However, it is, with the humpback, the smallest—averaging a little over five pounds—but the liveliest and the most handsome. In the Columbia River its back is blue and crimson when about to spawn. It is silvery below. It changes its color as it ascends the rivers; and its run begins later than that of the spring salmon.

The humpback travels about in schools, at the estuaries of the northern rivers, and is usually caught in traps and purse seines. Bluish above, silvery below, its flesh is pale or pink—hence its other name.

The coho and dog salmon are of less importance to the canners and to the Indians. The dog salmon or chum is a plump silvery fish, averaging ten pounds, whose flesh is pale and unsuitable for canning. Yet it is well-flavored when fresh, and it is put in cold storage or salted. The Indians up the river still capture and smoke or dry a fair number of them as a winter supply for their dogs, which explains the name of dog salmon. And the Japanese were partial to it, taking a large supply of them to their homeland for the winters.

The market value of the salmon is impressive, and it is put down by statisticians in rising and fluctuating curves varying from year to year.

At the cradle time of the industry, in 1878, the product of salmon fisheries in Alaska amounted to around forty-one thousand dollars; and in 1907 to more than nine millions. The purchase price of the whole Alaskan peninsula, in 1867, was only seven and a half millions. In 1937, the value of the salmon catch of Alaska and the United States was estimated at over seventeen millions; and that of British Columbia, for the same year, at

around twelve millions—a grand total for one year of
nearly thirty million dollars. It is no wonder, then, if
the salmon is tagged with the caption of "commercial"
fish.

In the early stages of the industry, the coast Indians
were true pioneers. In the capture of the salt-water fish
they used simple contrivances that sufficed to their ends:
hooks, spears, gaffs, and nets of nettle or fireweed fibers.
Their most effective device then was artificial lagoons,
somewhat in the same style as those of the Copper Eskimos at the mouths of Arctic rivers. While the tide was
low, the beach at a suitable spot was cleared of rocks
and a circular wall of stone was built, the ends abutting
to the shores. At flood tide, the fishermen kept on the
lookout for a school of fish in the neighborhood. As
soon as one was sighted, they maneuvered it toward the
enclosure and held it stationed there until the tide had
fallen. When successful, they trapped the whole school.
And this was said, at Port Simpson, to have originated
among the Tlingits of southeastern Alaska.

Fish traps are used by the Alaskan canneries. As they
are destructive, they do not meet with the same favor
on the Canadian side of the border. Nets of various
descriptions—gill nets and purse seines—are the most
common devices, being adapted to the various kinds of
salmon, and are controlled by the law.

The legalized fishing season, beginning with June and
ending in September, brings about a wholesale yearly
migration northward of fisherfolk and cannery hands
from the populated centers in the south, particularly
Seattle and Vancouver, or from the Indian villages within easier reach. The managers, storekeepers, wireless
operators, clerks, and their families, are the first, with

some mechanics, to arrive at the canneries. The fishermen in numbers come in later, many of them being Scandinavians, and, before the war, Japanese. Groups of Chinese, under the supervision of "bosses," reach their stations inside the plants. Thousands of local Indians, from the coast and river tribes, enlist every year and fish for the companies. When, later in August or in September, the active season is over, the native fisherfolk go to the neighboring towns to spend their wages while being entertained at fairs. Then, usually empty-handed, they migrate back home. The canneries close down and the "salmon pack" then filling the warehouses is ready for the holds of the coastwise steamship lines.

At the canneries, the number of which reaches into the hundreds, the life is well-regulated, quiet, and almost silent. The management is bent on efficiency, and it is controlled from the companies' headquarters elsewhere, in the United States, Canada, or Great Britain. The local manager ever hopes for a large catch and a profitable season, and accordingly marshals his personnel, which is of his own choice.

The size of the salmon run varies yearly, and competition is keen between the rival companies. A fisherman's income depends upon the salmon run and, not a little, upon his skill and industry, as he is paid for his catch. He often owns his own gasoline boat and tackle. The Japanese always owned theirs, and, of late years, they owned some canneries of their own, it is rumored, including some floating canneries.

A modern cannery is usually a big establishment. It is situated in a sheltered cove on an island or at the estuary of a river, and consists of several large buildings and sheds, wharves for the fishing craft and the coast steamers, and rows of small cabins in the close neighborhood for the Indians and their families.

The medley of races, the activities of each group of workers, the fishing boats as they scatter for the oncoming tides, the drifting and hauling of nets, the frequent cleansing of the equipment, all tend to make existence at a cannery, in its brief summer span, a unique feature of the North Pacific coast. It is worth seeing. The machinery for cutting up, canning, and steaming the salmon is the last word in modern ingenuity; for every improvement means economy. The episodes of group and even of individual lives are kept under the control of the administration. Yet at times it furnishes interesting diversions. The Indians, with Mongolian features, are picturesque and slovenly in their ways; the Japanese kept proudly to themselves, and chattered almost silently in their quarters, after the "drifts"; and the Chinese, when they are not busy "canning" or "packing" tins inside, scatter on the wharves, talk and laugh lightheartedly, hide to smoke long pipes, and fish for flounders, which they dry in the sun—a delicacy for them.

All this scenery, against a deep-green background which is ever moist and semitropical, is impressively exotic. The casual visitor, if he likes it, may nibble at blue or pink huckleberries and red or golden salmonberries, or salal, eat delicious crabs, drink saki (Japanese whiskey), taste leechi nuts from the Celestial Empire, listen to strange languages, and let his mind wander off into new spheres, toward Asia—which is not very far off.

WILD LIFE

VAST, diverse, and bounteous, has always been the
wild life of Alaska, in territories too immense and
inaccessible ever to be fully embraced by its scanty
population.

In prehistoric times, it never ceased to be a lure to the
roving hunters and fishermen of the Far North who
preyed upon it. All along the eastern edge of Bering Sea,
at the rear door of the New World, it drew on like a bait
the harassed or famished populations of Kamchatka.

The native seafolk and whalers on the Asiatic
coast, in skin boats, armed with detachable harpoons
with bladder floats, gave chase to the whale, the walrus,
the sea cow, the sea lion, the seal, and the sea otter,
wherever they found them, and this led them all the way
from the Diomede Islands, or the Aleutian Islands, as
far southeast as Vancouver Island and beyond, where
we recognize them in the Nootkas and the Coast Salish.

Siberians, from the interior, crossed the strait and
penetrated inland or ascended the rivers. There they
hunted the bear, the caribou, or the migratory fowl on
the tundras, and fished or trapped the salmon in the
streams. They traded the caribou skins with their former
kinsmen across the sea, with whom they maintained
yearly relations, and they went on making parkas in
Siberian style either for themselves or for export along
the northern trade routes.

Nearer our times, the ancient cultural features of

Alaska have been sensibly tampered with. In the wake
of the white man's excesses in the most exposed parts,
wild life has become shy and elusive; it shuns the eye of
the hunter and the fisherman. But it still retains its
perennial spirit, which is no less real than its externals.

It is both the spirit and the externals of this wild life
which is easily found on the lips of its own imaginative
folk, Indian and white, in their candid utterances by the
fireside. As these forest and river folk are part of this
wild life, they have seen it, captured it at times as part
of their own wandering existence. They will tell us here
of their activities in their tundras, forests, and mountains.

The pictures which their stories bring out with simple
words are often vivid, unforgettable; they belong to
sheer adventure. Some of these pictures, besides, conjure
up a long tale of the past—far longer, indeed, than may
at first be apparent. The skill of the storytellers, their
emotions, their retentive memory, and the curiosity of
the listeners, go hand in hand together to make the
truth feel actual, yet stranger than fiction.

For truth is at the core of all these narratives. Their
source is ancient racial experience, bringing man and
animal together for a clash or in a performance where
the narrator, the listener, and the beast in turn take
their cues in thrilling action.

Few countries on the globe offer such opportunities as
are found at every turn in Alaska for such encounters—
on the rookeries, with sea lion and walrus; at sea, with a
few species of whales; on the rivers and on the lakes,
with salmon, land otter, fisher, and beaver; on the high
plateaus in the interior, with ptarmigan and other northern birds, ground hog, pack rat, porcupine, wolverine,

deer, caribou, timber wolf, moose, wood buffalo, grizzly bear; on the mountains, with bighorn and mountain goat; on the islands within the Bering Sea, with Kodiak bear; and in the Arctic, with polar bear.

All these wild animals and many others, belonging inseparably to the Alaskan landscape, beckon to us in our quest for the unknown and mysterious. And, in spots, their numbers still are baffling. For instance, an observer for the Canadian government, pausing at an observation point in a valley east of Mount St. Elias and west of Kluane Lake—an important big-game country, near the place where the Alcan Highway recently was officially opened—counted no less than 12 grizzlies, 19 moose, 240 caribou, and 1,064 mountain sheep within the range of his binoculars—a mere sample out of the unseen.

The Indians, far more than the white people invading their territories, possess the gift of creatively portraying wild animals. Keen observers, they have known them from childhood, and they have inherited a great wealth of folklore about them. To the natives, the quadrupeds, the birds, and the fish of the forests, the rivers, the lakes, and the seas are not a mere suborder of creation. To them, the animals, however small and negligible, down to the wren, are endowed like human beings with thought and powers of reasoning and speech. Once they were people themselves, and their immortal souls, through some accident or misfortune, were reborn after their death into strange shapes outside the social framework. At times they re-enter the ranks, as it were, to be people as they once had been. This is according to the ancient belief in metempsychosis, or the transmigration of souls, which the American natives have received from their Asiatic forebears.

Father Petitot, who spent his life as a missionary among the Dénés of the frozen tundras, knew how to interpret them when he wrote:

The quadrupeds, the birds, the plants and the trees, own an animate life; they become superior genii who may converse with the people and reveal to them the secrets of the other world. In their quality of totems or *ellonhays*, they may bring to human protégés success in the hunt, a cure for illness, and a long prosperous life. The totem or *ellonhay*, in exchange for its gifts, requires its man-shadow to spare it in the hunt, never to kill it, never to eat of its flesh, nor to utter its name disrespectfully.

Earth Mother is said to live under the earth and to hold it up; She is the first of the hidden spirits. Although she is never seen, her presence at times is felt. When she grows tired, she moves a little, and the earth quakes.

On the immense bosom of Kralla, Earth Mother, the animal spirits at the beginning created everything that dwells on the land or in the water. The most powerful among them once spread six times over the world the magic veil of creation that was smooth and soft like the tanned skin of an elk. Every time they raised the veil, a new species of animal made its appearance, and then hastened away to the forest or the river or the sea.

"The trees standing around us:" [a northern Indian would tell the missionary], "the flocks of ptarmigans that swarm in the sky, the herds of caribou which the wolves track in the wilderness, were men like ourselves. No one knows why they were changed into their present selves, but they have the power to resume their human form, usually at night, when they become enemies and harry the living.

"Last winter, for instance, two of us went to visit our nets on the ice on Lake Kronayden. We lost our way at dusk, and headed for a point on the shore where the trees and the rocks seemed unknown to us. When suddenly we saw campfires close to shore under the open sky, we made for the camp consisting of many skin tents swarming with unknown people, who were gay and talkative. Their language, quite unknown to us, was light and bird-like. As they were roasting fish over the fire, they offered some to us, and invited us to sleep with them on the beaten snow.

The fervor of a medicine man rising to frenzy, he utters supplications to his guardian spirit PAGE 293.

"At dawn on the morrow, everything but ourselves had vanished from sight. The camp no longer stood there. We were sleeping alone at the edge of the lake. As we sat up, a flight of white partridges sprang from little holes in the soft snow about us, made a great noise of flapping wings, and soon disappeared behind a clump of firs away from sunrise.

"These people, our hosts for the night, we then realized, were not real human beings. In the darkness, they only behaved like people, spoke among themselves as they do. At the break of day, they had resumed their bird forms, to take their flight away. We had only deceived ourselves."

Indian tales of this kind are countless. They reflect beliefs and practices long familiar to the Indians. Much in earnest, a Déné would say to Father Petitot: "I have seen on the hard snow on the lake the tracks of a deer. These tracks, as I followed them, changed into a man's footmarks—once more, a caribou had become a man." Or, when a halo crowned the moon before a snowfall, another would remark: "Many deer will cross the steppe, for the white planet finds it worth while to put on her headdress, to hunt our enemies"—the deer being considered enemies of the Dénés, now victimized in the hunt into being their prey.

The spirits in the animals were collective rather than individual; this gave them superior powers. The eagle, the whale, the wolf, the bear, and a few others, stood over the rank and file; they were like minor divinities, yet not true gods, even in the eyes of the natives. It was in the power of benevolent spirits at times to become men and women, to appear to adolescents fasting in their seclusion at puberty, and, as guardian spirits, to give mystic powers that might endure a lifetime. Others, like the hawk, the otter, and the weasel, were the privilege of medicine men and sorcerers; they might serve a good purpose in curing disease, or do harm as they were directed in incantations.

A medicine man, for instance, may be called upon to use his power over a patient. After fasting, he dons a crown of grizzly-bear claws, a robe of hairy pelts, an apron of skin and deer hoofs, and he wields a round rattle or a large one-sided skin drum, to accompany his spirit song. His fervor rising into a frenzy, he utters supplications to his guardian spirit and conjures it to assist him with such incantations as this:

"I will sing to the lizard, the great one of the mountains. I will sing to the many lizards, his sons and daughters. Let them roll down the mountainsides, let them descend to me in the low valley! As they glide down, the trees under their weight are crushed to dust, the snow under their breath turns into water and the rocks are pulverized into grains of sand. Child, look at him coming, the great lizard! He is followed by his children every one. Now that they have arrived, they sit in a ring at the bottom, and the bands around their heads have fallen undone. The bands are blown upward by the wind from the canyon. Child, look and look with me! These bands have become rainbows. They stand up on the earth and reach far into the sky. The rainbows are the lizard's breath, the breaths of the many lizard spirits from the mountaintops, and this is what they sing, 'Child, the breath of our soul is a rainbow. The power of rainbows is what preserves our health. We are never, never ill. Look at us, look at the rainbow, child, and you shall be well again.' "

The profound belief that spirits animate nature is what has made the Indian mind what it has always been, keenly sensitive to hidden powers in things and

highly respectful of the laws of life impressed upon it
from time immemorial. Wild life in the care of a native was, for this reason, in no danger of destruction, as
it is now that the white man has taken control in his
hands. Any Indian unwise enough to ignore ancient
wisdom and violate taboos was, in the eyes of his fellows,
a renegade. He courted a punishment that re-estab-
lished a balance essential in the world of living beings.

Two examples, well known among the Alaskan tribes,
will bear this out: those of Bear-Mother, and of the
Painted Goats of Stekyawden; but they are too extensive for full quotation here. A bare outline will suggest
their contents and implications—for they have given
rise to songs, rituals, dramatic performances, and totems
on carved poles and wooden masks. The bear and the
goat are the clan totems of some of the leading families
of the Tlingits in Alaska and of the Tsimsyans and
Haidas in northern British Columbia.

The story of Bear-Mother is familiar among the Alaskans, the northwestern American tribes, and, no less,
among the Asiatics in eastern Siberia. It comes back to
the rovers on wild trails when they slip in the dung of
grizzlies and, on the spur of the moment, might vent
their annoyance, as a berry picker of the foothills once
did. "Hush, my dear! Don't scold, don't laugh—" an
old woman would reprove, "the bears might hear you!"

As soon as a remark like this is made in a household, the
listeners turn their brownish faces toward the story-
teller, their flashing dark eyes and white eyeballs showing
their eagerness. They know well that one must not laugh
at grizzly bears. Bears are mighty, they are fierce; like
spirits, they hear everything. That is why people, when
speaking of them, must be courteous and thoughtful—

The story of Bear-Mother as illustrated in native carvings.
PAGES 294-99.

else they may fear punishment. An old Nahannie elder, after a pause, would illustrate her point:

"Peesunt, long ago, was gathering huckleberries at timberline with two young women of her tribe. Instead of singing like the others, to keep the bears away without offending them—for the bears, too, live on berries, late in summertime—she kept talking and babbling while picking up berries. The bears in the end pricked up their ears and listened. Why did she always babble as if she were mocking at some one? they asked each other. Perhaps she was laughing at them. That is why they began to spy on her in the bush and to follow her down the trail, when she "packed" a large basket of fruit for the camp.

"One evening, all three young women one after the other paced the trail, stooping under their loads, which were held on their backs by 'pack-traps' from their foreheads. Peesunt, the babbler, was the last of the three, a short distance behind the others. Suddenly she slipped, nearly fell down, and her 'pack-strap,' loosened, let her basket hit the ground and the fruit spill on the footpath. She looked at her feet and burst out with angry laughter:

"'Boo with Naek—the bear-orphan! Here he has dropped his excrements!'

"She might just as well have said, 'You are fatherless, a bastard!' This insult to the bears one and all could not pass unpunished.

"Her 'pack-strap' broke and, while she tried to mend it, the others went on their way, leaving her behind, far behind. Ill-tempered, she did not sing as she should have, to keep off the bears, but only scolded and groaned.

"As it was now turning dark, she heard voices in the bush behind her, men's voices. Then two young men, looking like brothers, came toward her and said:

" 'Sister, you are in trouble, with nobody to look after you. Come with us, we will carry your berries for you!'

"Following them, she noticed that they wore bear robes, and were taking her up the mountain. After dark they arrived at a large house up a rockslide, and invited her to enter it with them. Around a log fire, a number of people, all dressed in bear robes, were sitting and looking at her strangely.

"The white mouse, Tseets [Grandmother], came to her and pulled at her robe, which was now coated with long gray hair, like a bear's. And the tiny one squeaked:

" 'Granddaughter, the bears have taken you to their den; from now on you shall be one of them, bearing their children.'

"As she heard this she became frightened, more so still when the chief's eldest nephew approached her and said:

" 'You shall live, if you agree to stay with me—my wife; if you refuse, you die.' "

The listeners then hear about Peesunt's life as a bear, among the grizzlies up in the mountains. Before the long story is finished, they learn that the young woman, as wife of the eldest nephew of the grizzlies' chief, bore him two children, perhaps three or four. These children assume the form of cubs at their own pleasure, or at times they are human, or only half-human.

One day in the early spring, the bears dozing in their den heard the yelping of a dog and the voice of Indian hunters down below. These hunters were Peesunt's brothers, looking for her and bent upon revenging her, unless she were retrieved alive from her captors.

The young chief in the den, unable to bestir himself, made up his mind to submit to fate. Bears henceforth would fall under the arrows and the spears of man. But there must be some atonement for the wastage in their own ranks.

Speaking a last time to the young mother about to return, with her mixed brood, to her people, the bear spirit said,

"Whenever the men in your tribe shoot and kill one of our own, let the hunters bend their head with regret over the kill and hum this dirge in sign of respect to our spirit!"

From the sorrowing chief in the den at the rockslide, Peesunt learned the dirge and sang it aloud. Her brothers, hearing it, would recognize her and spare her when killing the true bears. Then she pressed a handful of soft snow in her palm and let it roll down to her brothers. As they picked it up, they recognized the mark of human fingers on it, and hastened up to the den.

They speared the real bears and saved their own sister and her brood. They bent their heads low and chanted the dirge of the grizzlies, to beg their grace and forgiveness, just as every hunter has done ever since.

The kinsmen of Peesunt and her posterity, which is supposed to have branched off among the Tsimsyan, the Tlingit, and some of the Haida tribes, assumed the grizzly bear as their crest; they had it carved on their totems on the Nass and the Skeena rivers, and at Wrangell, where it is the leading emblem of Shaiks, the high chief—it squats at the top of a famous post in front of his house on the island within the bay. The Haidas, particularly those of Massett, have illustrated many episodes of this story on their house or grave posts or in their

argillite carvings. Their illustrations were masterpieces
of native art. Many of them are now treasured by the
museums of America and Europe.

The mountain-goat story shares some of the same
features: the disrespect and cruelty to the animals on
the part of reckless hunters forgetting the taboos; the
revenge of the victims through the spirit presiding over
the species; and finally the adoption of the animals as
emblems by those who first sang a dirge over the kill
and observed the rule that the brood be saved and no
more of the animals be slaughtered than should be
needed at one time.

The tale of the Painted Goat of Stekyawden Mountain is one of the most typical in the rich repertory of
the northern tribesmen. A few excerpts will serve here
as samples. In its preamble we hear:

"For ages our ancestors lived in peace. Their hearts
were pure as the fresh snow. Happy were their lives and
blessed with prosperity. Their homeland had become an
earthly paradise, the Eden of Temlaham, our birthplace.

"Their blissful existence might have lasted to this
day, had they obeyed the words of sky command for the
welfare of all, the words of the first precept: 'Do not
abuse animals nor ridicule them. Their lives are not unlike yours. Their spirit-selves, unless propitiated, stand
over them in readiness for retaliation. Do not waste
their flesh nor scatter their bones. Above all, spare
their broods, lest they visit their wrath upon you and
migrate from your hunting territories, leaving them
barren for your own ruin.' But our ancestors, no less
than the sinners in our midst, strayed from the high path
and met with their downfall in the end.

"After the victory over Kunradal, men no longer indulged in frivolous games. Skillful hunters, they resorted to their forest preserves, and returned home with much booty. Their choice sport was to hunt mountain goats in the high ranges above Temlaham, to hunt them and capture them in snares.

"In time, they grew careless, gave heed no longer to the rules of the chase. They slaughtered too many goats, and knew not what to do with the meat. Surfeited, they left the flesh bleeding on the ground, exposed to the sun, the bones scattered, unburned. They carried home only the kidney fat for food, and the horned heads, for trophies.

"The children at home, emulating their elders, made fun of the heads of the goats, tied them to their foreheads like masks, and danced impishly to songs that aped the ancient dirges.

"Yet, they should have remembered, young and old—sinners all—that the wild animals are intelligent like human beings, only more canny; that they are gifted and powerful, like the spirits themselves! The goats of the lofty crags beheld the bones of their kindred lying scattered in the dust, overheard the jests and the songs, and they were aggrieved in their hearts.

"Six cousins there were who caught many goats in their deadfalls, one spring, and with their bows and arrows destroyed the rest of the herd. They maimed the survivors and chased them away with jeers that sounded like curses. The only one spared was a kid, which they held in captivity, that their children might make sport of it as they pleased.

"The kid was much abused wherever it set foot. One evening, a crowd led it to the riverbank, and thrust it over the edge into the swift running waters. It swam ashore, clambered the slope, only to be thrown back over and over again. Never before had anyone beheld a goat swim a stream like a deer or a bear—a goat whose only known habit is to saunter and graze near the high peaks, and glide off in the twinkle of an eye beyond the crests.

"An old chief, passing by, nodded his head and gave warning, 'Stop your foolery, O thoughtless rabble! Beware the spirits!' They jeered only the more and knocked the kid headlong into the fire.

"Du'as [Raven-Feather] spied them and took pity on their victim. Wise and highborn, he could not stand by and suffer this indignity. Stepping forth, he reprimanded them, saying, 'Stop this! The kid is my pet,' and he carried it away in his arms to the lodge of his uncle, Nee-awks.

" 'Supernatural one,' he murmured, along his way, 'how sinful of them, how cruel!' He rubbed his hands softly on its body and anointed its burns. Dipping his brush in ocher dissolved in salmon roe, and parting the long hair around the kid's neck, he painted bright red stripes over the burns and drew red circles around the nostrils and the eyes in its white face.

"At night, Raven-Feather led his pet outside the village, led it to the foot of Stekyawden. 'Go, little one,' he urged, 'Go back to your home! You are free, O little friend!' Tottering on its legs, the kid disappeared in the shrubs."

The rest of this myth recounts the tribulations that befell Temlaham because of its impiety toward the goats — a rockslide so overwhelming that most of the people were buried underneath it, with the exception of Raven-Feather and his clan. This young chief escaped down the river, and later assumed as a crest the moun-

tain goat, as we still see it on the totems of at least two
nations of the North Pacific coast.

The mountain-goat story concludes with the dirge
that is still sung with reverence by the Indian hunters
who would not forsake the past in their mountains:

> The little spruce tree hangs aloft, hangs aloft. On the
> ledge it hangs till morn, then marches down the cliffs
> chanting "Kwisamaws, Kwisamaws."

> The puny Goat is my pet, the kid of the crags, the dear,
> snow-white one, whom I once saved from the swift waters,
> from the bonfires, who for my reward rescued me from
> peril, bestowed on me gifts aplenty.

> Behold the prince, proud and mighty! He sets his foot
> down, and the earth cracks to pieces, crumbles to dust. Be-
> hold the prince! He knocks off the flanks of Stekyawden
> with his hoofs, and the stone walls split asunder like clay
> baked in the sun. Behold our prince, the highest among
> the mighty! His eyes glitter like opalescent pearls, the
> pearls of Larhmawn, the far, deep sea.

For the Indians of the older generation the supernatural and the natural often merge into one, in the
fabric of their daily lives and their folklore. Even now,
when only a few shreds of their former selves are left,
they readily pass from realism to fiction, or the reverse,
sometimes to the point of disconcerting white listeners
unfamiliar with their peculiar turn of mind. This striking feature—the blending of truth with fiction—is in
part due to their Asiatic ancestry. They conserve a
hoard of past experiences and beliefs which, in taking
an abstract turn, has fostered in them a sense of mysticism; for the other part, they lapse into their own
recent or individual experiences, in which realism is

uppermost. The first tendency is profound, ancient, and racial; it could not easily be eradicated. The second, recent and dependent upon actual observation, opens the door to novelty and prepares the ground for tribal adaptation to ever changing surroundings.

Gamanut, the Gitksan outlaw who spent many years among the lost souls at odds with the white man's authority, in the Cassiar district at the Yukon border, is a good example of the modernized Indian thrown back upon wild life for a subsistence, who retained all the mental traits of his race. He could not consistently tell me "true" stories of the hunt, when I wanted to hear from him actual experiences concerning bears, caribou, salmon, and other wild creatures. He would begin right, with a recollection of an encounter with a fierce grizzly; but before the end of his tale, he would bring along a little white mouse low on the ground. The rodent had asked him to spare his life, and given him some good advice. The white mouse is a well-known character in the mythology of the Far North, on both sides of Bering Strait.

Other Indians as a whole prefer telling folktales to the delivery of truthful recollections. If you succeed in impressing upon them your desire to hear only "true" stories—that is, without human-like speaking animals— they may settle down, like a white man, to telling real adventures, in which we hear of fierce animals and sharpshooters engaged in mortal combat. But wild life in native storytelling always remains rather elusive; it never becomes crude and bloodcurdling.

The contrasting attitudes of three hunters in the following bear stories are an instance to the point—two of them white men, the third a native of the country.

One night in camp, on a trail in the Cassiar country, which is in the heart of the best hunting grounds for the grizzly, we began to talk bears. We had just seen fresh tracks of a grizzly near our camp. This topic is infectious, and whenever it is broached, from fresh experience, nothing else seems worthwhile. There were many bear reminiscenes in the air. Gamanut, the Indian guide in my party and former outlaw, Angus Beaton, the big-game hunter of Scottish-Canadian birth, and Gervais, the old French-Canadian prospector, were full of them, mostly from first-hand experience.

"Are grizzlies man-eaters?" was my first question, which started the ball rolling.

"Man-eaters? No!" answered Angus Beaton, who had hunted in the Cassiar for over thirty years, part of the time as a guide to American big-game hunters. He was the keenest observer of wild life I have ever met.

Gamanut, the Indian, shook his head, and argued:

"I have seen human hair caught between the teeth of a grizzly, after it was killed. The Stikine Indians had punished it, it was a man-eater. Our people are much afraid of grizzlies, and for good cause."

"There are bears and bears," advanced Gervais, who, in spite of his momentary low status (being our cook), had seen and shot many bears during his long adventurous life in the Klondike. (He was the discoverer of the La Valtrie gold mine, named after his wife, whom he had left at home.)

"What do you mean?" I wondered, "bears and bears."

"Never be too sure what a grizzly will do," he answered. "It usually runs away from you before you have seen it. But when it starts the other way, the trick is up to you!"

"In the first place," I wondered, just to make him speak, "where do you find grizzlies?"

"You find them with their food," instantly answered Beaton for Gervais. "And this varies according to the district. It doesn't matter how good a hunter or a trapper you are. As soon as you move into a new district, you find things a bit different—the bears, like the other animals. Before you discover your quarry, you have to catch on to the ways of the country. Up here in the North, the grizzlies, from the spring on, feed on the grass of the mountainsides. Then you get them in the hills, wherever wild fruits are ripe, or a bit before they get ripe. Grizzlies live in the berry country and burned timber until the early fall, when they go down to the rivers and grow fat on salmon spawning at the mouths of the creeks. Grizzlies also dig out ground hogs and eat them. No, they are not, as I have heard some people say, strictly vegetarians. Far from it, they like fish, and hunt for meat too."

"The best hunting ground for grizzlies is east of Groundhog Mountain," added Gamanut, who knew that country like his pocket—having lived there for many years after running afoul of the white man's law. "It is called Place-of-Grass [Larh-weeyip]. The bears there are quite fierce."

"They are, wherever you surprise them," Gervais said, "in the Klondike too. They will charge, unless *you talk to them*." And his index finger bent forth, as if to pull the trigger.

"A man, an Indian named Ahkwedzah, once was killed in the grassy hills of the Stikine," Gamanut resumed (he had a story to tell). "He shot twice at the grizzly but failed to bring it down, good hunter though

he was. The bear chased him back and forth, up and
down, till he became exhausted. Then it took hold of
him and killed him, while his brother, Larhay, helpless on
a cliff above, watched the fight. Aroused, the people
started on the warpath against the grizzly, to avenge the
death of their relative. For this retaliation they would
not use gun, only spears and long sharp knives.

"They did not travel far before they found the grizzly.
Infuriated, they piled onto the bear and killed it with
their spears. They examined its teeth to see whether
human hair could be found between them. There was
none. Yet the bear murderer was known to have torn
the scalp of the man it had killed and done away with
it; it must have devoured it. This then was the wrong
bear. They hunted till they came upon another grizzly,
and they brought it down. They must kill the killer;
that was the custom. But still they could find no human
hair between its teeth. They went on and on looking for
other bears, till they encountered a very large grizzly.
Like the others, it fell to their hands and they cut it to
pieces. Looking into its mouth, they found human hair
in its teeth. So this was the bear they were looking for—
the killer. They skinned it, dried its skin and stuffed it.
It looked as if it were alive. The Stikine hunters did this
for the sake of revenge, while I lived with them. And
the stuffed bear is still in Larhay's house. I saw it there
only last year."

"That sounds like an Indian tale," Gervais remarked
with a lack of diplomacy that was characteristic. "I
have never known a grizzly to be a man-eater."

"I know of one case when hair was found in the
stomach of a grizzly," said Beaton, as if to corroborate
the Indian's story. "But this was the hair of another

bear. For grizzlies at times fight one another. Two of them not so long ago were seen locked together in a death struggle. People looked on, from a distance; they had heard fierce growling down along the creek. After the bears had fought for a long time, they separated. One walked away and suddenly fell down, dead. The other disappeared. The people after a while went down and found that the body of the bear was badly torn. They skinned it, cut it open, and found some of the hide and hair of the other bear, chewed off, in its stomach. The bear had begun to eat the other one while it was still alive. The other bear was nearly dead when they found it, a few hundred feet away, in the brush."

Gamanut was positive that grizzlies often chased his people and killed them, particularly in the old days, when the hunters had only muzzle-loaders or spears to hunt them with. He told us of some hand-to-hand encounters between man and beast, usually to man's detriment. Yet, in one of them the Indian had defeated the bear by thrusting his left hand into its throat and holding its tongue while he stabbed it with his right. But that instance was a classic among the storytellers of the North.

"The grizzly is a hard animal to kill," said Beaton, in his turn. "He's vulnerable only at a few spots—at the back of the shoulder or under the shoulder right through the heart, in the neck or in the small of the back, to break the spine. Every other wound is only a flesh wound. A grizzly with three legs, his two hind legs intact, for one thing, is as good as with four. He will fight you standing on his hind legs. As to the skull, it's a hard nut to crack. You can do it only with a very powerful rifle, and I wouldn't try it. You're a good

shot if you manage to get the bullet straight into the eye
or into the ear. Half an inch aside is enough to make it
glance off on the thick skull, and there you are, worse
off than at the start. When you miss a grizzly with your
first shot, you get excited and you shoot wide of the
mark. That's not always healthy!"

"Neither can you always choose to run away," Gervais
chuckled.

"If you do," resumed Beaton, "take my advice: climb
a tree quick, the right one, big enough. For a grizzly
cannot climb. I have never tried it, 'pon my word. A
hunter seldom does. It looks foolish."

Gamanut laughed at the idea. It reminded him of
something. He said: "The bear waits there at the foot
of the tree until you fall into its mouth. That nearly
happened once, when I was still young, to my uncle,
Kail. He hunted the grizzlies with a muzzle-loader, and
it was quite a job. One day, on the trail, he shot a
grizzly, but didn't quite kill it. He ran, climbed a tree,
and stayed there. The grizzly stood up maybe ten feet
high, put his great arms around the tree and tried to
shake my uncle down, tried and tried. But the tree
was too big, and my uncle held fast.

"Kail stayed there a whole day in the tree. The bear,
at the foot, kept him good company. Most of the time
they looked at each other. Then they parted, the bear
getting tired of it first.

"When Kail arrived at the village and told of his
adventure, the people asked him: 'Why did you not,
when you were up there, shoot the bear right in the eye?
Had you not plenty of time to take your aim?'

"Kail answered: 'A bird's nest stood right in my way.
Because of the nest, I couldn't see the bear.'

The Painted Goat of Stekyawden and its protégé Raven-Feather
PAGES 299-302.

"He would not confess that in his haste he had left his gun on the ground. The people after that couldn't forget about the bird's nest; they found it too funny for words!"

Climbing a tree was not always done by the hunter alone, Gervais declared, as if to give a broad hint that grizzlies too can climb a tree when they choose. This was so clearly at variance with a common experience that both Beaton and Gamanut, surprised, turned around to look at him. Challenged, our old Klondike prospector at once was bent upon proving his contention. Of course grizzlies are not everywhere the same, he admitted, and the bear he had in mind belonged to the Klondike, where strange things have happened, and still happen.

"I was going up the Takina River in a canoe," he said. "As I paddled close to shore because of the current, I came up to a tree, a tall pine, leaning over the river. A noise in the tree startled me. I looked up and saw a bear, a grizzly. I didn't believe, at the time, that a grizzly could climb a tree. But there he was! Without thinking, I took my gun and fired at him, from under. Quite stupid of me!

"The bear tumbled right over and fell on his back into my canoe, at the bow. There he was caught fast, and, by Jove, still alive!

"I jumped into the river, and swam to shore. As soon as I touched solid ground, I remembered that, at other times, I couldn't swim. From there I saw my canoe drifting down, in midstream, with the head of the bear jutting out.

" 'Confound it!' I said, 'I still need my canoe, I must look for it.'

"The river a little below made a long turn, bending to the right. Cutting across the tongue of land through the trees, I ran for all I was worth. When I came to the shore again, below the curve, I looked up and down for the canoe and the bear. I could see neither.

" 'What's happened?' I thought, and waited. Nothing! Yet I was sure I was the first to reach there.

"After a while, I decided to walk upstream along the shore, looking for my canoe. Another tree, like the first one, stood in my way, bending over the river. As I was climbing over its trunk, what did I see, above?

"The bear was up there, in the forks, with my canoe still fastened to his back."

To that moment we had been listening intently to Gervais' story, Beaton with his mouth open. Awakening to his sense of humor, Beaton burst with laughter. "You're a damn liar!" he said. Then he helped himself for the second time to the bacon, with the words: "Enough of silly yarns for just one breakfast!"

From these stories, one may realize how grizzly-bear stories pass from mystic belief in Bear Mother and her semihuman cubs to verbal realism, in which infuriated beasts fight standing on their hind legs and, for a "show-down," swallow the scalp of a hunter far too busy to think of climbing a tree to escape.

After crossing the Bering Sea, the Siberian nomads did not lose the impetus that had thrown them forward into Alaska. They followed the course which the Yukon River, untold ages in advance, had mapped out for them. This huge river would lead them on east or south, as in other periods it had led whatever tribe had given itself up to it, out of the lands of the sunset.

Already vacated by most of the previous transients, who had not tarried long on their trek upstream, the Yukon River offered to the newcomers tantalizing opportunities. One after another they yielded to them, according to their own racial predispositions.

Seafolk naturally preferred the islands or the seacoast in the new country. But the hunters of reindeer and wild fowl, born rovers of the frozen tundras, headed for the hinterland, in the tracks of the caribou. And fishers, used to feeding on salmon in the Kamchatka rivers, looked for their familiar food up the Yukon tributaries which led them on far afield, over the divides, to the headwaters of the salmon rivers of the North Pacific coast.

The Siberian emigrants split into three main spearheads, all of them driving forward in different directions. The first headed down the west coast, the second went up and down the salmon rivers on the western side of the Rockies, and the third crossed the mountains eastward.

This eastern spearhead, that of the caribou hunters far inland, eventually broke up into two main halves. The first half found its way on the rolling tundras and marshlands across the Mackenzie River, keeping close to the Eskimos, with whom they mingled and fought at times —just as the Chukchees of eastern Siberia, their kinsmen left far behind, were doing.[1] Members of this forward

---

[1] Some Chukchee bands, at one time not so long ago, may actually have occupied the lower Yukon River. At least we were led to surmise it by the following statement of Cornelius Osgood ("Kutchin Tribal Distribution and Synonymy," *American Anthropologist*, XXXVI [1934], 177):

"The people on the Yukon River just below the True Kutchin are another problematical group who are at least partially extinct. My informants called them te tsci, Murray (p. 38) Tchuktchis (relating them to the Siberian Chukchees), and Richardson (1:398) Teytse or "people of the shelter." These are also, I believe, Dall's Tatsah (p. 30), which he said were wiped out by an epidemic of

group eventually reached the rivers emptying into Hudson Bay.

The other half of this eastern spearhead—Beavers, Sarcees, Navahos, and Apaches—turned south, to track the herds of caribou and the buffalo in the foothills. They proceeded by slow stages across the northwestern prairies. The Sarcees eventually remained on the Bow River (Alberta). The Navahos and the Apaches, at the present Canadian border when the discoverers first noticed them, journeyed onward until they reached Arizona and New Mexico. The Apaches were about to force their way into Mexico, to conquer the Corn Maidens, when they were stopped short of their goal by another intruder, the white man, who had come there to stay.

The traditions of all three Déné or Athabascan migratory waves reflect the twin aspects of their history: first, their higher cultural status of the past, on another continent; second, their present adaptability to new and arduous surroundings. Those three-pronged spearheads in time have spread far apart. Yet, for a retrospective glance, they can easily be gathered together.

To the Kamchatka spearhead, surging "out of the foam" (the ocean), belongs the Salmon-Eater and Selarhkons tribe now embodied in the Haida and the Tsimsyan nations of the west coast. Other offshoots of similar stock down the coast may go back to the same source, as they were of idential type. These sea hunters and fisher folk never ventured far inland, for they were old "salts," feeding on sea foods. Short, squatty, bow-

---

scarlet fever about 1863. The *Handbook* (11: 698) lists them as Tatsa and locates them around the mouth of the Tanana and up the Yukon river. The same authority (11:712) suggests the Teshin (now extinct) were a subdivision of the Chandelar River [Gens-du-Large?] tribe of True Kutchin, but I think they were more probably related to the Tatsa."

legged—from their prolonged habit of sitting in canoes
—they are characterized by flattish Mongolian faces and
slanting Oriental eyes.

Epic narratives tell of their former use (recently illustrated in crests) of skin bidarkas or canoes, of twin
dugouts tied together and linked by a planked platform,
of woven-mat sails, of cormorant-skin parkas and
spruce-root hats, and other typical Asiatic heirlooms.
They tell also of spirit or divine rivers and volcanic
eruptions.

From them and other forerunners have sprung the
typical North Pacific coast people who, to this day, look
Mongolian, quite at variance with the majority of North
American Indians.

The independent linguistic stocks to which some of
them belong—Tsimsyan, Kwakiutl-Nootka, and Salish
—should not obscure for us the plain strands of racial
origin; for languages are only like vestments, easily
changed or disposed of.[2]

In the Salmon-Eater tradition, for instance, a coast
people changed their language first into that of a native

---

[2] A most important extension of the Déné or Athapascan languages in northwest
America has recently been discovered by John P. Harrington, of the Bureau of
American Ethnology ("Pacific Coast Athapascan Discovered To Be Chilcotin."
Journal of the Washington Academy of Sciences, July 15, 1943. Pp. 203-13).

It has been previously established that Tlingit and Haida are divergent branches
of the same Siberian-American language of great magnitude on the maps of two
continents. Here are two of Harrington's conclusions, based upon extensive research and analysis:

"The so-called Pacific Coast Athapascan is composed of a string of Chilcotin
languages straggling down, and near, the west coast of the United States proper
from what is now southern British Columbia to almost within sight of San
Francisco, Calif. . . . Most satisfactory, were actually remembered traditions corro-
borating the linguistic evidence, which, although in part shading off into the
mythical, are clearly indicative that there has been a southern spread of
language-bearing ancestors, accomplished in war, opportunism, and peace, resulting
in linguistic supplanting in large just-inland and coastal regions, and that the
spread has been piecemeal, consisting of the throwing off of more southerly
linguistic neighbors by more northerly adjacent ones. These tying traditions are
10 in number."

Alaskan tribe—the Bear people, who had welcomed them into their domain. These newcomers again dropped their tongue to speak Haida, then Tsimsyan. A new language—which they called She-algyarh—was as easily accepted as it was later discarded. Their leading families, in two or three generations, passed from Tlingit to Tsimsyan, and to Kwakiutl; then a few of them reverted to Tsimsyan. Yet they were all originally of the same breed, mingling and intermarrying with their varied hosts. Out of their arrival new tribes quickly came into existence and produced new dialects.

Whatever language these seafolk accepted while on their way forward, they preserved some age-long aptitudes and customs. They went on reverting to ancestral mysticism and pattern-like notions of their more highly cultured forebears in Asia. This notable heritage impelled Father Petitot, the missionary among the northern Déné, once to declare: "Between their language and their intelligence [the one, collective and archaic, the other, recent and individual], there is an immense gap. This linguistic appanage is the gift of a noble past, whereas their present status is a sheer downfall." (Déné-Dindjié, p. 6.) [3]

The seacoast branch of this racial stock possesses as a foremost traditional feature the divine Raven, their maker and culture hero. A brief extract from this myth, referring to the appearance of Beaver and Salmon, is so

---

[3] "The situation may be summed up by the statement that a consideration of over five hundred traits shows a generally decreasing complexity in the cultures of the Northern Athapascans from west to east with a sharply distinctive break between the relatively rich culture of the Pacific drainage peoples and the essentially simple patterns of behavior of the aborigines of the Arctic coast. . . . There is generally among the groups of the Pacific drainage a dependence on salmon, which is entirely lacking among those of the Arctic drainage." Cornelius Osgood, "The Distribution of the Northern Athapascan Indians," *Yale University Publications in Anthropology*, Nos. 1-7, p. 21.

typical of their new lands west of the Rockies that it may
serve as an example here. The Beaver and Salmon episode
is a recent expansion of the Siberian myth of the supernatural Raven, who, at the beginning, placed the sun
and the moon in the sky and brought forth man and the
wild animals.

Having learned that Tsing, the Beaver, kept the Salmon in a
mountain lake where no one else could find it, the Raven flew away
from the islands to the mountains and, once more, turned himself
into a little boy. He wandered around the Beaver's house, at the
head of a river, and the old chief, seeing him, made him welcome.
As time passed, he adopted him as his son, for he was fond of him:
the child was so wise and skilful.

The Beaver and his adopted son, one day, partook together of a fine
fish—the red salmon from cold waters. To the boy who marvelled
about this find, the old chief did not mind revealing his secret. The
lake and the river flowing from it teemed with salmon which, every
season, proved an ample supply. As the young son was very helpful,
the Beaver chief brought him along to the lake and, growing quite
confident after a while, he sent him alone to fish salmon. The young
fisherman failed to return. Having gathered all the salmon he could,
in his bill and between his claws, he flew away to other lakes and
other rivers, and he dropped a few fish here and there for them to
multiply and be useful to all. Old Tsing no longer was the only one
to enjoy his possession. [*The American Antiquarian*, March, 1895.]

The Raven creator or transformer was injected, about
1875, into Haida plastic arts by a noted carver, Charles
Edensaw, who was fond of using this bird as a theme for
decoration. The Beaver and the Salmon, in the story of
creation and in illustrations by Edensaw, were also frequently brought out together. It is also a favorite theme
of Edensaw's contemporaries, Tom Price, engraver of
argillite plates and maker of miniature totem poles, and
of his disciple, Chapman, the cripple.

In one of those carvings by Chapman, for instance,

the Raven is seen holding a small bird in his bill. This bird is meant for his companion, the Eagle, as spoken of in the Skidegate stories of creation. In the Massett version, the Butterfly is the Eagle's substitute. The sitting Beaver, at the base of the totem pole, gnaws his poplar stick, while the head and wings of the Beaver, turned downward, occupy most of the space in front of the body. In the Raven's bill, the house of the Beaver is rolled up like a sheet of birchbark, and a tiny salmon head appears at one end of the bundle. Nowhere, even in the older Edensaw work, can we find a finer illustration of the Eagle or Butterfly and Beaver episode. The figures, all three, are admirably carved, as are most of the pictorial representations of the mystic animals of North Pacific mythology.

The same mystic animals, besides, were the object of stories and rituals that lifted tribal life from the low levels of daily activities to the superior plane of religious life and spiritual transfiguration. The Raven, the Beaver, and the Salmon, for instance, figure in this exalted self-expression. Large totem poles hold them up to reverence at many points on the coast and the adjacent rivers. First-fruit celebrations—in particular, that of the first salmon caught in the year—are meant to propriate the great spirits presiding aloft over the welfare of the animal species and of man feeding off them in earthly valleys below.

Of a different hue are the narratives and rituals of the northern Dénés, who, from inborn tastes and ingrained habits, chose for their stamping-grounds the hinterland of sub-Arctic America. Devoid of talent for plastic crafts, they were richly endowed with lyrical gifts. Their songs, in the Yukon area and on the northern plateau and lake areas, are lofty hymns to nature and the unseen spirits, or they are the moving outbursts of exiles endowed with an infinite nostalgia. The song of Kwiyaehl's is a typical example of loneliness outspoken, from the upper reaches of the Skeena River in the northern Rockies.

> *Hay, hawmiday!* They left me alone, all alone behind, the forgetful ones who went on their way. Like an orphan am I—poor, lonely, without friends, without relations any, *hay hawmiday!*

> Oh, how wretchedly they have treated me! Young and old went on their way alone, forsaking me, their kinsman, and their bosom friend. They abandoned me, empty-handed as I was, deprived of a living, anguished, forlorn, *hawmiday!*

> So weak are my limbs, so limp, that I may fall by the trail, *hadzaw!* My eyes can see no longer, cannot see my friends, cannot perceive my foes. I hit the trees as I walk, mistaking them for shadows. . . .

Wherever they journeyed in their poverty under remote stars, they kept on singing like bards, whose strain was reminiscent of greater days, now regretfully lost. A few songs noted by Father Petitot among the Hares of the Mackenzie River, bear this out (translated from Petitot's *Déné-Dindjié,* p. xxxiii):

> Younger brother, beware lest the reindeer in the sky
> lure you on to perdition!
> Young brother, come back to your earthly abode!

This dirge was to mourn the loss of a dear brother, who had vanished in the wilderness. Another chant deplores the death of a cherished sister:

In the river flowing around the great island,
My sister has, without warning me, drunk of the bitter
    waters, alas!
My younger sister has ignored the omen of the night owl,
    alas!

In a funeral chant over the body of a dead hunter, the mourners would chant:

On the stellar paths aloft, set your snares for the white
    reindeer!
Shoot your arrows at the mountain goats of the sky!
Why upon this earth have you ventured
And hunted the moose? Here you have met with your
    fate.

Even their clamors of victory rang with pain and nostalgia, like this boasting song over the death of an enemy:

The mists of the polar sea descend upon the waters,
The ocean in its immensity mourns your fate, alas!
For the foe from the barrenlands never shall go back home
    alive!

The bards of Alaska, the northern Rockies, the lower Mackenzie River, and their kinsmen of the Barren Lands and as far east as Hudson Bay, must have fallen heirs to a much higher civilization than actually was their own. For the refinement of their feelings, their language of abstraction, the loftiness of their minds, belong to an advanced culture. The gap between their present lowly status and their language, indeed, as Petitot pointed out, denotes an "immense loss." These outcasts remind us in a way of Adam and Eve expelled from an earthly paradise, which they have not yet forgotten to this day.

The remembrance of their downfall, in their lyric poetry and in their glorious myths, may be considered inherent. But it is also, otherwise, physical and to a certain extent historical. It is physical in so far as, bodily, they belonged to varied recognizable Asiatic types. Everyone who has seen them can vouch for it, and the same missionary who worked among them when they were less contaminated than they are now, spoke, for instance, of Master-Small-Hare, a northern Déné, as being typical *(un type vrai)* Lapp, with a complexion almost white, a small pointed face, canny and intelligent; and of War-Feather, a true Mongolian, coppery, suntanned, with chocolate-like complexion, small eyes slanting upward at the outer end, flat and shiny face, but honest, sweet, and always gay.

Pseudo-historical reminiscences abound in their copious lore. These lead us to infer that they have been the latest of all to cross Bering Strait into the unknown, for they have, more than any other tribe in America, brought with them distinct Asiatic traits and cultural features.

The Chipewyans (east of Mackenzie River) told Sir Alexander Mackenzie, in 1792, that they had originated on a vast western continent. There they had always journeyed eastward, endured an age of oppression and slavery at the hands of a cruel and blood-thirsty nation. To escape from tyranny, they had crossed a large lake, and on their path onward they had discovered shining metal and made it their own to carve and to use.

Sir John Franklin, the Arctic explorer of tragic memory, is even more explicit when he relates, from their own traditions, that these northerners had crossed a wide body of water before reaching these new lands. In spite of the

*The nomadic hunters of the tundras in their perennial pursuit of
"the meat"—caribou* PAGE 323.

passing of time and of great distance, they still treasured the racial memories of strange trees, now unknown to them, bearing large fruits, and of incessant tribulations in warfare, in which their pursuers had shaven heads. The Squinters (Loucheux) tribe spoke of armor and spears used in their ancient warfare. The Hares had not forgotten that once their ancestors had known of huge burden-bearing animals (elephants), serpents, and human-like animals perched on trees (monkeys).

All of these hunters of the tundras, so they themselves declared to Sir John, once had belonged to a single nation. Chased by the Shaven-heads, in a headlong flight toward the sunrise, they had for a time sojourned at the edge of a great eastern sea, but eventually had crossed it to the new land beyond, which they found quite empty. From one stopping place to the next they traveled onward in large numbers, until they had reached the mountains, where they had dispersed, never to meet again as a nation.

That these nomads "thought nothing of travelling a great distance" and had it "in their power to settle where they pleased," was vouched for, in 1795, by Roderick Mackenzie. He met a Chipewyan with his family and property, from Hudson Bay, at Bear Lake (longitude 125°N.), who went back home (a tremendous distance) in the course of three years. They could, should they want it, continue their course to Asia or Greenland, if they found it possible and suitable to their convenience and fancy."

This intrepid pioneer of the North West Company gave a remarkable instance of how a new tribe—also, presumably, a new dialect—would come into existence within a short span of years.

About eight years since, two Indians of different tribes deserted with women belonging to another tribe, and came to reside with a fourth tribe; where having met with a fair opportunity they destroyed the men of two families and carried away the *females,* or the youngest of them, and retired into distant regions—beyond the reach of those whom they had wronged. These four kinds, all speaking in some degree different languages, will form another compound of the whole and in the course of a century or two may be a distinct people—ready to make war upon the other descendants of their forefathers. . . .

The most impressive wild-life feature of the inland Dénés is their everlasting pursuit of what they call *ékfwen,* "the meat," or *étié,* "the food" or "life"; or again, *nontèli,* a name meaning "the nomads" or "migrants." These words mean just one thing—the caribou. Caribou to them, according to their habitat, may be of the Barren Land or the woodland varieties.

Yet they don't feed solely upon *ékfwen,* by any means, for they commonly rely upon smaller game—white hare, which they catch in snares, and snowy-white ptarmigan, said by Petitot to be "the Second Providence of these famished people."

The *ékfwen* of the Dénés (or *La Foule,* "the multitude," as it was called by the early fur traders) slowly moved across country while feeding on lichens, mosses, and browse. In its wake and around it gathered packs of timber wolves, and, here and there, the hunters and their families busy at the kill. In sheer intensity this unique phenomenon was comparable only to the buffalo hunt on the prairies and the salmon run and its parasites on the North Pacific coast.

The caribou are almost never stampeded by men or wolves, even nowadays, should they still exist in their former grandeur. When a few individual caribou, away from the main body, catch fright because of prowlers, they only rejoin "the crowd" or herd and feel secure again. This sense of security, which comes to the herd from its own size, is so strongly ingrained that hunters at the outskirts may shoot with arrows or guns and may kill as many heads as they desire, wolf packs may howl and may strangle their victims, and the caribou as a whole will seldom be moved to start on the run. But when it does it is a real avalanche. It becomes a mighty river, flowing sluggishly for days, now one way, then another, and almost never following the same course. This is the "great migration," a unique phenomenon of the North.[4]

The Nahannies, the Sekanais, the Yellow-Knives, the Beavers, and other Déné tribes[5] preying upon the caribou migrants, used to gather for the event and prepare in night-long vigils for the hunt. They expressed their thoughts aloud, recalling the largest migrations ever met with or heard of. And they relished the subject, for caribou migrations were part of their lives. They often followed them in their own progress. Caribou was the bread of their subsistence in winter, and Meat-Mother was their great female spirit, to whom they had incessant recourse.

The following morning the hunters would begin the slaughter, and then continue it for days. As the cold weather set in, most of the meat would be hung and frozen; but some of it, mainly the tongues, would be

---

[4] Cf. Rev. F. A. G. Morice, "The Great Déné Race," *Anthropos*, V (1910), 114, on hunting caribou.

[5] "The most important features of environment (for them) are the forest and the innumerable herds of wild caribou" (Kaj Birket-Smith, *Congrès international des Américanistes*, 1934, pp. 97-98). The many culture elements shared by both "must presumably be taken to be evidence of an ancient common culture foundation among Eskimos and Chipewyans."

The divine Raven steals the Sun from the lodge of the old fisherman and throws it into the sky PAGES 315-16.

smoked and made into a barter article for the trading
posts. The grease would be plentiful. It would be stored
in pouches made of stomach and guts, tied at the ends,
and put away in underground "caches." Truly this was
abundance and riches, and was the peak in a hunter's
life, at the end of a bounteous season and before the
long moon of scarcity.

Always addicted to songs and rituals to enhance their
mystic powers, most of them, along the whole length of
the Rockies from the Far North to California, would
sing throughout the nights preceding the slaughter, as
if to sharpen their senses and deepen their greed.

> Yazay, yazay! Wait, we shall see!
> Meat-Mother is mighty, she is witchlike!

The "meat" proved so tame that there was no sport
in killing it and cutting it up—merely work and butch-
ery that smacked of greed and surfeit.

The people at times seemed to experience a rebuke
from their conscience, for they had ready apologies for
their countless victims. Addressing their innocent prey,
they sang in singsong: "Who has taken your life?" and
volunteered the reply: "The Copper-Knives" (the Russians on the Alaskan coast). "Who has cut your head
off? The Stone-House people" (the British). "Who
has ripped your stomach open? We beg your pardon
for it; it was the Half-Breeds." And these apologies
were so frequently sung that all found themselves
chanting them.

After a time the hunters began to look bored and
jaded, and the dogs did not so much as sniff at choice
morsels. As the days passed these mild animals gazed at
their butchers with placid and confident eyes, and then

moved on slowly, grunting and grazing. They seemed to have souls, a language, and gentle social instincts.

In the wake of the caribou, swaying back and forth, north and south annually like a living tide, the wanderers of the hinterland slowly drifted onward, far away from their original stamping grounds. Never surfeited or finally defeated, they went on calling themselves Déné, or various forms of the same word—Tena, Tinneh, Na'a—meaning "People." In their own eyes they were "the People," the chosen people. Everywhere they were nomadic hunters, fearful and bold in their raids upon the larder of the earlier occupants whom they occasionally happened to stumble upon and whose preserves they coveted.

These invaders of the open steppes and the northern forests were a curse and a nightmare to those who stood in their path. There was no peace, no security anywhere, least of all where the food was most abundant— on the North Pacific coast and in the caribou and buffalo ranges. They were not, among themselves, immune to attack from behind. Their newly acquired riches often fell to other hands of the same remote extraction, the Nahannies striking at the Tahltans and the Tsetsauts; the Beavers, at the Sekannais and other tribes to the south; the Tsetsauts and the Sekannais, at the Gitksans.

The northern Athapascan tribes developed a characteristic, as a result of this pounding from behind, which was emphatic. In the winter they were addicted to fits of terror and hallucination: the terror of an unseen northern enemy that might massacre them at dawn. A medicine of their own making![6]

[6] "The two extremes of indomitable ferocity and pusillanimous meekness are to be found within the Déné nation." (Rev. F. A. G. Morice, "The Great Déné Race," *Anthropos*, II [1907], 14.)

Timid, cowardly, and treacherous though they were
when at rest, they must have food. So they crept nearer
to it step by step, and clutched it as soon as they dared.
When its possession was disputed, they landed in a
fight. Their backs to the wall, they usually made a good
showing, since perish they must one way or the other.
Read Father Petitot, the early missionary among them
on the tundras in the late 1860's and in the 1870's; or
Campbell, Murray, and any other early trader and explorer among them; or Rev. F. A. G. Morice, an
oblate missionary. I myself have recorded hoards
of reminiscences of this kind from some of their elders.
If one should remember anything of all this oral literature, it is the stress of southbound migrations, due to
hunger as a natural law in the sub-Arctic regions.

In other words, these invaders were of the breed of
Tamerlane and Genghis Khan in Siberia and Mongolia.
They plundered their way through distance and continents, until they were only half satisfied with their new
lot and went for one better. They never slept, if they
could help it, twice under the same star—and, if their
nerves were on edge at times, they had a knack, in a tight
corner, of showing courage and persistence.

Who will doubt this when it is remembered that the
warlike Apaches, of this Tartaric breed, were the vanguard of their thrust toward Mexico? Late as it was in
our age, Geronimo, their famous leader who became a
prisoner of state at the hands of the American government in the early eighties, was on his way to the conquest
of the Corn Maidens of the fertile southern lands. Left
alone to take care of himself, had he lived in prehistoric
times, he would have vanquished the peaceful reapers of
corn and squash and the city dwellers of the Pueblos,

perhaps without bloodshed, and settled among them with his famished warriors. A story of conquest, familiar in other parts of the world, would have repeated itself there. With his horde unchecked, this Attila of the New World would have grasped the seat of Montezuma and, tamed by a civilization which he was apt to assimilate, in his turn he might have become civilized and pushed culture a notch higher in the haphazard ladder of progress. Civilization does not require millennia to grow out of a fertile soil. Culture boils in the cauldron as soon as fire is set under it; just as it slumbers or recedes for the lack of the spark that does the trick.

With Geronimo at their back door, what would have happened to the civilized Mexicans in the absence of the Spaniards, in the past four hundred years? The answer can be only wild conjecture, yet with more than a grain of probability.

The Apaches and the Navahos, having overwhelmed the Mexican dynasty, would have spared its civilization for their own benefit, and fed upon its treasures. Instead of crushing it, as did the white man in his wanton greed, they would have absorbed it, as their kinsman Genghis Khan had done in China a few hundred years before, and as their brothers were about to do in a different way on the North Pacific coast—the totem pole culture being their recent creation. With new blood in their veins, they would, after a few generations, have started for a new conquest of Peru!

History goes on repeating itself. Once more it might have followed the same pattern, had the greedy Japanese been able to travel the Alaska highway at their own pace to their planned destination. The Aztecs a millennium before had journeyed down the Rockies, subdued the Mayas of Mexico, and the Central Americans had daunted the Incas of Peru.

Beware the barbarian of the North, whose dreams of conquest are tall and whose thirst is unquenchable! Like the Dénés of Alaska and the Yukon, he comes in as a thief at dawn, overcomes the previous occupants, and, appeased, sleeps the first nights with his boots on, in the bed of the princess, whose name is Culture!

BIBLIOGRAPHY

The bulk of the material utilized in this book was obtained at firsthand by the author among the North Pacific coast Indians, between 1915 and 1939, for the National Museum of Canada. It forms a small part of the vast collections now preserved in this museum. Extensive use has also been made of the printed and manuscript literature available to historians and anthropologists elsewhere.

The following is a brief list of the sources, whatever they happen to be. They are given according to the chapters.

THE HIGHWAY

The myth of Kronaydin and Ena-gwenee is drawn from Father Emile Petitot's *Dictionnaire de la langue Déné-Dindjié* ("Bibliothèque de linguistique et d'ethnographie américaines," Vol. II [1876], "Essai sur l'origine des Déné-Dindjié," pp. xxxvi-xxxvii).

The legends about Copper Woman or "Femme aux Métaux" are more than once discussed by the same author, particularly in his *Autour du Grand Lac des Esclaves* (1891), pp. 154-80.

On the volcanoes and geysers of Alaska, see: *The Origin and Mode of Emplacement of the Great Tuff Deposit of the Valley of Ten Thousand Smokes,* by Clarence N. Fenner (Washington: National Geographic Society, 1923 [Katmai Series, No. 1]); also *A Chemical Study of the Fumaroles of the Katmai Region,* by E. T. Allen and E. G. Zeis *(ibid.,* No. 2.)

Bearing on the encounters of the pioneer traders of the Hudson's Bay Company with the Alaskan or Russian Indians, consult: *Journal of the Yukon* (1847-48), by Alexander Hunter Murray, edited with notes by L. J. Burpee ("Publications of the Canadian Archives," No. 4 [1910]).

For the Western Union telegraph line, the sources are from manuscript records made after 1920 among the Indians and the white people on the upper Skeena River; also from a number of printed accounts and discussions, for instance: *The First Scientific Exploration of Russian America and the Purchase of Alaska,* by James Alton

James ("Northwestern University Studies," No. 4 [1942]), where we read: "The project of the Western Union Telegraph Company of an overland telegraph across Bering Straits to Europe was a failure but its greatest result was the annexation of Alaska."

The chapters of "Eagle Strikes" and the five following, including "Chanting Buddhist Dirges," are drawn from a great wealth of texts and materials recorded from many native informants, mostly among the thirty tribes or so of the Tsimsyans, for the National Museum of Canada, from 1915 to 1939, by the author and his assistant, William Beynon; also to a lesser extent from the several monographs by Franz Boas, Dr. J. R. Swanton, and other students, on the Tsimsyans, the Haidas, the Tlingits, published by the Smithsonian Institution, Washington, the American Museum of Natural History, New York, and other institutions.

One of the many versions of "The Story of the Bear and His Indian Wife, a Legend of the Haidas . . .," was published by James Dean (*Journal of American Folk-Lore* [1889], pp. 255-260).

The Selarhkons myth is given under this name in Dr. J. R. Swanton's "Contribution to the Ethnology of the Haida" (*The Jesup Expedition, Memoirs of the American Museum of Natural History*, Vol. V, Part 5). It appears under different names among the neighboring nations; it is the equivalent of the Copper Woman of the Dénés, and of the Frog Woman of the Tsimsyans.

See Waldemar Jochelson, "The Koriak" (*The Jesup Expedition*, VI, 198).

The Rev. J. B. McCullagh, missionary of Aiyansh, B.C., has written a little tract on the same volcano, containing a poem and some historical data (privately published): *Ignis . . . The Great Lava Plain . . . Nass River* (1918).

Dr. J. R. Swanton's monograph on the Tlingit is entitled: "Social Condition, Beliefs, and Linguistic Relationship of the Tlingit Indians" (*26th Annual Report of the Bureau of American Ethnology* [1904-1905]).

On the totem poles and myths of Temlaham of the Gitksans, see: "Totem Poles of the Gitksans," by Marius Barbeau (*Bulletin No. 61, National Museum of Canada* [1929], and *The Downfall of Temlaham*, by Marius Barbeau (The Macmillan Company of Canada [1928]).

On the volcanic eruption of the Nass River, the only geological report, very brief, is that of Dr. George Hanson; it is based upon incomplete observation in 1923. The Indians told him that they believed the eruption to have taken place about 150 years ago. He was under the impression that the volcano was "probably not older than 300 years" ("Tseax River Lava Flow, in Reconnaissance between Skeena River and Stewart, British Columbia," *Summary Report, Geological Survey of Canada* [1923], pp. 39a, 40a).

COPPER WOMAN

The Mongolian spot on children of Athapascan origin has been observed by Dr. Loman, Lovelace Clinic, Albuquerque, New Mexico. I quote from a letter of Langdon Kihn, dated November 17, 1942: "Dr. Loman told me that all Indian babies delivered in the hospital, the best one in the Southwest, and there are many [babies] have it [the Mongolian spot]." Sixty per cent of native American children in the Northwest have Mongolian spots, according to a recent compilation, recorded by Dr. Paul Rivet for the Paul Coze Expedition of 1931. See Dr. G. D. Darby's "The Mongolian Spot—British Columbia Coast Indians" *(Museum and Art Notes* [Dec., 1930]); also, "Mongolian Spot," by I. Brennemann *(American Anthropologist,* XI [1907], 12-30).

The last fight that broke out, in 1850, in front of the fort of the Hudson's Bay Company, is described in "Old Port Simpson," by Marius Barbeau *(The Beaver* [Winnipeg, Sept., 1940], pp. 20-23).

On Legyarh and the Tsimsyans, see: "Asiatic Migrations into America," by Marius Barbeau *(The Canadian Historical Review* [Dec., 1932], pp. 403-407).

A brief study of the Buddhistic dirges among the Tsimsyans, with examples, was published in: "The Siberian Origin of Our Northwestern Indians," by Marius Barbeau *(Proceedings of the Fifth Pacific Science Congress, 1933-1934,* pp. 2777-89); "Asiatic Survivals in Indian Songs," by the same author *(Musical Quarterly* [Jan., 1934], pp. 107-116; "Asiatic Survivals in Indian Songs," by the same author *(Scientific Monthly* [April, 1942], pp. 303-307).

On the topic of migrations of Siberian people across Bering Strait, see: "The Coming of Man from Asia in the Light of Recent Discoveries, by Ales Hrdlicka *(Annual Report of the Smithsonian Institution, 1935,* pp. 463-470). Here we find the following conclusions: "It is only too evident that all expectation of finding in Alaska, through systematic work, the remains of the early migrants to America across Alaska must practically be abandoned." The main reason for this is that "The Bering Sea region as well as the coast to the north of it are geologically alive, constantly cutting and building. The present coasts, the mouths of streams . . . were not there 500 years ago. . . . Examination on the spot of the Bering Strait region shows plainly that, once man arrived in northeastern Asia, the passing over to the visible American side was not merely possible but inevitable." The "much easier route over the water" would have been followed, had there been a land bridge between Siberia and Alaska (p. 465). "The coming of man over from Asia to America could never have been in the nature of a single or large migration. Rude and barren territory could never have accommodated any large population. . . . There could have been . . . but a few people passing over at any time. . . . There could never have been any large or continued migration into America . . . only small and interrupted dribblings over, but dribblings that went on over several millennia [p. 466]."

As to language, Dr. Hrdlicka wrote: "Unless it is accepted that there was but a single coming of man in America, and that by one homogenous group, the notion of the advent of but a single original language from Asia is impossible."

The evidence of the skeletal remains, according to the same authority, shows that in Alaska there is no homogeneity of type, therefore, no "unique original type. . . . We are steadily becoming more convinced that the course from Asia, though all of one large human stem, the yellow-brown, brought with it already considerable physical heterogeneity; and if this is true of physical characteristics, it is certainly true also of language and culture [p. 468]."

For the culture of a people on the frontier of the Alaskan Eskimos and the Tlingits, see *The Eyak Indians of the Copper River Delta, Alaska*, Kaj Birket-Smith and Frederica de Laguna (Copenhagen, 1938). The moieties of the Eyaks are described on page 123.

Most of the sources on the relations of the Déné-Athapascan languages and dialects, and the Na-Déné, are still unpublished. At the time of the elaboration of his theory of the Asiatic origin of Déné-Athapascan languages and of his Na-Déné studies, Dr. Edward Sapir and the writer were colleagues at the National Museum of Canada, and we frequently discussed various aspects of this fascinating problem. The writer, therefore, is well acquainted with the late Dr. Sapir's views. See his "Na-déné Languages, a Preliminary Report" (*American Anthropologist*, [N.S.], XVII [1915], 535-558), and his "Pitch Accent in Sarcee, an Athapascan Language" (*Journal de la Société des Américanistes de Paris* [N.S.], XVII [1925] 180-205.

In the latter, Dr. Sapir acknowledges that both Father E. Petitot and Father L. Legoff, the former French missionaries among the

Dénés, were aware of the existence of pitch accent among the northern tribes of the Athapascan stock. This distinctive feature in itself is enough to link the Athapascan dialects historically with Asiatic languages, in particular with Chinese.

That the Déné sublanguages were part of a much wider family of languages, the others being Asiatic, was a firm conviction of Father Petitot.

With an eye on the Asiatic sources of the Déné-Athapascan, Marcel Mauss, of the Collège de France and the Sorbonne, Paris, stated in the presence of the author, in 1931, that to his way of thinking the westernmost frontier of the root languages involved here extends as far west as the Punjab, in northern India—in other words, almost as far as the prototype of the *Hano!* dirge song of the Tsimsyans.

In connection with the same linguistic problem, see also Roman Jacobson's "The Paleosiberian Languages" *(American Anthropologist* [Oct.-Dec., 1924], pp. 602-620.

On the Paleosiberian tribes, see Ivan A. Lopatin's "The Extinct and Near-Extinct Tribes of Northeastern Asia as Compared with the American Indian" *(American Antiquity,* V [1939-40], 202-208). The indication here of the successive waves of migrants from the south into Siberia is particularly significant. For instance, "The New-Siberians of Mongolian stock immigrated into Siberia later than the Turks and the Tongus, the Buryat occupying their present habitat only after the northeastern migration of the Yakuts [p. 204]." "The immigration of the New-Siberians greatly aroused the Old-Siberian population, who were forced to vacate their old habitat for the inhospitable corners of their territories or, abandoning them altogether, to seek a new abode in remote unattractive countries.... The Old-Siberians had to move in northern and northwestern directions. This migration of the people of Siberia was gradual, the process being very slow and lasting for centuries.... Northeastern Asia was a place where many peoples were forced in from the south and the southwest. There was only one outlet by which the Old-Siberians could escape the pressure of the invaders—the Bering Strait [p. 204]."

In summing up, Lopatin concludes (p. 207): "Among the Old-Siberians the Mongoloid type greatly predominated. The medley of unrelated languages of the Old-Siberians had nothing in common with the New-Siberian languages (Turkish, Tungus, and Mongolian), nor with Chinese and Japanese. The general culture of the Old-Siberians also varied widely; some of them were advanced enough to pursue agriculture, while others were primitive hunters and fishermen. . . . The majority of the Old-Siberians lived in the conditions of the non-agricultural Stone Age. A great many diverse peoples aggregated in Siberia because of the severe pressure in population always existing in the south where the geographical environment favored growth. The pressure constantly forced peoples to migrate to the north, especially the northeast, where they found an outlet leading them to America. . . . The ancient American immigrant while still on Asiatic soil was linguistically heterogeneous. . . . Only the Old-Siberians could have been the immigrants into uninhabited America."

One of the outstanding studies of the Asiatic origin of the American Indians is Rev. A. G. Morice's "Northwestern Dénés and Northeastern Asiatics" (Transactions of the Canadian Institute, X [1912-14], 131-193). Here the writer accepts the theory of the "community of origin between the Asiatic and American aborigines"—the very conclusion I have myself reached after an altogether independent investigation. . . . "The ethnological unity of the Siberians and the North Americans [is] now admitted by all who have made an exhaustive study of the question."

Father Morice here quotes a letter from Dr. Hrdlicka, dated June 1, 1914, in which the writer states: "I have made a fairly long trip through Siberia and Mongolia, the results of which all tend to sustain the theory of the Asiatic origin of the Americans, while pointing to the utter improbability of a migration at any time in the opposite direction."

On the language of the natives on the Diomede Islands—connected with Alaskan Eskimo, or intermediary between Asiatic and American languages—see "The Chukchee," by Waldemar Bogoras (The Jesup North Pacific Expedition, VII, 20). According to Bogoras, the Chuckchee, Koriak, and Kamchadal are branches of a single linguistic family.

A list of sixty Japanese junks, wrecked on the North Pacific coast—a number of them with survivors aboard—is given in "Report of Japanese Vessels Wrecked in the North Pacific Ocean, from the Earliest Records to the Present Time" (Proceedings of the California Academy of Sciences, VI [1875], 50). And this list is incomplete. For instance, another junk was wrecked, in 1890, at Gold Harbor, Queen Charlotte Islands.

On the Paleosiberian people, their recent history, migrations, culture, in so far as they have a bearing on their relations with the Alaskan natives, consult the bulky monographs of Jochelson and

Bogoras in *The Jesup North Pacific Expedition*. There we learn that "The Mongol-Turk are the nearest neighbors of the Koriak," and that the Yakuts, of the same neighborhood, "form an isolated branch of the Turkish tribes."

Such words as *khama-san* or *kamba-tsan*, meaning "blizzard" among the Dénés of the Mackenzie (as recorded by Petitot), and the *kamshin* or "sandstorm" of the Arabs as far as the Sahara Desert, were originally the same; their wide diffusion can be explained only through common elements at the origin of the people themselves.

Jochelson *(The Koriak*, p. 348 writes: "The Yakuts are comparatively recent arrivals in the far north"; and: "The Tungus, before the Russians, were constantly at war with the Koriaks, invading Koriak territory after their subjection by the Russians." They even penetrated Kamchatka (p. 810). The Tungus, according to the same authority (p. 439), are related to the Manchus, and are supposed to have migrated northward from the Amur River. A part of the Mongol-Turk themes found in Koriak folklore was borrowed from the Tungus (p. 349). "The Yakuts ... constitute an isolated branch of the Turkish tribes; they have legends which bear traces of an origin from the folklore created by the civilization of Central Asia, which had reached a comparatively high state of development in early antiquity [p. 345].

Just as the Koriaks, according to Jochelson, appealed to the shamans of the Chukchees and the Tungus, their neighbors on both sides of Bering Sea must have exchanged ritual and mystic practices with one another. Certain cultural elements in this way may have filtered into Alaska even faster than the actual migrations of people eastward.

Among the early explorations of the Bering Sea and the North Pacific coast quoted here, mention of only a few can be made:

Bering's Voyages, by F. A. Golder, Vols. I, II, includes "G. W. Steller's Journal" (1743).

A Voyage to the Pacific Ocean . . ., by James Cook (1778-79).

Voyage de la Pérouse autour du Monde (1785-1788). Rédigé par M. L.-A. Milet-Mureau, Vol. II.

A Voyage Round the World . . ., by George Dixon (1785-88).

Voyages . . . Made in the Years 1788 and 1789, from China to the Northwest Coast of America, by J. Meares.

A Voyage of Discovery to the North Pacific Ocean and Round the World, by George Vancouver (1790-95).

Voyage round the World, by Etienne Marchand (trans.), (1790-92), (London, 1801).

Voyages and Travels in Various Parts of the World, by C. H. Von Langsdorff (1803-1807).

Voyage round the World, by Urey Lisiansky (1803-1806).

Narrative of a Voyage to the Pacific and Bering Strait, Part II, by F. W. Beechy (1825-28).

Narrative of a Journey round the World, by Sir George Simpson, (1841-42).

Travels and Adventure in the Territories of Alaska . . . , by Frederick Whymper (London, 1868).

On native metals in Alaska, see T. A. Rickard's "The use of Iron and Copper by the Indians of British Columbia" *(British Columbia Historical Quarterly* [Jan., 1939], pp. 25-50).

The full title of Petroff's monograph for the American government is *Report on the Population, Industries, and Resources of Alaska,* by Ivan Petroff (1882).

J. R. Swanton's report on the Tlingit is "Social Condition, Beliefs, and Linguistic Relationship of the Tlingit Indians" *(26th Bureau of American Ethnology* [1904-1905], pp. 393-483).

TOTEMS

On the subject of totems, the following publications of the author furnish extensive information:

"Totem Poles of the Gitskan, Upper Skeena River, British Columbia" *(Bulletin No. 61, National Museum of Canada* [1929]).

"Totem Poles: A Recent Native Art of the Northwest Coast of America" *(Geographical Review* [April, 1930], pp. 258-272); the same study was reprinted in the *Smithsonian Report* (1931), pp. 559-570.

"The Modern Growth of the Totem Pole on the Northwest Coast" *(Journal of the Washington Academy of Sciences* [Sept., 1938], pp. 385-393; reprinted in *Smithsonian Report* (1939), pp. 491-498.)

"Totem Poles: A By-Product of the Fur Trade" *(Scientific Monthly* [1942], pp. 507-14).

"The Southern Extent of Totem Pole Carving," by H. G. Barnes *(Pacific Northwest Quarterly* [Oct., 1942], pp. 379-389).

THE SALMON RUN

Many opportunities, from 1915 to 1939, have enabled the author to observe the features of the salmon run at firsthand, particularly on the Nass and Skeena Rivers, and along the adjacent coasts; also to visit, or stay at, various canneries in the same districts and around Prince of Wales Island, or as far north as Wrangell.

Among the printed information consulted, a few of the leading publications on North Pacific coast salmon are quoted at the end of the chapter. To these may be added Roderick Haig Brown's *Return to the River, a Story of the Chinook* (New York, 1941).

WILD LIFE

The author's sources here were in no small part secured at firsthand. Much information was obtained verbally in the course of many conversations with "old-timers"—white hunters. The printed literature on the various subjects was to a certain extent consulted.

A few published items bearing on the same subjects may be listed here:

Father Emile Petitot's *Exploration de la Région du Grand Las des Ours* (Paris, 1893); *Autour du Grand Lac des Esclaves* (Paris, 1891).

Indian Days in the Canadian Rockies (The Macmillan Company of Canada, 1923); *The Downfall of Temlaham* (same publisher, 1928); and *The Indian Speaks* (The Caxton Printers, Caldwell, Idaho, and The Macmillans of Canada, 1943); all these by the author, containing some of the oral literature and the songs of the northwestern natives.

Printed information on the Siberian migrations across Bering Sea into Alaska is to be found in:

"How Asia Used to Drip at the Spout into America," by the author *(Washington Historical Quarterly* [July, 1933], pp. 163-173).

On the Selarhkons myth of the Salmon-Eater group: J. R. Swanton's "The Haida" *(The Jesup North Pacific Expedition,* Vol. V).

A few traditions of the northern Athapascan were recorded by Sir Alexander Mackenzie in his *Voyages from Montreal through the Continent of North America to the Frozen and Pacific Oceans* (1789 and 1793); and by Sir George Simpson in *Peace River, a Canoe Voyage from Hudson's Bay to the Pacific* ... (1928), by Malcolm McLeod.

The Asiatic origins of whale hunting as practiced by the Aleutian Islanders and the North Pacific coast people are indicated by Elmo Paul Hohman in his *American Whaleman,* where he states that whale hunting was practiced first by the Siberian Tartars and the Japanese. And Robert K. Heizer *(American Anthropologist* [Jan.,

1943], p. 120) states: "... the Aleutian Eskimos invented, by a simple transfer process, a new and different method of whale hunting patterned after the technique of hunting sea-otter." This method consisted in hunting with spear or lance, tipped with a detachable, barbed point, cast from a baidarka, with an inflated bladder buoy or float.

Among the many Asiatic features of a technical nature which the American tribes of the North Pacific coast have preserved by way of inheritance or transmission are:

The semisubterranean round house in the shape of a beaver lodge, but with an exit through the roof by means of a notched ladder— that is, a log notched on one side, resting on the ground at one end, and passing through the opening in the roof. These dwellings are typical of the northeastern Siberian tribes, and they were the common type among the northwestern Athapascans, in particular among the tribes of the northern Rockies. Their advantage in the winter, in a country of deep snow and drifts, is that the entrance to the house is never blocked. This type of dwelling was the appanage of the Athapascans as far as they migrated—even into New Mexico. Dr. Frank H. H. Roberts, in his "Survey of South Western Archaeology" *(American Anthropologist* [Jan., 1935], pp. 28-29), writes: "The question of the two types of pit houses, the Hohokan and the Basket Maker-Pueblo, calls for consideration. ... In the earliest known form, the house is so specialized and bears such a striking resemblance to some of the structures in Northeastern Asia that the similarities would hardly seem to be the result of mere coincidence."

The stone lamp of St. Lawrence Island and of the Yukon type, according to Walter Hough, in "The Lamp of the Eskimo" *(Smithsonian Institution* [1898], p. 1038), is related to that of eastern Asia.

The manner of holding the arrow and the position of the bow in the hunter's hand before releasing the arrow are peculiar to the North Pacific coast; it is different from that prevailing elsewhere among the North American natives. The artist Langdon Kihn— who first made this observation—thinks it is Asiatic (for an illustration, see Harlan I. Smith's photo Neg. No. 56887).

The fortified villages or fortresses of the North Pacific coast tribes were so similar to those of the South Seas that the early navigators gave the same Polynesian name of *hippah* to one of them they observed on the west coast of Queen Charlotte Islands—Hippah Island. Jochelson, in his "Koriak" *(Jesup ...,* p. 564), states that rolling logs were also released upon the beseigers, among the Koriaks of northeastern Siberia, just as they were among the Tsimsyans of the Skeena River and adjacent islands.

Log and suspension bridges over the rivers and canyons of the North Pacific coast are—according to Lawrence J. Burpee, who was the first to draw attention to them—of the same type as those formerly built in northeastern Asia.

"Scrapers, called *tci-tho* in the upper Copper River Valley, are made and used in preference to iron blades at present, both in that region and in the Upper Tanana, for scraping skins. It is the most common implement in all Athapascan sites excavated. An oval or semi-lunar flake is struck from a water-worn boulder and then battered against a stone until crudely retouched. The same implement is reported by Hrdlicka from the lower Yukon; also by de Laguna from the lower Yukon and Cook inlet. The implement also occurs in collections from the Baikal region in Siberia" (Froelich Rainey, in "Archaelogical Investigations in Central Alaska" [*American Antiquity*, V. (1939-40), p. 301]).

"Natives on the lower Tanana and central Yukon inform me [Froelich Rainey] that their ancestors made pottery near Rampart Rapids where they had found a deposit of suitable clay. . . . I was further informed by the natives that pottery, made on the Yukon, was traded some four hundred and fifty miles up the Tanana as far as the mouth of the Delta River. At present, it appears that pottery was made by the historic Athapascans in the Yukon Valley as far inland as Rampart Rapids and that it was apparently traded some distance up both rivers above this point.

"The first collection excavated was described briefly by Dr. N. C. Nelson who observed that certain implements classed as end scrapers, semipolyhedral cores and small prismatic flakes struck from these cores are characteristic of pre-neolithic collections from the Gobi in Mongolia. He further observed that a definite similarity in the preparation process suggests specific proof of cultural relations between Asia and America. In a recent examination of epipaleolithic and neolithic material from the Lake Baikal region in Siberia, now in the museums of Moscow and Leningrad, I recognized not only the specific scrapers, cores and flakes, but also practically all the characteristic implements from the University of Alaska Site" (*ibid.*, p. 302).

"If we assume that inland people of Asia would follow in America a route of migration inland where the environment would be familiar to them, we may well expect to find evidence of late glacial or early post-glacial human migration from northeast Asia to continental

America in the Yukon and Tanana Valleys which were both ice-free corridors to interior Canada in glacial times. Some evidence of such migration has been found but it is certainly not conclusive, and this summary only pretends to point out methods of approach, and a frame-work for future research" (*ibid.*, p. 308).

The fits of terror and the hallucinations of the Dénés, caused by the dread of raiders coming behind them, are vividly described by Petitot in *Exploration de la Région du Grand Lac des Ours* (p. 285).

Genghis Khan, by Ralph Fox (New York, 1936), gives a good account of the fantastic career of this Asiatic conqueror. In its light we get a good perspective of the ethnic and social backgrounds in Siberia, at the time when the present northwestern tribes of America were beginning to trickle out of Siberia into Alaska.

The hypothesis of Fusang is expounded in: *Fusang or the Discovery of America by Chinese Buddhist Priests in the Fifth Century,* by Charles E. Leland (New York, 1875); and in *Ethnographie des Peuples étrangers à la Chine, ouvrage composé au XIIIe siècle de notre ère par Ma-Juan-Lin, traduit ... du Chinois ... par le Marquis d'Hervey de Saint-Denis* (Genève, 1876), "Fou-sang. ..." It consists of chronicles, in the fifth century, of Chinese Buddhist priests engaged in missionary work in foreign lands far away across the sea to the northwest or to the east.

On the origin and character of the Apaches and the Navahos much has been written. Of this literature, the "Handbook of American Indians" (*Bureau of American Ethnology, Bull. 30*) gives a good summary. Here we read: "There is no evidence that the Apache reached as far west as Arizona until after the middle of the 16th century. From the time of the Spanish colonization of New Mexico until within twenty years they have been noted for their warlike disposition, raiding white and Indian settlements alike, extending their depredations as far southward as Jalisco, Mexico" ("Apaches," Part I).

Of the Navahos the "Handbook" states: "For many years previous to the occupancy of their country by the United States, they kept up an almost predatory war with the Pueblos and the white settlers of New Mexico, in which they were usually the victors. When the United States took possession of New Mexico in 1849, their depredations were at their height. ... The story [their origin legend] gives the impression that these Indians wandered into New Mexico and Arizona in small groups, probably in single families. ... Hodge has shown that this Navaho origin legend, omitting a few obviously mystic elements, can be substantiated by recorded history, but he places the beginning at less than 500 years. . . . The [physical] appearance of the Navaho strengthens the traditional evidence of their very composite origin."

According to the "Early Spanish Accounts of the Apache Indians," by Donald E. Worcester (*American Anthropologist* [1941], pp. 308-312), "The Querechos [Navahos] passed the winter camped near the pueblos. . . . They relied upon the Pueblo tribes to supply them with corn, cotton blankets, and pottery, for which they exchanged salt, buffalo hides, and dried meat. The Querechos were great traders, whole rancherías of them going on trading expeditions. . . . Castañeda, a member of Coronado's expedition [in 1541], told of coming to settlements of people who lived like Arabs. . . . They travel like the Arabs, with their tents and troops of dogs loaded with poles and having Moorish pack saddles with girths. . . . They were sun-worshippers. . . . He saw mountain Querechos, possibly Navahos, who carried on trade with those at the settlements. . . . These Indians go forth through the neighboring provinces to trade and traffic with . . . hides."

This Déné-Athapascan way of creeping upon their neighbors and either trading with them, or fighting them, and the trade expeditions of the Navahos and the Apaches, are also the familiar traits of their distant kinsmen of the North Pacific coast—the Tlingits, the Haidas, and the Tsimsyans.

Quite possibly, at one time in the middle of the nineteenth century, large canoe parties of the Haidas, raiding the coast of California for slaves and booty, could have come upon the vanguards of Navaho trading incursions probing their chances for advancement across the Californian ranges. For both marauders of Athapascan-Mongolian stock, this chance encounter would have happened a few thousand miles south of their common starting point at Bering Sea. And all the way they had adhered to an ancestral cultural pattern going back to the Asiatic steppes and seacoasts far away and long ago.